More Advance Praise for *Creating Innovators*

"To combat the competitive threat from economies like Brazil, Russia, India, and China, we must develop empowered entrepreneurs and innovators. *Creating Innovators* is a masterful work that shows us how. Tony Wagner's case studies reveal more about these fine innovators than he may have realized. World leaders, business executives, educators, policy makers, and parents, take note!"

—Dr. Annmarie Neal, Center for Leadership Innovation, and former chief talent officer, Cisco Systems

"In my life I have met and worked with individuals who help create the world they live in—innovators. Their lives are so much more fulfilling than people who live in a world of someone else's creation. This book, in a clear, tangible way, explores how to help young people access skills of innovation and lead richer lives."

—Brad Anderson, former CEO, Best Buy Corporation

"A pioneering and invaluable work about what it really takes to build innovation capability in society—by planting and cultivating innovators, one person at a time."

—John Kao, chairman of the Institute for Large Scale Innovation and author of *Innovation Nation*

"Tony Wagner offers an indispensable guide to US education and economic strategy. Unless young Americans can create their own jobs, they face the prospect of limited economic opportunity. In delving into remarkable initiatives that foster innovation and deep learning, Wagner offers hope that we can retain global economic leadership in the twenty-first century. This book is a must for every parent, teacher, administrator, and policy maker in our country."

—Ted Dintersmith, partner emeritus, Charles River Ventures

Also by Tony Wagner

How Schools Change
Making the Grade
Change Leadership
The Global Achievement Gap

Films by Robert A. Compton

The Finland Phenomenon: Inside the World's Most Surprising School System
Two Million Minutes: A Global Examination

CREATING INNOVATORS

The Making of Young People Who Will Change the World

TONY WAGNER

With supplementary video material produced by

Robert A. Compton

SCRIBNER

New York London Toronto Sydney New Delhi

Video content is available at www.creatinginnovators.com.
Video content may not be available indeånitely.

Scribner
A Division of Simon & Schuster, Inc.
1230 Avenue of the Americas
New York, NY 10020

First Scribner trade paperback edition February 2015

Designed by Carla Jayne Jones
Cover photograph © Photodisc

Manufactured in the United States of America

5 7 9 10 8 6 4

Library of Congress Control Number: 2012007162

ISBN 978-1-4516-1149-6
ISBN 978-1-4516-1151-9 (pbk)
ISBN 978-1-4516-1152-6 (ebook)

For PJ—my muse and midwife to this book
And for my three wonderful children—Dan, Sarah, and Eliza—all innovating in their own way

Contents

Introduction

Recent events and new questions and insights have compelled me to write this book.

My last book, *The Global Achievement Gap*, published in 2008, described the new skills students need for careers, college, and citizenship in the twenty-first century and the growing gap between these skills versus what is taught and tested in our schools. Judging by the outpouring of positive responses to the book from diverse audiences and the many subsequent speaking requests I received from all corners of the world, it would appear that I got a number of things right in that book. But I now see that the new skills I described—which I call the Seven Survival Skills—while necessary, are not sufficient.

The world has changed profoundly since 2008. The economies of the West are in shambles. In the United States, the combined rate of unemployment and underemployment is more than 15 percent, and in some European countries it is far worse. Many economists say the solution is for consumers to start spending again, thus creating new jobs. But most consumers can no longer borrow money as easily as they once did. And because many fear for their jobs, they are now saving at a far greater rate than just a few years ago. It is not clear when—or even if—our consumer-driven economy and accompanying low unemployment rates will ever return. Meanwhile, both economists and policy makers are caught up in fierce debates about whether to reduce debt or provide more economic stimulus, which would in the short term increase government debt.

Most leaders agree on one thing, however. The long-term health of our economy and a full economic recovery are dependent upon creating far more innovation. New or improved ideas, products, and services create wealth and new jobs. Business leaders, in particular, say that we need many more young people who can create innovations in the areas of science, technology, and engineering. Many argue that so-called STEM education (science, technology, engineering, and mathematics) is increasingly important to the future of our country. Republicans, Democrats, and Independents alike say that for our young people to be better prepared for high-wage, high-skilled jobs, they must all graduate from high school "college ready" and earn a two-year or four-year postsecondary degree—preferably in a STEM-related field. Thomas Friedman and Michael Mandelbaum take the argument even further in their recent book, *That Used to Be Us,* asserting that only the jobs of innovators and entrepreneurs will be immune to outsourcing or automation in the new global knowledge economy.

At the same time as these arguments have gained traction, there has also been a growing concern about the cost of a college education and whether college students are learning very much in their classes. In 2010, college debt—estimated at $1 trillion—exceeded credit card debt for the first time.[1] And in early 2011, a new study revealed that, after two years of college, nearly half of all students were no more skillful than when they began their studies, and fully one-third showed no gains after four years.[2] Statistics show college graduates earn far more than high school graduates. But is that because they are actually more skilled or because the credential has become a simple way to weed through the forest of résumés?

Given the near consensus on the vital importance of innovation in today's economy, I decided to explore the question of how you educate young people to become innovators. What are the capacities that matter most for innovation, and how are they best taught? I became especially interested in what truly constitutes a meaningful STEM education.

The question of how teachers can develop those students skills that matter most for our country's future has become even more urgent for me as I have followed the recent education-reform debates in the United States and elsewhere. I am frankly appalled at the idea, now widely held, that the best measure of teachers' effectiveness is students' performance on standardized, multiple-choice tests. I am not a fan of teacher tenure, and I believe strongly in accountability for improved student learning. However, most policy makers—and many school administrators—have absolutely no idea what kind of instruction is required to produce students who can think critically and creatively, communicate effectively, and collaborate versus merely score well on a test. They are also clueless about what kind of teaching best motivates this generation to learn. And the tests that policy makers continue to use as an indication of educational progress do not measure any of the skills that matter most today. We need more profiles of quality instruction—and better sources of evidence of results—to inform the education debate.

Since the publication of *The Global Achievement Gap*, I have been inundated with e-mails from concerned parents. They know their children's schools are not teaching the skills that they will need, and the parents want to know what they can do. I have my own experience as the father of three wonderful children, now grown with children of their own, but that hardly seems like a sufficient basis for giving advice to other parents. How *do* parents nurture some of the important skills and attributes of their children? I began to wonder.

In the last few years, I have had opportunities to work with highly innovative companies such as Apple, Cisco Systems, and Scholastic, as well as with senior leaders in the US Army. I have been fascinated by how these leaders see the world and deal with the accelerating pace of change. I became interested in what the best employers do to develop the capacities of young people to be innovators. I also recently met with education leaders and visited schools in Finland, whose education system is considered the best in the world. It is also credited with helping to produce one of the most innovative economies in the world. I wanted to explore what lessons we might learn from Finland's success.

Finally, I have continued to be intrigued by this so-called net generation—the first to grow up as what Marc Prensky calls "digital natives." I interviewed a number of twentysomethings for the last book, but felt I had only scratched the surface of understanding this generation. Since then, the debate about this generation's work ethic—or lack of one—has continued to rage. So I wanted to better understand how they might be differently motivated, and what kinds of teaching and leadership they respond to most positively.

Out of all these disparate influences and questions an idea for a new book began to emerge. I resolved, first, to take a leap and become a student of innovation—something about which I knew little until a few years ago. I have tried to understand what the skills of successful innovators are and why are they so important to our future. I interviewed highly innovative twentysomethings and then studied their "ecosystems"—the parental, teaching, and mentoring influences that they told me had been most important in their development. I wanted to see if I could discern patterns of parenting that contribute to the nurturing of young innovators. And what about the teachers whom these innovators identified as having been most important in their development—were there any similarities in their methods? Are there colleges or graduate programs that do an excellent job of teaching the skills of innovation, and if so, how might they be different? I also sought to learn what the mentors and employers of young innovators had to say about how these capacities are best fostered.

I've interviewed scores of diverse young innovators—budding engineers, scientists, artists, musicians, and other individuals who have started companies or worked for some of the most innovative companies in the world, as well social innovators and entrepreneurs who are seeking better ways to solve societal problems. I then interviewed their parents, teachers, and mentors. I observed classes and conducted interviews at several colleges and graduate programs that have an international reputation for graduating innovators. Finally, I interviewed business and military leaders who are dealing with the challenges of developing organizational capacities to innovate. In all, I conducted more than 150 interviews for this book.

It has been an utterly fascinating project, but also challenging because of its scope and complexity. For this reason, I decided to limit the innovators whom I profile in this book to young people between the ages of twenty-one and thirty-two who fall into one of two categories: individuals who are doing highly innovative work in so-called STEM fields, and individuals engaged in social innovation and entrepreneurship. The former are critical to our economic future, the latter to our social and civic well-being. I have also chosen to combine the categories of innovators and entrepreneurs. I am well aware that not every young innovator is an entrepreneur or vice versa. However, I discovered that the majority of the young people whom I interviewed aspire to be both, and that young innovators and entrepreneurs—regardless of their areas of interest—share some common roots.

Describing how I found the people I interviewed would take another book. Research for this project has been much like the process of following hyperlinks on the Internet. Several of my student researchers suggested names of young people whom they had met or read about, while angel investors and venture capitalists introduced me to others. Some individuals—such as General Martin Dempsey—found me. One source would take me to another and that one to the next. I make no claims to a "scientific" sampling. However, based on all that I have learned in the last three years, I have a high degree of confidence that the innovators whom I profile in depth are a representative sample.

I am enormously grateful to the innovators I write about here, as well as the ones whom I had to leave out for space reasons, and to all of their parents, teachers, and mentors. Everyone gave me hours of their time—often over several interviews and in follow-up e-mails—and allowed me complete access to their life and family history.

Thanks to the persistence and hard work of Bob Compton, you will not only meet many of these people between the pages of this book, you will also be able to see and hear them on camera. Bob—who himself has had a remarkable career as a high-tech innovator, entrepreneur, and angel investor—has recently focused his energies on producing an outstanding set of videos about education. His first, *2 Million Minutes*, was screened by all of the presidential candidates in 2008 and has sold more than twenty thousand copies. We met at an Investment in America Forum at West Point several years ago, and we recently collaborated on a film about Finland's education system, *The Finland Phenomenon: Inside the World's Most Surprising School System.*[3] When I told Bob about plans for this new book, he urged me to make it a truly innovative book in its format—and not just a book about innovation. So throughout these pages, you will find a series of cues that direct you to a website where you can watch special video content.

Whether you are a parent, teacher (preschool through college), mentor, employer, or policy maker, I think you will find that the print and video profiles of these young innovators, as well as the ecosystems that have helped them to develop their capacities, have a great deal to teach us all. I know that I was—and continue to be—inspired by the people whom I interviewed for this project. So I invite you to read, watch, listen, learn—and then to reflect, share, and discuss with your friends and colleagues. For if we are to create a strong economic future and a sustainable way of life for our children and grandchildren, we all have much that we can and must do together.

VIDEO CUE:

Wagner on Why I Wrote This Book

Go to www.creatinginnovators.com
to watch the video.

Chapter One
A Primer on Innovation

Why Is Innovation Essential to Our Future?

As a country, we face intertwined economic and social challenges. A growing number of our good-paying blue-collar and even white-collar jobs are now being done in other countries that have increasingly well-educated and far-less-expensive labor forces. Since the Great Recession of 2008, the combined unemployment and underemployment rate in the United States has remained stubbornly high—more than 15 percent as I write this—and many others have given up looking for work altogether. According to 2010 US Census Bureau data, the percentage of American adults who now work has dropped to 58.2 percent, the lowest percentage since women began entering the workforce in large numbers.[1] Young people have been hit especially hard by this recession. In 2010, employment among young adults sixteen to twenty-nine was 55.3 percent, compared with 67.3 percent in 2000. It's the lowest number since the end of World War II.[2]

Our social challenge parallels the economic one. Because so many jobs are being off-shored or automated, people who may once have made $30 an hour on the shop floor now consider themselves fortunate if they find a $7-an-hour job sweeping the Walmart floor. According to the most recent research, real median household income has declined nearly 11 percent in the last decade.[3] With a disappearing middle class, income inequities continue to grow in the United States. More than 37 percent of young families—defined as under thirty—are living in poverty, the highest level on record, and they are disproportionately African-American, Hispanic, and Native American.[4] The total number of Americans living in poverty, both old and young, is now more than 15 percent of our population—the largest figure in the fifty-two years that poverty estimates have been published.[5]

Another world war isn't likely to save our economy and put people back to work this time, as it did in 1940. Nor is more consumer spending going to save us, as it has with the last several recessions. The easy credit that has fueled America's recent spending sprees is gone, and those that do have jobs are fearful of losing them and so now save rather than spend. Deficit reduction is essential, but by itself it is unlikely to jump-start the economy. We cannot spend or save our way out of this problem. We need a different answer.

Over the last hundred years, the locus of job and wealth creation in the United States has transitioned from agriculture, to manufacturing, to services, with innovation playing an important role throughout our history. Today, many worry that our economy has become too dependent on consumer spending as the engine of economic growth and source of job creation. It comprises more than 70 percent of our economy. Up until the Great Recession, our consumer-driven economy was increasingly fueled by people spending money they did not have to buy things they might not have needed, while threatening the planet in the process. It now appears that this economy is no longer economically or environmentally sustainable.

What we urgently need is a new engine of economic growth for the twenty-first century. The solution to our economic and social challenges is the same: creating a viable and sustainable economy that creates good jobs without polluting the planet. And there is general agreement as to what that new economy must be based on. One word: innovation.

We have to become the country that produces more ideas to solve more different kinds of problems. We have to become the country that leads the way in developing the new technologies for a sustainable planet and affordable health care. We have to become the country that creates the new and better products, processes, and services that other countries want and need. We can no longer create wealth by outmanufacturing or outconsuming the rest of the world. We must outinnovate our economic competitors.

But this is not a book about economics. This book is about how we can develop the capacities of many more young people to be creative and entrepreneurial. This book explores the new challenge of parenting, teaching, and mentoring young people to become the innovators that our country and our planet need to thrive in the twenty-first century.

In *That Used to Be Us*, Thomas Friedman and Michael Mandelbaum summarize our challenge today:

> Going forward, we are convinced, the world increasingly will be divided between high imagination-enabling countries, which encourage and enable the imagination and extras of their people, and low imagination-enabling countries, which suppress or simply fail to develop their people's creative capacities and abilities to spark new ideas, start up new industries and nurture their own "extra." America has been the world's leading high imagination-enabling country and now it needs to become a *hyper*-high-imagination-enabling society. That is the only way we can hope to have companies that are increasingly productive *and* many workers with jobs that pay decent salaries.[6]

VIDEO CUE:

Friedman on the Innovation Imperative

Go to www.creatinginnovators.com
to watch the video.

When explaining America's historical leadership in the area of innovation, economists are quick to list factors such as our strong patent and copyright protection laws, availability of venture capital, modern infrastructure, government investment in research and development, and an immigration policy that has traditionally encouraged the world's most talented individuals to come learn and live in the United States. Our nation's leading universities are also sometimes mentioned, but as we will see, many of the practices and incentive structures in our best research institutions are actually part of the problem when it comes to developing young people's capabilities to be innovators. And little—if anything—has been said about the parenting practices that cultivate budding innovators.

In reality, only a small portion of our population has been truly innovative—and up until now, that was all we needed to maintain our economic advantage. But our lead in innovation—and thus our economic vitality—is rapidly eroding. Other countries are catching up—and quickly. In 2009, 51 percent of US patents were awarded to non-US companies.[7] A recent report by the Information Technology and Innovation Foundation concluded that "The United States has made the least progress of the 40 nations/regions [studied] in improvement in international competitiveness and innovation capacity over the last decade."[8] In the 2010 *Bloomberg Businessweek* annual rankings of Most Innovative Companies, "15 of the Top 50 are Asian—up from just five in 2006. In fact, for the first time since the rankings began in 2005, the majority of corporations in the Top 25 are based outside the U.S."[9] China now requires that every college in the country teach the skills of entrepreneurship, and their current K–12 education reforms are aimed at deemphasizing standardized tests and doing more to teach creativity. So if we are to remain globally competitive in today's world, we need to produce more than just a few entrepreneurs and innovators. We need to develop the creative and enterprising capacities of all our students.

Over the last few years, the number of speeches, articles, and reports about the importance of innovation to our future, the future of countries around the world, and the future of our planet has grown exponentially. They have come from individuals and institutions of all political persuasions. Below are a few examples:

- According to a 2008 Conference Board report, "U.S. employers rate *creativity/innovation* among the top five skills that will increase in importance over the next five years, and *stimulating innovation/creativity and enabling entrepreneurship* is among the top 10 challenges of U.S. CEO's."[10]
- In a 2010 McKinsey & Company global survey, 84 percent of executives say innovation is extremely or very important to their company's growth strategy.[11]
- A 2010 report entitled "Rising Above the Gathering Storm, Revisited: Rapidly Approaching Category 5," prepared for the presidents of the National Academy of Sciences, National Academy of Engineering, and Institute of Medicine, asserts, "America's competitive position in the world now faces even greater challenges, exacerbated by the economic turmoil of the last few years and by the rapid and persistent worldwide advance of education, knowledge, innovation, investment, and industrial infrastructure." The report calls for "an urgent national dialogue to ensure the future competitiveness, innovation capacity, economic vitality, and job creation in the opening decades of this century."[12]
- In April 2011, Captain Porter and Colonel Mark Mykleby, who worked as special strategic assistants to Admiral Mike Mullen, the chairman of the Joint Chiefs of Staff at the time, published a paper about the future of US security that has gained considerable attention. They argue that we must move from a policy of containment to one of "sustainment." To increase our national security, our first priority should be "intellectual capital and a sustainable infrastructure of education, health and social services to provide for the continuing development and growth of America's youth. . . . We are losing our traditional role of innovation dominance in leading edge technologies and the sciences."[13]
- In his 2011 State of the Union address, President Obama was clear about the most urgent priorities of this country: "This is our generation's *Sputnik* moment. . . . We'll invest in biomedical research, information technology, and especially clean energy technology—an

> investment that will strengthen our security, protect our planet, and create countless new jobs for our people. . . . In America, innovation doesn't just change our lives. It's how we make a living. We need to outinnovate, outeducate and outbuild the rest of the world."[14]

Perhaps the most significant survey related to innovation was conducted in 2011 by GE, which interviewed a thousand senior business executives in twelve countries. They found that "95% of respondents believe innovation is the main lever for a more competitive national economy and 88% of respondents believe innovation is the best way to create jobs in their country." But the most stunning findings were about the *kinds* of innovation that will be most important—and the differences between the innovations of the past versus what they are likely to be in the future. A remarkable 69 percent of the respondents agreed *"today innovation is more driven by people's creativity than by high-level scientific research."* And 77 percent agreed, "*the greatest innovations of the 21st century will be those that have helped to address human needs more than those that had created the most profit . . .*"; 90 percent believe innovation to be the main lever for greener national economies; 85 percent are confident innovation will improve environmental quality; 58 percent said creative people on the team was the number one factor in helping companies innovate."[15]

One of the most compelling spokespersons for innovation is the internationally renowned inventor Dean Kamen. "Innovation is the only thing that can save our country," he told me. "Commodities made elsewhere are much cheaper. Today, we need to create intellectual property in order to create wealth. A pill that cures cancer is worth $1 million an ounce. The real value is now in the creation of ideas that are scalable, that don't consume resources, that aren't a zero-sum game. You come up with a cure for cancer; I come up with a way to create energy without pollution. We each started with one valuable idea; we each now enjoy the wealth of two ideas."

VIDEO CUE:

Kamen on What Drives the Human Spirit

Go to www.creatinginnovators.com
to watch the video.

In the midst of the growing demand for more innovative people, studies tell us that our children's creativity is on the decline. The cover of *Newsweek*'s July 10, 2010, issue was headlined "The Creativity Crisis," and the corresponding article cited research that documents the deterioration of creative capacities among young children since 1990. According to authors Po Bronson and Ashley Merryman:

> It's too early to determine conclusively why U.S. creativity scores are declining. One likely culprit is the number of hours kids now spend in front of the TV and playing videogames rather than engaging in creative activities. Another is the lack of creativity development in our schools. In effect, it's left to the luck of the draw who becomes creative: there's no concerted effort to nurture the creativity of all children.[16]

They conclude with an ominous warning: "While our creativity scores decline unchecked, the current national strategy for creativity consists of little more than praying for a Greek muse to drop by our houses. The problems we face now, and in the future, simply demand that we do more than just hope for inspiration to strike."[17]

Parents, teachers, mentors, and employers—we all have urgent work to do.

What Is Innovation?

Innovation is a hot topic these days, and many books have been and continue to be written about it. John Kao's 2007 book, *Innovation Nation:*

How America Is Losing Its Innovation Edge, Why It Matters, and What We Can Do to Get It Back, is widely cited, as are two more recent books: *Little Bets: How Breakthrough Ideas Emerge from Small Discoveries* by Peter Sims, and *Where Good Ideas Come From: The Natural History of Innovation* by Steven Johnson. These and others offer definitions of innovation that have informed my thinking. However, to develop a definition of innovation for this book, I thought it more interesting to find out how senior executives from both the for-profit and nonprofit world answer the question of what is innovation.

In a *Wall Street Journal* interview, Sir Andrew Likierman, the dean of the London Business School, which has inaugurated a new Institute of Innovation and Entrepreneurship, was asked for his definition of innovation and replied, "I don't define it technically because it's a term of art. It's about the process by which . . . new things take place. I look at innovation as an approach. However, [the institute] uses the standard definition, which is about novel and creative ways to create value through new products and services, or new business models or new processes."[18]

Rick Miller, president of Olin College of Engineering, offered this take: "Innovation may then be defined as the process of having original ideas and insights that have value, and then implementing them so that they are accepted and used by significant numbers of people. By this definition, a major innovation is one that is so successful that soon after its introduction few people can even remember what life was like before the innovation was introduced."[19]

Ellen Bowman, who recently retired as director of external relations for Procter and Gamble, told me in a recent interview that her definition of innovation is simply "creative problem solving." She said, "Problem solving without the creative element is not truly innovative." And creativity that is not applied to real world problems cannot be considered innovation either. Innovation is our lifeblood at P&G—but not just innovation for its own sake. It's about taking real needs and creating a bridge to a solution."

Brad Anderson, former CEO of Best Buy Corporation, agreed with

Bowman. "There isn't anyone that doesn't need to be a creative problem solver," he told me.

I had an opportunity to visit the Apple campus and talk to Joel Podolny, who is vice president of human resources at Apple and dean of Apple University. Joel earned a PhD in sociology from Harvard, and he has taught in both Harvard's and Stanford's business schools. Prior to joining Apple in 2008, Joel was dean of the Yale School of Management. Joel also talked about the importance of value creation.

"You can be a viable ongoing economic enterprise either because you are very good at value creation or you're really good at capturing the value that others create," Joel explained. "Succeeding through creation often requires innovation—figuring out how to put together and add value to things that just weren't there before."

Joe Caruso, a retired business executive who now coaches young entrepreneurs, observed, "Innovation doesn't have to be about creating the next iPad. It can be the way you treat a customer."

Annmarie Neal, who is chief talent officer and vice president of the Cisco Center for Collaborative Leadership, told me that leaders at Cisco Systems encourage innovation in two arenas. "At the core of the business, it is about being better, smarter, faster with our primary products and service offerings. Innovation at the edge, on the other hand, is about new business models, and new go-to-market strategies."

VIDEO CUE:

Neal on Disruptive Innovation

Go to www.creatinginnovators.com
to watch the video.

Annmarie's comments aligned with what a number of people said in interviews—that there are essentially two very different kinds of innovation in both the for-profit and nonprofit arenas: incremental and disruptive. Incremental innovation is about significantly improving existing products, processes, or services. Disruptive or transformative innovation, on the other hand, is about creating a new or fundamentally different product or service that disrupts existing markets and displaces formerly dominant technologies.

Clayton M. Christensen's seminal work, *The Innovator's Dilemma*, describes the evolution of a number of disruptive innovations, including how Sony's tiny, portable transistor radios eventually disrupted the vacuum-tube radio market dominated by Motorola and how DEC's mini computer market was eventually cannibalized by the IBM PC. In recent years, Apple has introduced at least three new products that have radically transformed the marketplace in their respective categories: the iPod, the iPhone, and now the iPad. Apple stores have transformed the retailing of high-tech products, as well. Apple's consistent ability to "disrupt" the marketplace explains why it enjoys a reputation as the most innovative company in the world.

Innovation occurs in every aspect of human endeavor. Martin Luther King is an outstanding example of a "disruptive" social innovator who successfully adapted Mahatma Gandhi's strategies of nonviolent passive resistance to the American civil rights movement, for which he was awarded the Nobel Peace Prize in 1964. More recently, Muhammad Yunus and the Grameen Bank were awarded the Nobel Peace Prize in 2006 for their work to alleviate poverty through microcredit lending. Many of the Peace Prize recipients have been social innovators who have changed the course of history.

So-called social innovation and social entrepreneurship are areas of rapidly growing interest, especially among twentysomethings. The idea for Teach For America—a radically new way to bring talented young people into teaching in high-poverty school districts—grew out of Wendy Kopp's 1989 Princeton undergraduate thesis. In 2010, forty-six thousand individuals applied to Teach For America, including 12 percent of all seniors at Ivy League schools. The number of applications was 32 percent above the previous year's.[20] And Teach For America alums have, themselves, gone on to create important new social innovations. For example, in 1994 after completing their TFA commitment, Dave Levin and Mike

Feinberg founded the Knowledge Is Power Program (KIPP), which today is the largest network of charter schools in America. KIPP has received international recognition for successfully educating economically disadvantaged minority students who would otherwise be left behind.

Leaving the problem of education aside for a moment, we clearly need both incremental and disruptive innovations going forward. Using consumption of carbon fuels as an example, we need to incrementally improve everyday products, such as building insulation and windows to significantly reduce energy use. Indeed, for Rick Hassman, director of corporate applications at Pella, continuous improvement is a passion. "Where innovation comes in," he told me, "is in figuring out the right problem to be solved, the right question to ask, and then figuring out a better way to solve the problem. You can't just come up with a solution for today's problem. Nothing stays the same."

However—important though they are—significantly improved products, services, and processes will not be enough to radically reduce our dependence on carbon fuels. Better windows will certainly help, but we will also need new green sources of energy—such as solar and wind. And all-electric vehicles will most likely be a necessary and a disruptive innovation. Shared-car-ownership models such as Zipcar and shared-ride programs such as GoLoco are examples of other kinds of economic and social innovations that are growing out of the need to reduce our carbon fuel consumption. (You will meet Robin Chase, the founder of both companies, and her husband and daughter in chapter 6 of this book.) Capital Bikeshare—a new effort that makes bikes available at more than one hundred rental stations in the nation's capital—is yet another example of a recent social innovation.

Innovation, then, comes in many forms. In my interviews with scores of twentysomething innovators, I have been stunned at the variety and imaginativeness of their many innovations. Their mastery and creative use of new media—from Facebook to YouTube to Twitter—represent entirely new ways of thinking about innovation, and indeed of fermenting and managing revolutions, as we learned in the Arab Spring of 2011.

What Are the Skills of Innovators?

In my last book, *The Global Achievement Gap*, I described the new skills all students now need for careers, continuous learning, and citizenship in an increasingly flat world.[21] I called these the Seven Survival Skills. They are:

1. Critical thinking and problem solving
2. Collaboration across networks and leading by influence
3. Agility and adaptability
4. Initiative and entrepreneurship
5. Accessing and analyzing information
6. Effective oral and written communication
7. Curiosity and imagination

Since the book's publication, I have consistently heard from leaders in the for-profit, nonprofit, and military spheres that, indeed, these are the skills that matter most in their worlds. But as I have researched what is required to be an innovator, I've come to see this list of skills as necessary but not sufficient. Curiosity and imagination are undoubtedly wellsprings of innovation. One cannot imagine any kind of innovation happening without these capabilities—as well as the other skills I outlined. However, the list doesn't touch on some of the qualities of innovators that I now understand as essential—such as perseverance, a willingness to experiment, take calculated risks, and tolerate failure, and the capacity for "design thinking," in addition to critical thinking. So let me introduce you to some new thinking on the skills of innovators.

Founded in 1991 by David Kelley, IDEO is a global design firm "that takes a human-centered, design-based approach to helping organizations in the public and private sectors innovate and grow."[22] It has been recognized as one of the most innovative companies in the world by both *Fast Company* and *BusinessWeek*. Perhaps equally important, IDEO's leadership has contributed significantly to a greater understanding of the innovation process—and the qualities or skills of highly innovative adults. David Kelley, a professor at Stanford University, also established the Hasso

Plattner Institute of Design, also known as the d.school, where teams of students and faculty learn to apply what IDEO calls "design thinking" to a range of social problems. (We will learn more about the d.school in chapter 5 of this book.) Tom Kelley, David's brother and managing director of IDEO, has written two influential books: *The Art of Innovation* and *The Ten Faces of Innovation*. And Tim Brown, who is president and CEO of IDEO, has recently written a book called *Change by Design*. IDEO's concept of "design thinking" is widely regarded as a way of viewing the world that is fundamental to any process of innovation.

VIDEO CUE:

Kelly on Innovation and Empathy at IDEO

Go to www.creatinginnovators.com
to watch the video.

In a *Harvard Business Review* article, Tim Brown described five characteristics of what he calls "design thinkers." The first is *empathy*, which is the ability to imagine the world from multiple perspectives and having an attitude that puts people first. *Integrative thinking* is to be able to see all aspects of a problem and possible breakthrough solutions. *Optimism* is also essential, Brown argues, because design thinking begins with the assumption that, no matter how challenging the problem, a solution can be found. But solutions can be achieved only through what Brown calls *experimentalism*, a process of trial and error that explores problems and possible solutions in new and creative ways. Finally, Brown writes that design thinkers are, above all, *collaborators*: "The increasing complexity of products, services, and experiences has replaced the myth of the lone creative genius with the reality of the enthusiastic interdisciplinary collaborator. The best design thinkers don't simply work alongside other disciplines; many of them have significant experience in more than one. At IDEO we employ people who are engineers and marketers, anthropologists and industrial designers, architects and psychologists."[23]

In another recent *Harvard Business Review* article, entitled "The Innovator's DNA" (and in a new book by the same title), Jeffrey H. Dyer, Hal B. Gregersen, and Clayton M. Christensen report on the results of a six-year study "to uncover the origins of creative—and often disruptive—business strategies in particularly innovative companies. . . . Our goal was to put innovative entrepreneurs under the microscope, examining when and how they came up with the ideas on which their businesses were built. We especially wanted to examine how they differ from other executives and entrepreneurs: Someone who buys a McDonald's franchise may be an entrepreneur, but building an Amazon requires different skills altogether."[24] The authors considered the habits of twenty-five innovative entrepreneurs and conducted a survey of more than three thousand executives and five hundred individuals who had started innovative companies or invented new products.

Dyer, Gregersen, and Christensen discovered that five skills separate innovative from noninnovative individuals: *associating; questioning; observing; experimenting;* and *networking*. They divide these skills into two categories: *doing* and *thinking*:

> **Doing**
>
> *Questioning* allows innovators to break out of the status quo and consider new possibilities. Through *observing,* innovators detect small behavioral details—in the activities of customers, suppliers, and other companies—that suggest new ways of doing things. In *experimenting*, they relentlessly try on new experiences and explore the world. And through *networking* with individuals from diverse backgrounds, they gain radically different perspectives.
>
> **Thinking**
>
> The four patterns of action together help innovators *associate* to cultivate new insights.[25]

To get a more "on the ground" view of the skills and dispositions of an innovator, I interviewed Judy Gilbert, who is director of talent at Google. Apple and Google are ranked number one and two on the list of most innovative companies in the world.[26] They are also the top two companies recent college graduates most want to work for—additional evidence of this generation's passion for innovation.[27] Judy's job is to think about how to "grow" the people who come to work at Google—as well as to help the company consider what kinds of skills it needs for the future.

I asked Judy to describe the most important skills Google looks for in hiring. "Of course we look for smarts," she told me. "But intellectual curiosity is more important. The person needs to be good at what we are hiring them to do—writing code or finance—but we also expect everyone to be a leader—someone who will take control of the situation versus waiting to be led. People who are successful at Google also have a bias towards action—you see something broken and you fix it. You are smart enough to spot problems, but you don't whine about them or wait for somebody else to fix them. You ask, 'How can I make things better?' And collaboration is so essential to everything that we do—we prize the ability to recognize and learn from people around you, who have very different kinds of expertise."

Can Innovation Skills Be Learned?

I am struck by the interrelationship and overlap between lists of skills identified in the two articles quoted above and what Google looks for in its employees. The "DNA" of innovators might be considered a set of skills that are essential elements in design thinking. One cannot have empathy without having practiced the skills of listening and observing. And integrative thinking begins with the ability to ask good questions and to make associations. There is also a kinship between collaboration and networking. And what all three lists have in common is the importance of experimenting—an activity that, at its root, requires a kind of optimism, a belief that through trial and error a deeper understanding and better approaches can be discovered.

Putting the research together, some of the most essential qualities of a successful innovator appear to be the following:

- curiosity, which is a habit of asking good questions and a desire to understand more deeply
- collaboration, which begins with listening to and learning from others who have perspectives and expertise that are very different from your own
- associative or integrative thinking
- a bias toward action and experimentation

But as an educator and a parent what I find most significant in this list is that *they represent a set of skills and habits of mind that can be nurtured, taught, and mentored!* Many of us tend to assume that some people are born naturally creative or innovative—and others are not. But all of the experts whom I've cited share the belief that most people can become more creative and innovative—given the right environment and opportunities. Indeed, Judy Gilbert's job is to continue to develop the capacities of Google employees to become more innovative.

Tim Brown writes, "Contrary to popular opinion, you don't need weird shoes or a black turtleneck to be a design thinker. Nor are design thinkers necessarily created only by design schools, even though most professionals have had some kind of design training. My experience is that many people outside professional design have a natural aptitude for design thinking, which the right development and experiences can unlock."[28]

Dyer, Gregersen, and Christensen agree. In the conclusion of their article, the authors argue, "Innovative entrepreneurship is not a genetic predisposition, it is an active endeavor. Apple's slogan 'Think Different' is inspiring but incomplete. We found that innovators must consistently act different to think different. By understanding, reinforcing, and modeling the innovator's DNA, companies can find ways to more successfully develop the creative spark in everyone."[29]

So DNA, then, turns out not to be the right term, after all. *It's not primarily what you are born with that makes you an innovator*—though clearly some people are born with extraordinary gifts. These authors seem to agree that *what you have learned to do is more essential.* Yes, there's nature—but there is also nurture, what the environments around us encourage and teach.

But here's the problem: It is often difficult in our society to "act differently in order to think differently." To do so requires radically altering our adult behaviors. When Dyer and Gregersen were interviewed in a blog about their research, Hal Gregersen talked about the loss of creative capacity. "If you look at 4-year-olds, they are constantly asking questions and wondering how things work. But by the time they are 6½ years old they stop asking questions because they quickly learn that teachers value the right answers more than provocative questions. High school students rarely show inquisitiveness. And by the time they're grown up and are in corporate settings, they have already had the curiosity drummed out of them. 80% of executives spend less than 20% of their time on discovering new ideas. Unless, of course, they work for a company like Apple or Google."[30]

Gregersen is hardly alone in his views. Sir Ken Robinson's recent book, *The Element*, and his TED Talks describe many of the ways curiosity and creativity are discouraged—"educated out of us," he often says. Dr. Robert Sternberg, a psychologist who has studied creativity, agrees. He writes, "Creativity is a habit. The problem is that schools sometimes treat it as a bad habit. . . . Like any habit, creativity can either be encouraged or discouraged."[31]

How Is the "Innovation Generation" Different?

A growing number of books and studies focus on the so-called Millennial Generation—and the controversy about them continues to grow, as well. Some authors claim they are the "dumbest generation" in history, and others write that they are the most innovative. I reviewed a number of these books in *The Global Achievement Gap*. Rather than do so again, I will briefly summarize the ways in which I think this generation is growing up differently and then turn to a discussion of how some business and military leaders whom I interviewed see the challenges of mentoring and managing them.

Anyone who has spent time in an elementary school classroom knows that every student starts school with unbounded imagination, curiosity, and creativity—until he or she learns that knowing the right answer is far more important that asking a thoughtful question, as Gregersen observed. What is profoundly different about today's youth, however, is that most of them have also gone to "school" on the Internet. They are the first generation to be what author Marc Prensky calls "digital natives." On average, young people between the ages of eight and eighteen now spend more time on their electronic devices than they do in classrooms.[32] And most young people today frequently find the Internet to be a far more compelling teacher than the ones who stand in front of them during the day.

Significant challenges come with the use of these new technologies, and I think the potential for misuse and excessive dependence is real and must be addressed by adults. Indeed, parents of some of the most innovative young people whom I interviewed for this book carefully monitor and limit "screen time." Nevertheless, the result of this new form of learning is that many of our youth, whom I call the Innovation Generation, have extraordinary latent talent for—and interest in—innovation and entrepreneurship, likely more than any generation in history.

On the Internet, unlike in their daytime classrooms, young people act on their curiosity. In interviews for my last book, many young people told me that they "google stuff for fun" and love following hyperlinks to see where they may lead. While some young people themselves worry about the addictive quality of Facebook, Twitter, YouTube, and so on, they have nevertheless learned to create, connect, and collaborate on the Internet—far more so than they are ever allowed to do in school. Uploading photos, videos, and music and blogging on the Internet is second nature for many in this generation. They have also been exposed to world events sooner and more vividly than any other generation in history, as a result of both television and the Internet.

Highly conscious of and concerned about a wide range of social problems and proficient in the use of technologies that enable them to learn, to express themselves, and to network, many of the Innovation Generation long to put their mark on the world. Are many of them overly ambitious and naive? Perhaps. Impatient? Definitely. But they are our future, and I believe that we must learn how to work with these extraordinary young people: learn how to parent, teach, and mentor them—and learn from them, as well.

Many of the Innovation Generation are deeply worried about the future of the planet, seek healthier lifestyles, and want to make a difference more than they want to make money. But they are swimming against the tides of tradition. A lot of parents still harbor hopes that their children will pursue prestigious careers and be economically better off than they are. Too many teachers and employers still reward the "old school" behaviors of deference to authority and striving for "success," conventionally defined—and count on carrots and sticks for motivation. The result is that many in the Innovation Generation are skeptical of adult authority and the institutions that their elders have presided over. School is a game the Innovation Generation knows they have to play to get "credentialed," but they do it with as little effort as possible. Most have no desire to climb the corporate ladder and wait twenty years to do something interesting or worthwhile. They have no patience with worksheets or busywork. They have dreams and ambitions that demand time and space—and active nurturing.

The problem is that many of us in our forties, fifties, and sixties who work in established institutions don't make time and space for the younger generation's dreams and ambitions. Leaders of conventional schools and businesses don't know what to do with this Innovation Generation. These young people have different dreams, different aspirations, from their elders.

Bob Compton, my collaborator on the videos for this book, is a high-tech venture capitalist and graduate of the Harvard Business School. He described his experiences with today's twentysomethings:

> Managing and motivating this cohort of young employees is almost overwhelmingly frustrating. All of the tools and techniques I learned at Harvard Business School, and all of my training and experience since, are ineffec-

> tive at best. What's worse, traditional motivators—stock options, commissions, bonus payments—are often counterproductive with this generation. They take offense at being managed. As one of my young employees remarked when I offered stock and bonus payments as incentive for accelerating product development, "I'm just not coin-operated, Bob." Not "coin-operated"? Well, how are you "operated"? It is still baffling to me.

Brad Anderson, who relied heavily on the skills and passions of twentysomethings to grow the Best Buy Corporation, told me he does not agree with those who say this generation is unmotivated. He, like Bob Compton, has found that they are *differently* motivated. "Lack of work ethic? That's nuts," he exclaimed. "The problem is lack of leadership. Sure, this generation is spoiled in a lot of ways. But they are looking for things to engage and interest them. Many are hyperengaged, but in order for them to commit themselves, the bar is higher. If you can get them engaged, the results are extraordinary. But if you want them to do Henry Ford assembly-line kinds of stuff—where they are expected to show up with their bodies, but not their minds—you won't engage them."

Annmarie Neal also sees this generation as differently motivated. "First, they are much more flexible. They tend to go out to ask questions versus having to have the answers. Personal branding is not about what they know, but who they know and what connections they can use to find answers. They are also more globally minded and have been exposed to more things out of the US. Finally, they are much more comfortable with collaboration. The boomers were socialized for individual achievements. It's less important to this generation. There is much more *we* in their language."

VIDEO CUE:

Neal on a Differently Motivated Generation

Go to www.creatinginnovators.com
to watch the video.

Keith Miller is manager of environmental initiatives and sustainability at 3M Corporation, which has long been recognized as one of the most innovative manufacturing companies in the world. He is also the father of two twentysomethings. "I deal with motivating this generation daily at home and at work," he told me. "Both of my children had good grades, but the learning was much more important to them. They didn't see the value in doing something just to get a better grade. Five points extra credit—why bother? My generation did things we may not have wanted to, but we did it to get ahead.

"Younger employees at the company want to have meaning in what they are doing. A lot of young people are interested in sustainability and wondering what they can do. It's a huge challenge for my generation. I came up through 3M when you had to put in your time before you got the good projects. You had to prove yourself. This generation comes in wanting to have an immediate impact. The challenge is to connect them with projects that have value and impact for the company."

Ellen Kumata, who is managing director and partner at Cambria Consulting, works closely with senior executives in Fortune 100 companies. She told me that big corporations are "really nervous about the Millennial Generation. They work differently—and are not as focused on individual achievement. They don't want to 'make it' and see themselves in multiple jobs. The real question is, will organizations be able to capture their strengths?"

Cofounder and executive director of the Technology and Entrepreneurship Center at Harvard, Paul Bottino described some of the strengths to which Ellen alluded, as well as some of the challenges of managing the Millennials: "There is a glimmer of insubordination in this generation. The belief in centralized authority has changed. In communications, they can hold their ground, make a case in a public setting, and have an ability to say, 'That's your thing, this is mine, and that's okay.'"

Leslie Andresen, a senior executive at General Dynamics, recently told me that her company's greatest challenge was how to keep the twentysomethings whom they hire. "They ask questions I never imagined asking," she said. "They want to know what they are contributing—what is the larger significance of their work. And if you can't give them a satisfying answer, they're gone."

These characteristics of the Millennials represent a particular challenge for leaders in the military. General Martin Dempsey is chairman of the Joint Chiefs of Staff of the US military. When I first met him, he was in charge of all training programs for the US Army. "We're at risk of losing this generation when they come back [from the war]," he said. "Unlike previous generations, they are unpersuaded by the twenty-year business case [the appeal of retiring at half pay after twenty years in the military]. They believe what we told them: 'Be all you can be.' They want to continue to be developed, and we must do that in order to keep them."

It isn't just employers and the military that need this generation to stay involved and to be effective. It is all of us. The Millennials are our future. They are the generation who can and must create a healthier, more secure, and sustainable way of life. While some of them might not care to admit it, they also need us in order to succeed. They need our expertise, guidance, mentoring, and support, but we have to offer our help in a new way. Our schools, our places of work, and our habits of parenting all must change if we are to actively encourage the Innovation Generation to create an economy and a way of life based on innovation—one that cultivates habits and pleasures of creative adult "play," rather than mindless consumption.

In the past, our country has produced innovators more by accident than by design. Rarely do entrepreneurs or innovators talk about how their schooling or their places of work—or even their parents—developed their talents or encouraged their aspirations. Three of the most innovative entrepreneurs of the last half century—Edwin Land, the inventor of the Polaroid instant camera; Bill Gates; and Mark Zuckerberg, founder and CEO of Facebook—had to drop out of Harvard to pursue their ideas. Apple's Steve Jobs; Michael Dell of Dell Computer; Larry Ellison, founder of the software giant Oracle; and the inventor Dean Kamen are other famous high-tech college dropouts.

So what would it mean if we were to intentionally develop the entrepreneurial and innovative talents of all young people—to nurture their initiative, curiosity, imagination, creativity, and collaborative skills, as well as their analytical abilities—along with essential qualities of character such as persistence, empathy, and a strong moral foundation? What can parents do to nurture these qualities? What do the most effective teachers and college professors do, and what can they—and the young people themselves—tell us about how schools and colleges need to change to teach these qualities? Finally, what can we learn from those who successfully mentor aspiring entrepreneurial innovators? These are the driving questions in this book.

How Do We Develop Young People to Become Innovators?

If we agree on the need to develop the capabilities of many more youth to be innovators, and if we agree that many of the qualities of an innovator can be nurtured and learned, the question now becomes, what do we do? Where do we start as parents, teachers, mentors, and employers?

I recently attended a colloquium at Olin College—a fascinating new school of engineering about which you will learn more later in this book. The invited group of business and education leaders—as well as the college's trustees—were asked by the college president, Rick Miller, to discuss the question of how to create environments that support innovators. When the question was posed by the moderator in my group, the room fell silent—until finally a senior executive at IBM said, "It's a lot easier to name the things that stifle innovation like rigid bureaucratic structures, isolation, and a high-stress work environment." Others agreed that it was easy to talk about how to kill creativity, but identifying how best to develop capacities of young people to innovate was far more difficult.

In research for this book, I explored the work of Teresa Amabile, currently professor of business administration and director of research at the Harvard Business School. Dr. Amabile's first profession was as a chemist. She subsequently returned to graduate school to complete her PhD in psychology at Stanford—and then her MBA at Harvard. For the past thirty-five years, her research has focused on topics related to creativity, productivity, and innovation. She is the author of two books and scores of published articles and book chapters.

One of her most influential articles is entitled "How to Kill Creativity." What's wonderful about the article is that Amabile goes beyond the attention-grabbing title to describe a framework for understanding creativity in the business world and the management practices that both discourage and encourage creativity. I find the framework that Amabile offers (see diagram) to be compelling for several reasons. It shows that the capacity for creativity is the result of an interrelationship among three things: expertise, creative-thinking skills, and motivation. But I think her framework is equally useful for understanding the essential elements of innovation. We can substitute the word *innovation* for *creativity* in the middle of Amabile's intersecting circles and have a useful starting point for understanding how best to develop the capacities of young innovators: [33]

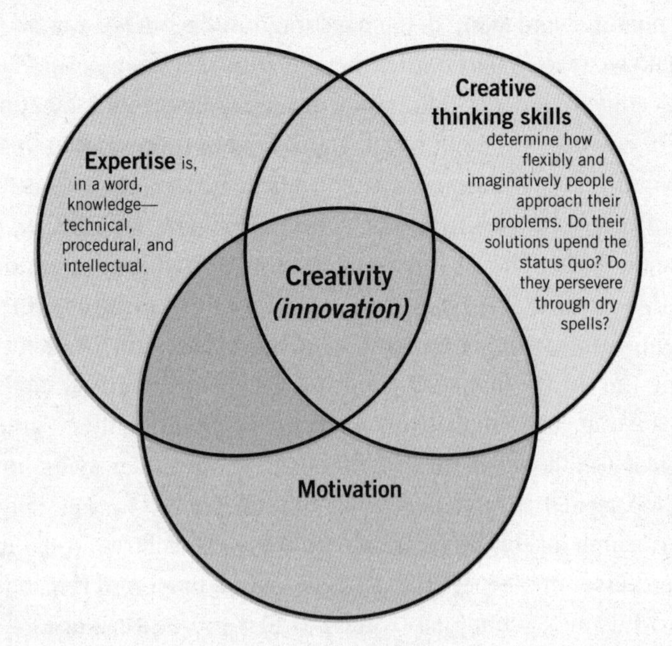
Expertise is, in a word, knowledge—technical, procedural, and intellectual.
Creative thinking skills determine how flexibly and imaginatively people approach their problems. Do their solutions upend the status quo? Do they persevere through dry spells?
Creativity (innovation)
Motivation

Expertise: You cannot innovate from nothing. You must have expertise—knowledge—though how much knowledge you need, when you need it, and how best to acquire it are important questions that we will consider later. *Creative-thinking skills:* To produce real innovations, knowledge in and of itself is necessary but not sufficient. You also need what Amabile calls "creative-thinking skills"—the innovator's skills described in this book and by Brown and Dyer, Gregersen, and Christensen that allow you to ask the right questions, make connections, observe, empathize, collaborate, and experiment. Finally, you need *motivation.*

Here's where Amabile's work gets even more interesting—even disruptive! She believes that motivation is far more important than either expertise or skills. She explains, "Expertise and creative thinking are an individual's raw materials—his or her natural resources, if you will. But a third factor—motivation—determines what people will actually do." Amabile distinguishes between *extrinsic* and *intrinsic* motivation. She writes:

> All forms of motivation do not have the same impact on creativity. In fact, it shows that there are two types of motivation—extrinsic and intrinsic, the latter being far more essential for creativity. . . . Extrinsic motivation comes from outside a person—whether the motivation is a carrot or a stick. If the scientist's boss promises to reward her financially should the blood-clotting project succeed, or if he threatens to fire her should it fail, she will certainly be motivated to find a solution. . . . Money doesn't necessarily stop people from being creative. But in many situations, it doesn't help either, especially when it leads people to feel that they are being bribed or controlled. More important, money by itself doesn't make employees passionate about their jobs.
>
> But passion and interest—a person's internal desire to do something—are what intrinsic motivation is all about. For instance, the scientist in our example would be intrinsically motivated if her work on the blood-clotting drug was sparked by an intense interest in hemophilia, a personal sense of challenge, or a drive to crack a problem that no one else has been able to solve. . . . People will be most creative when they feel motivated primarily by the interest, satisfaction, and challenge of the work itself—and not by external pressures.[34]

What is intrinsic motivation, then, and how do we encourage it? Is it merely "passion and interest," as Amabile suggests? I don't think so. My research, work as an educator, and experience as a parent suggest that there are three interrelated elements to intrinsic motivation: play, passion, and purpose. Whether—and to what extent—parents, teachers, mentors, and employers encourage these qualities makes an enormous difference in the lives of young innovators.

Play

Research shows that human beings are born with an innate desire to explore, experiment, and imagine new possibilities—in a word, to innovate. Alison Gopnik, author of *Scientist in the Crib*, *The Philosophical Baby*, and numerous other publications, is a professor of psychology at the University of California at Berkeley and is an internationally recognized leader in the study of children's learning and development. Her recent research and the work of other cognitive scientists whose work she draws on "demonstrates that babies and very young children know, observe, explore, imagine and learn more than we would ever have thought possible."[35] She writes:

> We've found out that even very young children can already consider possibilities, distinguish them from reality, and even use them to change the world. They can imagine different ways the world might be in the future and use them to create plans. They can imagine different ways the world might have been in the past, and reflect on past possibilities. And, most dramatically, they can create completely imaginary worlds, wild fictions, and striking pretenses.
>
> Conventional wisdom suggests that knowledge and imagination, science and fantasy, are deeply different from one another—even opposites. But the new ideas . . . show that exactly the same abilities that let children learn so much about the world also allow them to change the world—to bring new worlds into existence—and to imagine alternative worlds that

> may never exist at all. Children's brains create causal theories of the world, maps of how the world works. And these theories allow children to envisage new possibilities, and to imagine and pretend that the world is different.[36]

How do children learn such skills? In a word—through play.

What do you suppose the founders of Google, Larry Page and Sergey Brin; Amazon's founder and CEO, Jeff Bezos; Wikipedia founder Jimmy Wales; Julia Child; and rapper Sean "P. Diddy" Combs all have in common? Gregersen's research, cited earlier, uncovered an extraordinary commonality among some of the most innovative individuals: they all went to Montessori schools, where they learned through play. The research about the importance of play in children's development spans many decades. In the twentieth century, Maria Montessori, Lev Vygotsky, Jean Piaget, and others did groundbreaking research on the ways in which children learn through play. Montessori integrated her understanding of the importance of play into her curriculum for schools. Today, Montessori schools can be found around the world.

And it's not just infants and children who learn through play. Joost Bonsen, who is an alumnus of the Massachusetts Institute of Technology and currently serves as a lecturer in the world-famous MIT Media Lab, talked about the importance of the famous tradition of pranks at the university.

"Being innovative is central to being human," Bonsen told me. "We're curious and playful animals, until it's pounded out of us. Look at the tradition of pranks here at MIT. What did it take to put a police car on a dome that was fifteen stories high [one of most famous MIT student pranks], with a locked trapdoor being the only access? It was an incredible engineering feat: They had to fabricate the car, get it to the base of the dome without getting caught—and then the real challenge was to get it to the top of the dome, and get yourself down without getting caught or hurting yourself. In addition to everything else, you had to track security, create diversions. To pull that off was a systems problem, and it took tremendous leadership and teamwork.

"Pranks reinforce the cultural ethos of creative joy," Joost added. "Getting something done in a short period of time with no budget, and challenging circumstances. It's glorious and epic. They didn't ask for permission. Not even forgiveness."

These students were playing—just doing something for the fun of it. Play, then, is part of our human nature and an intrinsic motivation.

VIDEO CUE:

MIT Pranks, Hacks, and Creativity

Go to www.creatinginnovators.com
to watch the video.

Passion

Passion is familiar to all of us as an intrinsic motivation for doing things. The passion to explore, to learn something new, to understand something more deeply; the passion to master something difficult. We see these passions in others all around us and have likely experienced them for ourselves.

Malcolm Gladwell, in his recent book *The Outliers*, writes about the importance of working at something for ten thousand hours in order to achieve mastery—or, in Amabile's framework, expertise. He describes the circumstances that enabled famous innovators—or outliers, as he calls them—to achieve their breakthroughs. But he doesn't talk about motivation. What drove a young Bill Gates or a Steve Jobs—or more recently a Mark Zuckerberg—to put in the ten thousand–plus hours that they did as young people to achieve a level of mastery? None of them had a "tiger mom"—author Amy Chua's description of herself as a mother—who threatened and bribed them to stay up night after night learning to write computer code. What they had was passion.

When asked his advice for young entrepreneurs in a Smithsonian oral history interview, Steve Jobs said, "A lot of people come to me and say, 'I want to be an entrepreneur.' And I go, 'Oh, that's great, what's your idea?' And they say, 'I don't have one yet.' And I say, 'I think you should go get a job as a busboy or something until you find something you're really passionate about because it's a lot of work.' I'm convinced that about half of what separates the successful entrepreneurs from the nonsuccessful ones is pure perseverance. . . . So you've got to have an idea, or a problem or a wrong that you want to right that you're passionate about; otherwise, you're not going to have the perseverance to stick it through."[37]

In more than one hundred and fifty interviews for this book—lengthy conversations with scores of innovators and their parents, teachers, and mentors—*passion* was the most frequently recurring word.

Purpose

Daniel Pink, author of the book *Drive,* writes about the importance of autonomy, mastery, and purpose as essential human motivations. He distrusts the word *passion* as suggesting something that is fleeting or driven mainly by emotions. For every positive example of a passion, we can likely site examples where the pursuit of a passion led to serious trouble.

Pink is partially right, I think. Pure passion, by itself, is not enough to sustain the motivation to do difficult things and to persevere—in love or in work! In my research, I observe that young innovators almost invariably develop a passion to learn or do something as adolescents, but their passions evolve through learning and exploration into something far deeper, more sustainable, and trustworthy—purpose.

The sense of purpose can take many forms. But the one that emerged most frequently in my interviews and in the interviews by the authors of "the Innovator's DNA" is the desire to somehow "make a difference":

> Throughout our research, we were struck by the consistency of language that innovators use to describe their motives. Jeff Bezos wants to "make history," Steve Jobs to "put a ding in the universe," Skype cofounder Niklas Zennström to "be disruptive, but in the cause of making the world a better place.". . . Embracing a mission for change makes it much easier to take risks and make mistakes.[38]

In the lives of young innovators whom I interviewed, I discovered a consistent link and developmental arc in their progression from play to passion to purpose. These young people played a great deal—but their play was frequently far less structured than most children's, and they had opportunities to explore, experiment, and discover through trial and error—to take risks and to fall down. Through this kind of more creative play as children, these young innovators discovered a passion—often as young adolescents. As they pursued their passions, though, their interests changed and took surprising turns. They developed new passions, which, over time, evolved into a deeper and more mature sense of purpose—a kind of shared adult play.

Throughout this journey from play to passion to purpose, they learned what Amabile calls "creative thinking skills" and gained real "expertise," but most often in ways that encouraged intrinsic motivation. They also learned the importance of taking certain risks and persevering—and why IDEO's motto of "fail early and fail often" is so important. When asked about the role of failure in his learning, one Olin College engineering student said, "I don't think about failure—I think about iterating."

But these young innovators did not learn these things alone. They received help from parents, teachers, and mentors along the way. Their evolution as innovators was almost invariably facilitated by at least one adult—and often several. What these parents, teachers, and mentors did that was so helpful may surprise you. Each of these adults, in his or her own quiet way, is often following a different, less conventional path in his or her role as a parent, teacher, or mentor. They acted differently so that the young people with whom they interacted could think differently.

In chapter 2, we take an in-depth look at what "creates" an innovator: the parenting, teaching, and mentoring practices that mattered most for a remarkable young person. We shall see if the framework I've proposed for understanding what is important in the development of an innovator holds up.

Chapter Two

Portrait of the Innovator as a Young Man

So what goes into the "creating" of a young innovator who becomes a product manager for Apple's first iPhone? How do you parent such a child? What and how do you teach such a young person? What are the most important influences in a young innovator's life that develop the capacity to make new things? And what might we learn from a close look at a portrait of the innovator as a young man? These are some of the questions we will explore in the following pages.

VIDEO CUE:

Introduction to Kirk Phelps

Go to www.creatinginnovators.com
to watch the video.

Kirk Phelps is a high school *and* a college dropout. Kirk left Phillips Exeter Academy (an elite private boarding school in New Hampshire) at the end of his eleventh-grade year to pursue his passion for science at Stanford University, then left Stanford a few credits shy of earning both a BS and an MS degree to work on the first iPhone for Apple. Now, at age twenty-nine, he's working for a start-up company, SunRun, that wants to transform the way electric power is generated and sold in this country.

Reflecting on his education in our recent conversation, Kirk said, "What you study is not that important. Knowing how to find those things you are interested in is way, way more important. . . . I've got this momentum, and the idea is to figure out what interesting opportunities there are around you and use them to get to the next point. It's like how I would imagine navigating a satellite through space. You're headed off with a velocity, and, oh, there's a planet over there. I'm going to orbit it a couple of times, and then shoot off somewhere else. How to pick the things you are bouncing off of is really about integration—integration at a personal level. What do I like, what tools do I want to add to my toolbox, and how can I use my current velocity and heading to go in a new interesting direction.

"It's a good analogy for how my parents supported me," Kirk added. "Here's what he's interested in *now*—he has a velocity and a heading. That's what matters."

Parenting an Innovator

R. Cord Phelps and Lea Phelps, Kirk's parents, have always been very intentional about their children's learning, but their involvement went way beyond merely choosing summer programs and schools for their kids and talking with their teachers a few times a year. They took a kind of evidence-based, trial-and-error approach to parenting.

"Kirk is the oldest of four, and he experienced firsthand all of our mistakes," Cord Phelps explained to me one weekend afternoon several months after I'd met Kirk. (After a career at Hewlett-Packard where he worked in information technology, Cord is now involved in a health-care start-up.)

"We tried to put them in as many situations as possible related to their interests. Almost like moving them through a buffet of opportunities. Try this, if you don't like it, you might like this over here."

"What were some of Kirk's buffet items?" I asked.

"Being involved in soccer at a young age was one. He had some interest and obviously had some skill. I saw that there was an interesting path to take that corresponded with a couple of objectives I had—one was to get our children out of their privileged enclave. So rather than enroll Kirk in the suburban soccer league near us, we went down to a blue-collar neighborhood, where everyone spoke Spanish, and Kirk played in their league. It gave Kirk an opportunity to become involved to a limited extent in another culture. I didn't care if he was on a winning team or even a starter—I just wanted him to develop his interest in sports and to experience other kinds of people."

"What about his early school years?"

"Of course, we wanted the best schools and teachers for our kids, and so we went down the private-school path. We quickly realized that it would serve a lot of Kirk's needs, but also that there were real limitations. I bought a whiteboard and put it up in this space we called 'the homework room,' which had a big table they could all work around. I imagined myself as this prescient teacher—that I could probably do a better job than the system could—that was my pipe dream. I played the role of teacher and made them cry. I realized that I was a terrible teacher and backed off that. It lasted for a week.

"I was always experimenting—I saw what the school was offering, but I was wondering how can I improve it—augment, enhance. I was always tinkering.

"One of my real interests since college has been American history. I've always been fascinated with the two renaissance periods in our history—the 1850s and the 1960s. When Kirk was young, I was obsessing about *Moby-Dick, Robinson Crusoe,* Jack Kerouac, Alfred Hitchcock, Jimi Hendrix. I talked to my kids about those books, about the ideas. I had them listen to Jimi Hendrix.

"At one point about nine years ago, we were all going to take a trip to New York. And I thought this would be great for them. I would take them to Ellis Island, where my wife's family came in from Italy. We're going to go to the World Trade Center site; we're going to go see Yankees and Mets games; we're going to see *Oklahoma* and *Les Misérables.* I had this thought that as a history teacher I could help them understand what it means to be an American.

"In preparation for the trip, I tortured them by reading them bits of *Les Misérables,* I talked to them about the Oklahoma land rush, I talked to them about integration. I was just trying to do my best in preparing them for this really exciting trip."

"So what finally happened on the trip?"

"It was hugely successful at Ellis Island, somber at the World Trade Center. The Mets and Yankees games were fantastic. *Oklahoma* they couldn't tolerate; *Les Misérables* they had a hard time with—I was enthralled with Jean Valjean, they were not!

"Mixed results, but maybe that's my style of being in a parent," Cord reflected. "You do what you can to discover how the black box works, and sometimes you hit a dead end and need to turn around.

"I had a lot of books about incredibly creative people around the house. Kirk devoured them. A couple about Richard Feynman, the physicist at Caltech; a book called *Drawing on the Right Side of the Brain,* about creativity; another called *Art and Physics;* and another, *Mathematics and the Imagination,* which had some great puzzles and ways to think about problem solving; my *Beowulf*; *Teaching the Buddha.* Kirk would read pretty much anything I gave him. He was always walking around with a book.

"None of the kids really had a problem with their homework or getting their homework done. We never had to stand over them."

"What made you decide to send Kirk to Exeter?"

"That again was a struggle for us to decide the right thing to do—Kirk being our firstborn. A teacher I knew was touting their science program—they were building a new science building with gazillions of dollars of resources that went into science. Kirk's interest in science was well developed by then—he'd been helping out in research labs in the summers at Stanford. He was just cleaning beakers and doing other trivial tasks in the labs, but it was hugely satisfying and awakening for him. Because of his interest in science, we thought Exeter was a good idea from an academic perspective, but we were incredibly torn. We wondered whether this meant our role as parents was over, and that we can't really contribute to his development anymore.

"Looking at the problem from multiple sides, we thought he could go to Exeter, but there was nothing to say that we couldn't go with him. At the time I was doing a lot of traveling for my work, my boss said it didn't matter where I was based, so we went to live in Exeter, New Hampshire, for his freshman year.

"We rented a house just down the street, and we all experienced New Hampshire for a year. The other kids went to the local school. Weekends Kirk came off campus, and so he was almost like a day student, but he wasn't a day student—he was living a couple blocks away in the dorm.

"We started getting this close-up, magnified look at Exeter, and we began to realize that maybe the stuff about private schools is not necessarily true. We began to question whether the system was the right one or whether it was fulfilling its objective to help Kirk discover what was truly interesting to him. Their approach to science was not very creative—far too rote.

"Every class had a path that they are trying to take you on. They tout the Harkness method [a Socratic approach to learning, where students sit together with the teacher at a large oval table],[1] but there was not too much innovation in thinking about the objectives of the classes. Even though there was good dialogue through the Harkness model, at the end of the day the results of the class were pretty predictable."

Lea Phelps, Cord's wife and Kirk's mother, joined the conversation now and explained why Kirk left Exeter to go to Stanford at the end of his junior year. "Kirk felt that it was a fairly rigid curriculum that didn't really allow for much innovation or for him to go as fast as he wanted to go. He had already completed all of his required courses and was ready to move on. He wasn't feeling challenged."

When I'd talked to Kirk previously, he'd offered a slightly different explanation. "I was really interested in biochemistry then. I thought I wanted to be a scientist. I was taking all the classes that I could there, playing on two varsity sports teams, and I wanted to do more. The school had unbelievable resources for high-school-age science students. There was another science class that I wanted to take during a free period in my schedule, and they wouldn't let me do it. At the time, I was being my indignant high school self and I thought that was unjust. So I applied to Stanford and got in and left."

"Exeter was very offended," Lea told me. "They threw every roadblock in front of him. They did not want him to leave because they thought it was a commentary on them. They did not want the colleges to think that there was a child who was bored at Exeter. They said, 'Oh, he'll never get into Stanford.'"

In fact, after completing eleventh grade at Exeter, Kirk was admitted to Stanford without his high school diploma for a combined bachelor of science and master of science degree program. Kirk then ended up leaving Stanford as well—just two courses shy of receiving both his MS and BS degrees.

Very different from most middle-class parents with children enrolled in elite institutions I'd encountered, Kirk's parents supported his unconventional and seemingly risky decisions to drop out of both high school and college. I asked Cord and Lea if they sometimes felt they were going "against the grain" as parents. "Most parents I know would have told their children to stop complaining, buckle down, and do what they have to in order to complete their degree," I elaborated.

"We always kind of thought we were doing things differently," Lea replied. "We always went to bed very early. We had a regular, extremely early bedtime for the kids until seventh or eighth grade. And when they weren't doing school, they had a lot of outside, unstructured time. A child has to get bored before he can figure out how to get himself out of boredom, and a lot of that happens out of doors. Other mothers scheduled their kids into all sorts of activities. Our kids spent a lot of time outdoors—making things, kicking balls, climbing trees. Other kids would flock to our house and act surprised: "You're playing outside!" A lot of them were inside their houses with nannies, playing with computers, and I remember neighborhood kids thinking our house was really different.

"Another thing that we did which was very different was to have an hour of enforced free reading a day. The kids have said to us that they're going to do that with their kids because it was such an amazing thing. We did it no matter how much schoolwork they had—always a quiet hour of reading, with a book that had nothing to do with schoolwork."

"Part of the reason why we did this was that we wanted to create an alternative to the pressures of school where teachers were always saying memorize that, do these problems. It's different when you can pick something up that you've chosen and move at your own pace," Cord explained.

"What about TV?" I wondered.

Cord laughed. "I tried to get them to watch soccer on the Spanish-speaking TV station on Sunday mornings, but that was not one of my more successful experiments."

"On Friday nights, we had something called TGIF, where after the sun went down, we would make popcorn and all sit on the couch and watch two or three shows together," Lea said.

"As a mother, I believe the combination of out-of-doors, unstructured time, where you have to figure out how to entertain yourself without a lot of bought toys, and reading on a regular basis are extremely important to children's development. LEGOs kits were important to them, as well, but I think parents need to take away all the mindless toys, all the latest and greatest things—like a PlayStation or Xbox—that kids are passively doing on the computer and say, 'Okay, go outside.' Of course, we were fortunate enough to live in a place where kids could get outside. I realize lots of kids don't have the opportunities ours had."

Lea continued, "On weekends, a lot of parents would go out and play tennis or golf with their friends. But we really loved being with our kids. That was another thing that was different. A lot of parents didn't seem to think it was very much fun to hang out with their kids, and we did.

"Parents with all the best intentions sign their kids up for the 'right' activities and get them in the 'best' schools. For me the piece that a lot of parents are missing is the quantity of time that they spend with their kids. It's important that when a child speaks, there is an adult who listens, when they look out, there is someone looking back at them. We didn't think of spending time with the kids as a sacrifice. We just found our kids to be very interesting human beings, and we spent a lot of time with them. A lot of people undervalue that. When the kids were young, I started a company, and I bought into the idea of 'quality time' for a while: I'm going to come home and spend forty-five minutes of quality time, but a child is not going to give you quality time unless you have already put in the quantity."

Play

How did Kirk come to understand that "knowing how to find those things you are interested in is way, way more important" than the specific things you study? I am struck by how Kirk's parents considered play an essential element of childhood. Lea and Cord gave their children a great deal of structure and clear rules related to reading time, screen time, and bedtime. But they were adamant about children using playtime as an unstructured opportunity to discover, explore, and experiment. And while they insisted on the structure of an hour a day of reading, the choice of what to read was the children's to make—so long as it wasn't schoolwork.

Unlike many of her neighbors, Lea chose not to fill up her children's out-of-school time with additional classes and lessons, preferring that they have more unsupervised time playing outside. Lea believed that children needed to learn to entertain themselves. The choice of toys—LEGO blocks, which allow you to build anything you can dream up, versus video games, which require no imagination—also reflects the parents' belief in the value of free-form play.

Cord contributed to his children's "play" by exposing them to lots of different and new things. He choose a Hispanic soccer program in a working-class neighborhood over the one that was closer in his suburban "enclave"—as he called it—to expose Kirk to another culture and language. He gave Kirk a wide variety of very different kinds of books to dip into and to explore. The way Cord prepared the children for the trip to New York also shows how he intentionally and methodically exposed them to new ideas and experiences. Cord talked about putting a "buffet" of opportunities in front of his children—not just to entertain them, but to help them, and him as a dad, discover what most interested them: what was in the "black box," as Cord said. In other words, what truly and intrinsically interested and motivated them.

But to be clear, Cord and Lea did not tell their children to "run along and play" as a way to get them out from underfoot. There was nothing indulgent or lackadaisical about their encouragement of their children's play. To the contrary, they clearly enjoyed their children's company and cherished their family playtime.

For parents to give children more unstructured, unsupervised playtime is to take a risk. Many parents worry about the potential for an accident—their kids will climb a tree that's too high, fall out and lose a tooth or break an arm. Or they may poke an eye out playing with a stick. Or far worse—that someone will come along and snatch their child. As a parent of three children and now with two grandchildren, I deeply empathize with those fears. But I think that what we learn from Cord and Lea is that the potential advantage of giving children more free playtime is worth the risk. Not only did Kirk learn what his interests were and how to pursue them, I think he also learned self-confidence. He learned to trust and to follow his instincts—perhaps one of the most important qualities of an innovator.

That self-confidence did not come just through play. Cord and Lea radiated confidence in their children. I asked the Phelpses how they thought about Kirk's future—were they concerned that he was now involved in a risky start-up business?

"Both Cord and I grew up back East—Rye and Greenwich," Lea explained. "And the thinking is very different out here, where there are many more ways to be creative, many paths to success.

"A few years ago, Kirk said to me, 'You know, we make the pie here on the West Coast, and back East they just cut it up into pieces. I'm not interested in cutting up the pie. I'm always going to want to *make* the pie.'"

From Passion to Purpose

Where and how did Kirk learn that "making the pie" versus merely cutting it up was his calling? How did his youthful passion for science morph and evolve into what he's doing now? I talked to Kirk about why he went to Stanford, his years there, and what he calls his "transformational experience" that set him on a clear path.

"My parents were very encouraging of me to do things outside of school that were related to my intellectual interests. I was way too serious in high school, but that was what I wanted at the time, and so they were really focused on helping me to be creative and think outside of the constraints of the academic environment—either to reform it in a way that worked for me or to find opportunities outside. When I wanted to take an additional science class at Exeter, as an example, they completely supported me. But they didn't care all that much about *what* I was interested in; they were far more interested *in the process* of my finding out what it was that I was interested in.

"When kids think about creation generally, first thoughts are often about explorers and scientists. When I was young, I just wanted to create stuff—I liked the idea of creation—to me that meant being a scientist. I identified as a science person, and I spent my entire elementary-school and junior-high experience learning as much as I could about science. But when I got to college, I realized I wasn't really a scientist. The more solitary aspects of thinking deeply about problems and designing experiments weren't really what turned me on. It was more the collaborative 'let's go build something' aspects that I liked. Very early on in my Stanford career, I realized that's what engineering was.

"I didn't know what kind of engineer I wanted to be. So I picked computer science because it seemed like the most general-purpose tool that I could use to solve a lot of different problems, but I was really a closet mechanical and electrical engineer. I could never see myself wanting to write code for Google. Writing code on a server that no one will ever see and no one will ever interact with didn't really appeal to me. I wanted to create products for people that they could hold and use.

"I was looking for ways to teach myself about that, so I started exploring robotics. I worked on surgical robotics in the labs at Stanford's computer science department and in Italy.

"For my master's degree, I took mostly mechanical and electrical engineering classes, and that was where I found the embedded systems design sequence of classes, called Smart Product Design, which was the turning point in my academic career—or my 'project career,' as I like to think about it. Smart Product Design basically means robot building.

"These classes were formed to teach mechanical engineers enough electrical and software engineering so that they could build embedded systems. An embedded system is anything that is a computer that doesn't sit on your desk: your car, an airplane, an electric toothbrush—all these things that are fundamentally computers, but take physical forms that are specific to the task.

"The courses are the longest and hardest sequence in Stanford's engineering program—not because they are intellectually the deepest, but because the classes require the most dedication. You have to really want it.

"The classes were transformational for me not because of the content, but because of the people process. Up until that time, my experience in Stanford engineering had been solitary—especially in computer science. You go write this code, but you couldn't be any further from the reality of real-world engineering. Real-world engineering is all about teams: How do I solve a political problem, a social problem, and a technical problem all together to deliver something.

"I've never been the deepest person in the room or even the smartest person in the room, but I'd discovered that where I wanted to add value was at the intersection of things. Being a PhD never appealed to me. I never wanted to spend five years becoming really deep in one area. I wanted to find ways to add value at the margins. What that means practically in engineering is being an integration engineer—you're going to bring these pieces together to create a product. This class was great for me because I got to work in teams on these multidisciplinary problems that required bringing together a set of tools to create a solution.

"So taking the classes was really important, but in looking back on it, what happened afterwards was even more important in setting me on the path that I'm on today. I was asked to be a TA [teaching assistant] for the class the next year. It was that experience that enabled me to set a vision for myself. It was also how Apple found me.

"I really liked the process of helping people understand an ill-defined problem and put some structure around how they could potentially solve it. Being a teacher in this integration-project class is the closest you get to real-world engineering in an academic environment. All of the people I ended up hiring at Apple were former TAs from these classes."

In chapter 1, we explored the importance of intrinsic motivation as an essential aspect of the desire to create and to innovate. I suggested that the developmental arc of moving from childhood *play*, to adolescent *passion*, to adult *purpose* was fundamental in the development of intrinsic motivation. As a child, Kirk was encouraged to explore and to discover the world and what most interested him through *play*. Along the way, he developed a *passion* for science—and for creating things. But what was important, I think, is that his parents did not then assume that he would become a scientist and try to manage him toward a career, as I've seen many parents of precocious children do. They continued to encourage him to explore. As Kirk said of his parents, "they didn't care all that much about *what* I was interested in; they were far more interested *in the process* of my finding out what it was that I was interested in."

I think it was this constant encouragement to pursue his interests that allowed Kirk's passion to evolve through his college years. He discovered that science wasn't really his passion, then tried computer science, and that didn't quite fit him either. Finally, through this remarkable sequence of courses called Smart Product Design, he discovered a new passion—to work with others to make tangible things. And, it seems to me, it was the experience of being a teaching assistant that allowed his passion to blossom into a deeper sense of *purpose*.

This sense of inner purpose and intrinsic motivation continued to develop and deepen through his experience working at Apple. What's fascinating about Kirk's Apple story is that it is both a profile of a purpose-driven individual who is developing his capacities and a company that seems to build the demand for innovation into the designing and manufacturing of a new product by intentionally creating conflict. The story that follows sheds light, I think, on the culture of one of the most innovative companies in the world, the skills that Kirk needed to succeed in that environment, and how he grew as a result of the demands placed on him.

Creating the iPhone

"The opportunity to be a part of the first iPhone team at Apple came through an alum of the Smart Design class," Kirk told me. "The class created a kind of supernode—a network of people who are unusually good at creating or training people who have affected the world positively. People who come to this program from all over the engineering school do it because they want to create, and they want to create in groups, and they want to create now.

"The common thread between what I did at Stanford in Smart Product Design classes and what I did at Apple was that in both environments people made irrational sacrifices. In both places, people worked incredibly hard, not because of any compensation package, but because they believed in what they were doing.

"The day I signed at Apple, they sent me a plane ticket. My first day on the job I was in Osaka. By the end of my first year at Apple, I had three hundred thousand frequent-flier miles to China and Japan, and I'd lost ten pounds. And I was a pretty lean guy to begin with.

"It was a really rough job. My team and I were making sacrifices that most people would not consider making. If I'd had a plant, it would have died; if I'd had a dog, it would have run away; if I'd had a girlfriend, she would've dumped me. It was the same for the rest of the team, but it was what we wanted at the time.

"If you are leading a team that makes those kinds of sacrifices, you've got to understand what makes them tick and support them in a way that addresses their fears. I wish I'd paid more attention to developing that side of my personality earlier—the political and social side. But the problem is that places like Exeter are not very useful for developing those capabilities.

"As a product manager, it's not your job to execute the product. It's your job to understand constraints and define the problem in a way that allows the team to understand what those constraints are, and then make cold-blooded, unemotional, and precise trade-offs. In order to facilitate that process, you need someone who is multilingual—someone who wants to understand lots of things and how they come together.

"The only reason I could do my job as a product manager at Apple was that I could talk to the optical engineers, the mechanical engineers, and the electrical engineers, and the firmware guys; the industrial designers, the packaging engineers. I couldn't do any of these guys' jobs, but I knew enough about what they did to have an intelligent conversation and to represent their interests when things were inevitably in conflict.

"Conflict resolution is fundamental to what it means to do good product. A lot of companies that are supposedly innovative still don't make great products. It's because they believe that in order to create new products, you have to remove constraints. But without constraints, you have no forcing function, which makes you think deeply to simplify—and to innovate.

"This is what Apple does better than anyone else in the world. Creativity is more a commodity than you think. Apple is not successful just because it has the ability to conceptualize new products better than anybody else. It's because they have an engineering and design process that's all about creating conflict."

"Can you give me an example of what you mean by conflict?"

"Every part of the design and engineering of the iPhone involves conflict. I will tell you about the first one. iPhones have a dimension that early in the process was identified as critical—and that's the distance between the edge of phone and the edge of the display. The display going almost to the edge makes it look as though the entire phone is nothing but display. It makes it look magical.

"Bringing the edge of the phone as close as possible to the display was enormously difficult. Glass breaks from preexisting micro-cracks in the edges. If you want to bring the display to the edge of a device, you have to have a strong display. How you build a strong display is by having really clean edges. One of my first tasks at Apple was to work with display suppliers to understand how they could make cleaner cuts in the glass.

"When we told them that's what we needed, they looked at us like we were crazy. No one else had ever asked them to do that before. Japanese display vendors were convinced of their own awesomeness—and they are some of the best engineers in the world, but they were offended: 'Why are you asking me about this? It's not your business.'

"But Apple makes it their business to know the business of all their suppliers. Their products are always at the bleeding edge of what is possible because Apple doesn't take the word from vendors. You go ask a vendor, 'What's the best you can do?' And then Apple says, 'Let's try to do twenty-five times better than that, and here's how we think we can do it.'

"The only way you can push the suppliers to do more is that you have enabled young punks like me who go around saying, 'What if we do it this way or that way?' I tell this story because it begins with a very high level goal—a very senior-executive-level goal—to create this really thin border. Invariably that creates conflict. Step one is learning more about the display supply chain than anyone else in the industry.

"But the goal of having the display very close to the edge of the device created another problem—it's going to be impacted when you drop the device. So now the conflict was, how do you build a device that's strong enough to protect the glass? The solution was to put stainless steel around the rim.

"Other technology companies will never build a part like that because that one part costs more than most people's phones—and people believed it couldn't be done in volume. Apple said, 'Screw that, we're going to buy an army of CNC machines and use that advantage to create products that no one else can create.' [A CNC is a machine tool that uses computer programs to automatically execute a series of machining operations.] They spent six months buying every CNC milling machine of the type they needed in the world. The existence of those CNC machines also enabled Apple to build unibody Mac laptops—which no one else builds, still.

"Apple has big dreams, and they buy strategic capability so they can execute products that no one else can execute. Imagine that you are [a senior executive] sitting in the C-suite of a technology company. Job one is knowing what's cheap and keeping it cheap. That's why most smartphones are made out of plastic. The executive's job is to come in and say, 'That design is not cheap enough.' The job of an executive at Apple is knowing what is great, what's best for the product, and making it cheap.

"Of course, there is a huge amount of great engineering and design in the iPhone, but it's enabled by an executive who saw his job as not just cost reduction—but building great products. My team developed the first glass-front products, but that's only because Apple was willing to spend an inordinate amount of effort, time, and money figuring out how to cut and paint and strengthen glass.

"Everyone in the organization understands Apple's core values about building great products. And people at Apple have beliefs about what defines greatness in Apple's products. All the conflict and conflict resolution stems from that vision. So you can have Engineering go out there and advocate for building stainless parts that cost more than people's phones and Operations isn't happy about it, but there's a conflict-resolution process that enables the values of the organization to get expressed in the way decisions are made and the way people work together."

Teaching an Innovator

The turning point in Kirk's young life was the Smart Product Design class, as we heard him say. The set of experiences he had in these classes helped him develop his sense of purpose, learn new skills, land a job at Apple, and succeed there. I wanted to know more about these courses. But I discovered it wasn't so much the classes as the person who taught them that had made the real difference in Kirk's life—and in the lives of many other young innovators. "Ed Carryer was both my teacher and my mentor," Kirk told me.

"There was a joke about our Smart Design Class. If Ed wanted to go to Mars, he'd shine his Batman light into the sky, and his alums would come from all over the world, and he'd be on Mars in six months. Hands down, he's the best teacher at Stanford. He and his classes were seminal points of my college education.

"He's an interesting character at Stanford. He's not a research professor. Research universities tend to look down on people like Ed. They think about these guys as trade school guys. His class was about how to build stuff, nothing truly academic about it, but he creates more value than the research guys. Name any significant company in Silicon Valley, and in two degrees of separation you'd find your way back to his program at Stanford—Tesla Motors, many people from the Apple team, the list goes on and on—all people who are driving product creation in the valley. He's been teaching the class for twenty years. Yet he struggles for funding every year—scrounging around for donations from alums to keep the program alive. He's completely unsupported by the academic culture."

Ed Carryer is director of the Smart Product Design Laboratory (SPDL) in the Design Division of Mechanical Engineering at Stanford University. His title is consulting professor. He received a BSE from the Illinois Institute of Technology in 1975, then worked in industry until 1986, when he came to Stanford, graduating with a PhD in mechanical engineering in 1992. His industry experience is widely varied. He's designed water-treatment facilities for coal and nuclear power plants and the electric controller for the Arctic Heated Glove under contract to NASA. He also spent eight years in Detroit working in the auto industry on electronic engine-control systems and continues to have an active design consultancy.

"The Smart Product Design Lab is a place where mechanical engineers—predominantly master's degree students—learn about a field called mechatronics, which is at the intersection of mechanical engineering, electrical engineering, and computer science," Ed explained to me.

"The majority of the students in my classes are mechanical engineering students who need to learn about electronics and software. There are a few students, like Kirk, who come in with a computer science background and are interested in applying computer science in a less traditional way—in embedded systems and products."

"What do you do in your class?" I asked.

"My goal is to empower them. I want them to feel like they've taken command of a body of material and can do things with it. We have lectures, and they are jam-packed—always overflowing—but the real learning goes on when they get into the lab, where they have to actually apply what they have been hearing and reading about—build circuits, write software, make it work. And most importantly integrate all of these pieces together. I take a very hands-on, application-oriented approach to the material.

"The integration part really happens in open-ended team projects that are part of the three courses that are the core of the master's sequence in Smart Product Design. The projects get incrementally more complex and take up a larger and larger fraction of the time in the class. As they learn more, they can take on more challenging tasks."

"Can you give me an example of some of the kinds of projects students have done?"

"By the time students get to the third class in the sequence, they are ready to use multiple processors and focus more on wireless communications between an interaction device and an action device. So last semester the theme of the project was 'the world's most dangerous job.' It turns out that crab fishing is incredibly dangerous on a per capita basis.

"The students built crab boats and remote controllers for these boats. We put 'crab pots' in a pond right next to our lab. Each crab pot had an RFID [radio frequency identification] tag, so the boat had to go up and communicate with the RFID reader to find out how many crabs there were in each pot. Then they had to harvest the crabs and go back to the dock and unload their catch.

"There are always options for teams to compete—though winning doesn't in any way affect their grades. So in this class if your boat got swamped—that is, got water into the water sensor that was in each boat—you had to go back to the dock and get repaired. One team called themselves Greenpeace. They decided to not play the competition of how many crabs you could catch at all. Instead, they went around to the pots and, after filling their boat with crabs, they devised a way to squirt water onto their own water sensor, which required them to free their crabs and go back to the dock 'for repairs.' Because the crabs had been released from the crab pots, they could not be harvested by the other boats. They were saving the crabs."

"The class sounds like a lot of fun!" I said admiringly. "It really gives students a chance to play."

"That's something I learned a long time ago. Having an element of whimsy in the project is really highly motivational. If you give them a task that has a real and obvious connection to some industrial thing, it doesn't feel like it's fun to do. They are going to perceive it as boring—even though it has all of the same educational content as these games that we put together. It doesn't resonate, it doesn't hook them.

"We come up with new projects every year. I have a team of coaches who are former students in the class. We come together and brainstorm for four to six nights to create a draft project description. We begin with the goals of the project and the elements that we need and then ask ourselves what would be fun to watch. Are there interesting ways that we can incorporate new technologies?

"It's important that students are not doing the same project that students did the year before. Then, of course, there are the usual bragging rights: My project was a lot harder than your project."

I asked about the percentage of women in the class.

"It's not great, but it's much higher than the percentage of women in the overall program—perhaps because the course has a reputation for being empowering."

"You've mentioned the word *empowering* several times," I observed. "Can you say more about what you mean by that and why it's important?"

Ed paused and reflected before answering. "It really goes back to my educational experience. I felt like I had learned how to solve a lot of problems that the professors gave me—problems on tests, based on the material we had learned in class—but I had no confidence that I could design something from scratch. In the real world you get presented with a problem that requires you to draw from all that you know. I figured out how to do that pretty much on my own.

"To me, empowerment means students can go out and apply what they've learned to the problems that they've never seen before with parts that they've never used before."

"Your classes are far more interdisciplinary and hands-on than most," I observed. "Can you talk about some of the challenges of teaching in this way in Stanford's academic environment?"

"There's no problem with how the courses are viewed. That's because when students who've taken the Smart Product Design classes go on for a PhD at Stanford, they can do things in their labs that the rest of the students who have not taken the courses can't do. They're a bit more fearless about diving into things."

"So in a sense they are providing you with cover—they are living evidence that your classes get results."

"Exactly," Ed replied.

"What about challenges beyond the classroom?" I asked.

"I am a consulting professor. For a long time, I was the only consulting professor. I don't have tenure. I'm on a year-to-year contract."

"And I assume that means a greatly reduced salary compared to tenured professors?"

"If I was in it for the money, I would definitely be doing something else. What I do is not the traditional academic stuff. I don't have a research program, though I've participated in a number of colleagues' research projects. My focus is on teaching and making sure the course sequence stays both fresh and just back from the bleeding edge of technology. I want them to feel that the stuff they are learning is current."

"All of the work you do to know what's current, and to be just back from the bleeding edge in your courses, is not considered research?" I asked.

"It isn't. I understand what research is, and I've done it before, but it's not what I find to be the most exciting or rewarding thing to do. It's a mixed bag. I get to work with incredibly bright students. At various points, I've toyed with leaving Stanford and always come back to the combination of the set of colleagues I have in the design group and the quality of the students we have here."

I asked Ed to speculate for a moment: "What would universities have to do to create more of a reward or incentive structure for the kind of teaching you do?"

"Research One universities [Research One refers to the Carnegie Foundation's rating system for universities]—places like Stanford, MIT, Georgia Tech, Michigan—all share a really strong emphasis on PhD research. Here at Stanford, at least half of the student population is graduate students. And so the requirements for tenure are that you be a world-class researcher and a good teacher. But the clear emphasis is on the research. You can't be a world-class teacher and a good researcher and get tenure."

"What does this emphasis on research mean for undergraduate programs?"

"My concern about undergraduate education in Research One universities is that they tend to be focused on preparing students for PhD programs—rather than the more practically oriented master's programs. There is less emphasis on application. You don't know where students are going to end up, and so I think it is an educational disservice not to prepare them broadly. You can teach the same body of material with an emphasis on applications or an emphasis on theory. In many cases, it's easier for the professors to teach it from their perspective, which is theoretical."

I was disturbed by what Ed was saying and couldn't help remarking, "But when you look at the future of our country, what stands out for me is that we don't need more PhDs, we need more students like the ones you're graduating."

"I have a biased view, but I think the biggest impact in engineering is being made by master's degree students. We get a large number of students in this program who are here to learn the skills they need to start their own company. It attracts the students who think they would like to be entrepreneurs. They get supported here—not just with technology courses like mine—but also with entrepreneurship courses. The excitement of creating new products is what drives many of the students here."

"What can you tell me about Kirk? What drove him as a student?"

"A standout student—he was a great student in my class and then a great TA. Very enthusiastic, very sharp guy. Very much jazzed by what he was learning and what he could do with it. He had a pretty good idea of where he wanted to go early on. While he was at Apple, I got the impression that he was looking at it not as a job but as a learning experience for the future.

"I'm on his case about finishing his degree, though. Maybe he's gone far enough so that he won't need it, but you never know when someone from HR will say, 'We can't hire that guy. He doesn't have a degree.'"

Motivating Innovators

Ed's story tells us a great deal about the essential elements of educating young people to become innovators: the value of hands-on projects where students have to solve a real problem and demonstrate mastery; the importance of learning to draw on academic content from multiple disciplines to solve a problem; learning to work in teams. What most intrigued me, however, was his use of two words: *empowerment* and *whimsy.*

I rarely hear a teacher at any grade level talk about wanting to empower their students, and I certainly didn't expect to hear it from someone teaching a graduate-level course. But as Ed explained the deficiencies of his own education—where he learned the content needed to pass his professors' tests, but couldn't do anything on his own—the goal of empowerment made more sense to me. Academic content is not very useful in and of itself. It is knowing how to apply it in new situations or to new problems that matters most in the world of innovation. It strikes me that when Ed empowered his students, he was doing two things: teaching them skills by giving them experience in solving progressively more complex problems, and developing their self-confidence. Ed observed that his students, when they went on for a doctorate, were "a bit more fearless about diving into things." We certainly saw that fearlessness in Kirk.

But whimsy? I can remember the last time I'd even heard someone use that word. On reflection, I suppose I shouldn't be surprised, though. Whimsy is a kind of play, after all—adult play. It reminds me of why the MIT students are so fond of their tradition of outrageous pranks, as Joost told us in chapter 1—they're whimsical, too. So it would seem that the element of play is every bit as important in adults' learning as it is in how children learn. Play, then, may be an element of passion and purpose, as well as an intrinsic motivation that stands by itself.

I was also struck by Kirk's description of Ed's classes as something you "had to really want." It seems students in his courses are not motivated mainly by the desire to get a good grade. They are motivated because they are a part of a team; they are motivated because they have to solve an interesting problem that requires integration of learning from many sources, as well as new learning. And they are having fun. From what I had heard, it sounded as though they were far more *intrinsically* motivated than the students I see in most classes.

One other theme in the conversation with Ed was both surprising and disturbing: his description of what Research One universities do and do not value. I had begun the work for this book with the conventional belief that our major research universities such as Stanford, MIT, and Harvard and their graduate schools are one of the true sources of innovation and wealth creation for America—and hence the envy of the world. And now Kirk's experience had planted a seed of doubt.

Kirk had said not one word about the many academic courses he'd taken at Stanford. His best teacher and most important mentor was an outlier at the university: Ed Carryer—a PhD from Stanford with decades of experience in industry as a designer—has been on a year-to-year contract since 1992, with no chance of promotion or tenure, and he has to scrounge money for his lab every year from his famous alums. Ed's description of Stanford as being far more focused on churning out PhDs, rather than people who will make and create things, was unsettling.

An Expanding Sense of Purpose

In a recent conversation with Kirk, I explored why he left Apple and what he has been doing since. I discovered that he now evaluates everything he does not just in terms of what he might learn—which has always been a passion of his—but also what he can contribute. My sense is that he is developing a deepening sense of purpose.

"I left Apple in the summer of '08, because I was excited to take my product-development learnings from Apple and apply them to new areas. You want to keep your learning rate high. Where and when I was born has given me lots of access to learning opportunities that I really value. Hanging out in a job for a decade seems like a wrong move. I want to keep adding tools to my toolbox, though I don't quite know what I want to do with them yet.

"I went to work for Foundation Capital [a small venture capital firm] because the founders were all former 'doers'—guys who had long careers working for real companies prior to their jobs in venture capital. These were the type of people I wanted to learn from, but I always knew it was an intermediate spot. At Foundation Capital, my job was looking for my next job, while I scouted new investment opportunities for the company and provided coaching and support to our investees.

"SunRun is one of the start-ups Foundation Capital had invested in. I interviewed with them and discovered both a great team and an exciting market opportunity." Kirk joined the small company as senior product manager in the summer of 2010.

"SunRun has an opportunity of a very rare magnitude to change the way consumers think about the energy services they buy. It is a home solar company that owns, installs, insures, and maintains the solar panels so all families have to do is pay a low and controlled monthly rate for the power they use. We call this a solar power service, and the goal is to be the largest provider of energy for American homes within twenty years. Often, families will save between ten to fifteen percent right away on total power bills, plus more over time as utility rates continue to rise.

"Feedback we often get from customers—we're literally obsessed with getting to know customers and what makes them happy—is that they love how the best thing for their wallet is also the best thing for the planet. We're creating a new kind of environmentalist—one that does it because it's a smart environmental decision and not necessarily because they are a die-hard environmentalist.

"At SunRun, I'm focused on designing and delivering fundamentally better customer experiences around renewable energy."

Reflections

Kirk's story provides some fascinating insights into how one young person has come to be a significant contributor to some highly innovative enterprises. His parents, Cord and Lee Phelps, looked and dressed in ways that appeared similar to that of their suburban neighbors. But, as we learned, their philosophy of child rearing—the time they spend with their children, their focus on learning as discovery through trial and error, their interest in their children's process of learning, and the unusual combination of both structure and freedom that they allowed their children—was an essential element in the development of Kirk's capacity to innovate. Above all, it seems to me their focus on nurturing Kirk's self-confidence and intrinsic motivation to learn and to explore was critical. Learning, for them, was not a means to an end—a way to get into a good school or job—it was an end in itself.

I was also deeply moved by their unquestioning support of their children's decisions—even when they may have seemed unconventional or risky, such as when Kirk decided to leave Exeter before finishing his high school diploma, and then to leave Stanford before he'd finished his MS or BS. Kirk's brother is a gifted athlete, I later discovered, and when he wanted to leave private school and go to a public high school to increase his chances of getting into a Division I college for sports, his parents totally supported him in that decision—as well as in his aspirations to become a professional athlete, which he is today. Finally, I was struck by their emphasis on the importance of giving back—to "contribute," as Cord said in an e-mail to me.

In looking at Kirk's education experience, the opportunity to go to an elite private high school does not appear to have been an important factor in the development of his innovative capacities. You'll recall that Cord said, "Every class had a path that they are trying to take you on. . . . At the end of the day the results of the class were pretty predictable." His and his parents' dissatisfaction with his experience at Exeter was not surprising to me, though, as I have both researched and taught in some of our country's most highly rated public and private high schools. In my last book, *The Global Achievement Gap,* I documented the ways in which learning and teaching in many of our best high schools fall far short of their reputations.

Kirk's college experience was more ambiguous. It is now widely believed that every high school student should graduate "college-ready" and that sending many more young people to college is the key to their individual future and our future as a country. Additionally, Bill Gates and other CEOs advocate that more students take STEM courses in college—classes in science, technology, engineering, and mathematics—to better position our country to compete in these spheres of enterprise. Yet Gates, Mark Zuckerberg, Steve Jobs, Michael Dell, Dean Kamen, Paul Allen, and many other brilliant innovators had to drop out of college to pursue their new ideas—as did Kirk. To borrow a phrase from Henry Rutgers, their schooling was interfering with their education. According to Jobs, the course that he did take in college that had the most impact on the design of the first Apple Macintosh computer was not a STEM-related course at all—it was a course in calligraphy![2]

Referring again to Teresa Amabile's three factors in developing individuals' capacity to be creative, Kirk's story suggests that *expertise* was the least important of the three in his case. Kirk, himself, downplays the importance of content expertise—saying at the beginning of this chapter that "what you study is not that important." This is not to suggest that academic-content knowledge and expertise are unimportant. Ed Carryer's courses did teach academic content, and Kirk no doubt had to master a lot of academic content in all his other courses at Stanford. This knowledge gave him a foundation for continuous learning and problem solving, but his ability to *apply* the knowledge—and to learn new things, such as how glass is cut—was far more important than the academic content by itself.

Kirk's story leads me to question the wisdom of urging students merely to take more STEM-content courses. What Amabile calls *creative-thinking skills*, as well as what Kirk calls people and political skills, seemed far more important to his contributions at Apple than the academic expertise he'd acquired. And his intrinsic *motivation* and sense of purpose may have been most important of all. Of all the courses that Kirk took, it was Ed Carryer's that made the greatest difference in his development.

Creating a Culture of Innovation

In Ed's classes, intrinsic motivation and creative-thinking skills are far more essential than mere technical knowledge. Additionally, the academic content learned in his classes is contextual, not isolated—it is a means to solve a problem, a tool, not a stand-alone goal. The final "exam" in his classes is not based on having memorized academic content, but rather is an assessment of how well students have used their content knowledge to solve the problem they were given. Additionally, Ed's classes demand teamwork and use multiple disciplines to solve problems. His courses, then, have a *culture* that is very different from the academic STEM classes most students take in college.

Most conventional high school and college academic courses share three fundamental cultural traits that are radically at odds with the culture in Ed's classes: First, they reward individual competition and achievement versus Ed's focus on teamwork; second, traditional academic classes are organized to communicate and test very specific subject content expertise versus the problem-based, multidisciplinary approach in Ed's classes; third, conventional classes rely heavily on extrinsic incentives—grades and GPA—unlike Ed's, which rely more on the intrinsic incentives of exploration, empowerment, and play—or what Ed calls whimsy.

Teamwork, interdisciplinary problem solving, intrinsic drives, and a kind of empowerment that gives individuals the confidence they need to take risks—these were also what Kirk described as essential to the culture at Apple. Common sense suggests that the classes that best prepare students for work in innovative companies would create a culture that most closely resembles what they will encounter in the workplace. Kirk, himself, observed, "This integration project class is the closest you get to real world engineering in an academic environment."

How might we put together this idea of the *culture of innovation* in a class or school with Teresa Amabile's three elements of creativity—expertise, creative thinking skills, and motivation—that I have adapted as a way to think about developing the capacities of an innovator? You will recall her three intersecting-circles visual representation from chapter 1. What if we assume that the *culture* of a classroom or a school—values, beliefs, and behaviors— is what *surrounds* these three requirements for innovation and deeply influences how expertise and creative-thinking skills are acquired and how motivation is developed? Taking the idea of culture into consideration, a revised framework for developing the capacities of young people to become innovators might look like this:

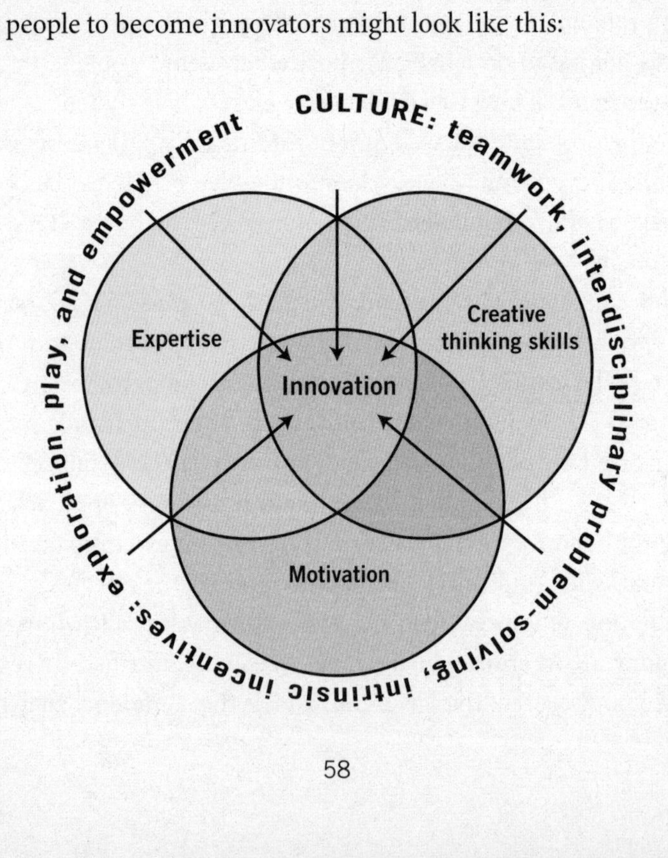

New Questions

So how important is college in the development of young people's capacities to be innovative? Do we merely need students to take more STEM courses in college, or will they most benefit from a different kind of teaching—more like the way Ed Carryer teaches?

What similarities and differences might we find among the development of young innovators who don't have the good fortune of growing up in an affluent suburb and going to private schools, as Kirk did? Will we see some similar patterns among parents from diverse backgrounds in how they help their children to develop?

These are some of the questions we will explore in the next chapter, where I profile the lives of four additional STEM innovators.

Chapter Three
STEM Innovators

Shanna Tellerman

Shanna Tellerman is an artist—and has been since she was a child. "She would sit in my office and make tissue-paper people—action dolls," her father, Kenneth Tellerman, told me. "We went on a hike in the woods one day, and when we got back, she created a panorama in a shoebox that re-created the feel of walking in the woods. She was seven or eight at the time." Little did her parents or Shanna know how prescient her first 3-D creation would be. In 2006 at the age of twenty-four, Shanna founded Sim Ops Studios, a start-up company that developed a web platform for 3-D design, called Wild Pockets. Her company—and her team of designers and engineers—was acquired by Autodesk in the fall of 2010, where she now works as a product-line manager. Autodesk is a world leader in 3-D design, engineering, and entertainment software. Wild Pockets lives on as an open-source game-design website, whose tools are available for anyone to use.[1]

VIDEO CUE:

Meet Shanna Tellerman

Go to www.creatinginnovators.com
to watch the video.

"Democratizing 3-D design was my goal when I started Sim Ops Studios," Shanna explained in a recent conversation. "But now I am able to work in a much larger space: I'm not just impacting the digital world, I'm impacting the real world: how to design buildings and factories that are sustainable, efficient, with less waste and huge cost savings. The products we're working on at Autodesk enable architects and engineers to go out into the field with a handheld device, stand in a half-built room, pull up digital design and simulation software that resides on far more powerful servers in the cloud, and visualize how various parts and the design will come together."

Shanna grew up in Baltimore, Maryland, the eldest daughter of Kenneth Tellerman, a pediatrician, and Donna Bethrens, a registered nurse whose focus is program and policy work in school-based health care. "We made the decision early not to use Baltimore City public schools," Donna told me. (The Baltimore school system then had an extremely high dropout rate and was considered one of the most troubled urban districts in the nation.) "She went to Jewish day school through eighth grade. When Shanna started looking for a high school, she told us, 'After being in a Jewish school, I can't go to a school with no values.' Her friends were applying to many of the elite private schools in the area, but Shanna only applied to Baltimore Friends, a Quaker school that aligned with her values."

"Friends School also helped nurture her art interest. One art teacher took particular interest in Shanna," Ken added.

Shanna agreed. "The best part was that I was able to take art as a major in high school, which meant I could have an art class almost every day of the week. My teacher really individualized her approach to different students, so I was able to grow in the areas of art that interested me the most. I remember many days going up to the art studio in this small, attic-like space and losing myself in a warm room with dramatic shadows. Having an hour or ninety minutes of quiet and the total focus I got when doing art was a wonderful break in the day."

Applying to colleges was the hardest part of high school, Shanna told me. "Many middle-class white girls in Baltimore who went to private schools, played sports, and worked hard were also applying to all the schools I wanted to go to. There was nothing so unique or differentiating about me except for maybe my art, but most schools don't really care about art as a differentiator. I had my heart set on UPenn, and I had applied to Yale as a wild card. Both had art programs I thought I would really like. I was rejected from both and felt totally dejected. After so much hard work I felt like I wasn't good enough. Carnegie Mellon on the other hand had reviewed my art at a portfolio day, and the art school had basically accepted me right after. CMU also recruited me for their soccer team and gave me a scholarship. The decision was easy, although I was not superexcited about CMU at the time."

I asked Shanna's parents how they'd felt about their daughter's decision to be a fine arts major in college.

"Neither of us is artistic. I draw stick figures. We recognized these gifts when they were young and tried to breathe life into their interests," Ken explained. (Their other child, Rachel, a daughter who was born ten years after Shanna, is a gifted artist as well.) "We had an extra room, which used to be their playroom, and we turned it into a studio. Shanna could go in and close the door, and she'd come alive. She'd come out covered in charcoal or paint. It was so clear that it was something she loved doing. We basically let Shanna show us where she wanted to go. We had a sense of trust that she'd figure out what she wanted to do and would be happier for having made her own decisions. We never said she can't earn a living with art."

"We thought it, though, and held our breath," Donna added. "It's walking a fine line—providing boundaries within which children can explore. She had a sense of having to earn a living and be responsible for herself. Yes, follow your passion, but within parameters—clean your room, work every summer, be a part of the community and our country.

There's no clear-cut road map for this kind of parenting. We never said, 'Oh, you're artistic, that's great.' It can't be just about what you want to do.

"We would never have predicted that her interest in art would lead to what she's doing now," continued Donna. "A big part of it is that Shanna has a very strong social conscience. Her motivation to start a business had nothing to do with business. What she initially developed in graduate school—post 9/11—was an amazing program to train first responders and that could help them do a better job. Shanna never saw herself as being CEO of a start-up, but she had a vision and she couldn't find any other way to do it."

VIDEO CUE:

Tellermans on Parenting

Go to www.creatinginnovators.com
to watch the video.

From Fine Arts Major to CEO

Shanna told me the story of her journey from fine arts major to CEO of a start-up:

"During my senior year at Carnegie Mellon, I took a course with Randy Pausch, called Building Virtual Worlds. It was the best class I've ever taken. For me it was an eye-opening experience that changed my entire direction in life and thoughts about a career—everything I was doing. The course is now taught by Jesse Schell, who is also an incredible teacher. Jesse was my adviser for the project that I spun off into Sim Ops Studios, and he was one of the cofounders of the company. Both of these guys were very, very influential for lots of people.

"The course was a boot camp experience. Your team had two to three weeks to complete different projects—virtual-reality experiences, like little worlds and games that people would immerse themselves in, with headsets, hand sensors, goggles, see in 360, be in 3-D space. After each project, you had to showcase your work to the entire class for critiques. There was a campus-wide presentation at the end of the semester, where guests from industry came from all over the country to see students' best work. I had three of my projects—out of five that I did during the semester—chosen for the final presentations.

"The part of the course that was most compelling to me and that changed my interest was the collaboration. I really loved working with people with such diverse backgrounds—computer scientists, fine artists, sound designers, 3-D modelers. We had to come up with an idea, execute, and keep the team on track and motivated during very compressed development timelines. My experience in the show at the end of the semester was supercool, but really I'd fallen in love with the whole experience—working in tight timelines, with visual experiences, and diverse people—it was the people that drove me."

In 1999, Shanna's teacher Randy Pausch, who was then a professor of computer science, teamed up with Don Marinelli, a professor of drama, to co-found the Entertainment Technology Center (ETC) at Carnegie Mellon. They developed a unique interdisciplinary master's degree in entertainment technology.[2] (Randy died of pancreatic cancer in 2008, at the age of forty-seven. His "last lecture" has been viewed more than 13 million times on YouTube and was adapted into a bestselling book.[3]) Jesse Schell, who has taught in the ETC since 2002, described its origins for me. "The program was founded by the schools of fine arts and computer science, but reports to neither. It was started by two iconoclasts who had no interest in the status quo. They made a deal with the university: 'You stay out of our hair, and we'll pay for ourselves.'"

VIDEO CUE:

Randy Pausch's Last Lecture

Go to www.creatinginnovators.com
to watch the video.

Shanna's experience in Randy's course was so compelling that she decided to apply to the master's program he'd developed and was accepted. She continues her story:

"Everything in grad school was project-based—one project per semester for the entire two-year program. There were no classes or tests. Teams were usually given a real-world client or problem to solve. Grades were determined by the presentations we did at the beginning of our project, halfway through, and then at the end when you'd showcase your project to everyone in the program to be critiqued.

"My second-semester project in 2003 was called Hazmat Hot Zone. The goal was to use video game technologies to allow emergency responders to train in simulated environments. When I got started on the project, I made a connection to Tony Mussorfiti in the New York Fire Department, who taught a course on hazardous materials for first responders. We showed him our early prototype and he said, 'That's nice, but let me tell you what we really need.'

"The department had lost so many people in 9/11—especially senior-level people—that they needed a way to quickly train younger people, only now they had to teach about a much wider range of threats, beyond just fires. Hands-on, live drills were their best means of training, but they were expensive and time-consuming. The alternatives of videos, textbooks, and PowerPoints just weren't good enough. The idea was that video games might be a better option—a very immersive experience without the expense. He wanted to be able to choose a scene and a threat and be able to change factors while the simulation was going on, then pull people together to debrief what happened and go back through it again, if they needed to. We built a prototype that semester—initially he was doing us a favor by giving a couple of hours of his time, but when he saw what we'd built, he became passionate about the project.

"Often what happens at the end of a semester is that projects get put on the shelf and not continued. That summer I went to work at Electronic Arts on the *Sims 2* game. I could have stayed there and continued to work for academic credit, but I had this feeling I wanted to go back. I'm so glad I did. The faculty let me work on the Hazmat project for both semesters of my second year. There was a lot of interest in what we were doing, and after I graduated, the university hired me to figure out if there was a way to fund the project. I applied for tons of grants, but it was kind of a hopeless cause. The likelihood of landing a big grant was small, especially with zero experience.

"During this time, I sat in on classes at the Tepper School of Business at Carnegie Mellon. I figured I should know something about organizing and managing projects, and I began to think more about how what we'd been working on might become a business. I got connected to a small investment group there. One person in the group urged us to start a business, and I incorporated Sim Ops Studios in January '06. I knew absolutely nothing about starting a company or entrepreneurship—I didn't even know Silicon Valley existed. Our earliest investor was an economic development fund in Pittsburgh called Idea Foundry. After a couple of years, we got connected to very experienced investors in Silicon Valley. We got additional funding on the condition that I would move to San Francisco so that the investors could give hands-on help. I lived on a friend's couch for six months while we were waiting for the funding to close."

What follows in Shanna's story are five long years of trying to make a go of the start-up in the midst of the worst economy since the Great Depression. Her team quickly learned that most emergency departments didn't have enough money to purchase the software they were developing. Shanna's vision evolved into a different product: to make the creation of a 3-D environment something anyone—including teachers and nonprofit organizations—could do at a reasonable cost and without a great deal of expertise. Jesse Schell, Shanna's teacher at the ETC who had co-founded the company with Shanna and whose own company, Schell Games, had acted as an incubator for her start-up, described the qualities that enabled Shanna to persevere under difficult conditions. "She has an indomitable quality—to just go figure things out. She's unafraid. Incredibly persistent."

By the time Autodesk acquired her company in the fall of 2010, Shanna had raised and spent nearly $3.5 million of capital. She and her team of nine, who still worked back in Pittsburgh, had created and validated the product, but they had still not found a revenue model. That's when Autodesk stepped in. Five months after the acquisition, I talked to Mike Haley, director of emerging platforms and technologies at Autodesk.

"Shanna's company came across our radar screen two years ago," Haley told me. "When I sat down with her for the first time, I came away very impressed—not so much with her technical skills as in the breadth of her thinking. But we were looking at other companies then, and they had just received a heavy round of funding. A couple of years later, the group was doing contract work for the cash flow, and we hadn't had any luck with the other companies we'd been looking at. So I went to Pittsburgh and met with the entire Sim Ops team and was very impressed. They had a great balance of engineering and design capabilities."

I asked Mike to describe how Shanna had fit into the culture of Autodesk, her strengths and weaknesses, and how he saw her future.

"The most important aspect of being in an innovative environment is not being afraid to fail. Shanna loves the creativity and doesn't let failure get her down. She has a strong vision, too, and a lot of leadership qualities come from that. Her opportunities for growth are around team development and setting up the right processes to get things done—it's the least compelling part of the work for her. Shanna has learned a lot in five months here, though. She's a real sponge. But after a few years, there won't be a lot left to sponge up here. She will be confident, and there will be things she will want to tackle. My guess is probably not entrepreneurial, though. She doesn't have that driving, single-minded passion. She's much more creative. She could end up as a senior exec in a major company—running a large business unit—or a CEO of a small company."

When I asked Shanna about her future at Autodesk, she was clear about what she wanted.

"My best experiences so far in life have been those moments when I'm working with people with an idea coming together—it's an amazing feeling! Building, sharing, laughing. It's addictive—the sense of accomplishment that comes from it. I didn't understand that before taking Randy's class because so much of my schooling and even my art was solitary. Even group projects in school weren't like that because you didn't really build something together.

"I wasn't sure what I would think of working in a large company. I was wary. Walls? Roadblocks? Taking forever to make decisions? These are things you hear. But what's great about being at Autodesk is that it's like being in a start-up again—only you have services like HR that we never had. What I'm loving is all these teams working together on a very interesting goal that's important to the company—a business team, an engineering team. Everything is teamwork with brilliantly smart people. The collaborative aspect is the same as in grad school: building things we could never even imagine on our own. I am open to staying and continuing to evolve my career here so long as I can still do innovations. If it slows, I'd go to another company or do a start-up again."

I asked Shanna why innovation was so important to her.

"To me, it means doing things that are meaningful in the world, that people are impacted by, excited by. I see two kinds of companies. There are the archaic companies that function well, but at a slow pace. They know what they are doing, they have systems in place, and they do things a certain way because it works. Then there are some companies that are continuously disruptive—Apple is run like a start-up. It is a company that is continuously innovating, through rapid prototyping and iterating. Rethinking what the future will be. Yes, you have to make a profit to build a successful company, but real success means putting that profit back into continuous innovation."

Similarities Between Kirk's and Shanna's Experiences

What is striking to me about Shanna's story is the many similarities to Kirk's. Both sets of parents actively encouraged them to pursue their passions without worrying about where they might lead in terms of a career. In doing so, they were developing their children's intrinsic motivation. Both also allowed their children to make significant decisions about their schooling as adolescents. They trusted their children's judgment. Finally, the parents encouraged their children to think about how they were going to "give back."

It is striking, too, that both Shanna and Kirk had experience with a transformational project-based course that was hands-on, interdisciplinary, required teamwork, and encouraged risk-taking. For both, the opportunity to collaborate and build real products with others was the most exciting and motivating part of their education—and something they had never previously experienced. These courses enabled their passions to evolve into a deeper sense of purpose. In the model of how the qualities of innovators are developed that I introduced at the end of the last chapter, the *culture* of these courses continued to develop their *intrinsic motivation*, as well as their *creative-thinking skills*, and *expertise*. And both courses were taught by iconoclasts who did not fit the conventional academic mold.

Shanna and Kirk have each worked for a large innovative company and a small start-up. Both are innovators with a strong entrepreneurial streak who want to make a difference in the world.

Finally, both the Phelpses and the Tellermans are solidly middle class. What about the children of families with different cultural or socioeconomic backgrounds, though? Will we continue to see similar parenting values? And will this pattern of a radically different college course having a transformative impact on a young innovator continue to hold? In the rest of the chapter, we will learn the stories of two innovators in their early twenties and a third innovator/entrepreneur who is now in his early thirties. All three of their childhoods and adolescences were quite different from Kirk's and Shanna's.

Jodie Wu

Jodie Wu graduated from the Massachusetts Institute of Technology with a BS in mechanical engineering in 2009. She turned down a full scholarship to the University of California at Berkeley to start her own business in Tanzania. Today, at the age of twenty-four, Jodie is president and CEO of Global Cycle Solutions, whose motto is "transforming the bicycle into a vehicle of innovation."[4]

VIDEO CUE:

Meet Jodie Wu

Go to www.creatinginnovators.com
to watch the video.

"My parents came to the US from Taiwan in 1980, seven years before I was born," Jodie explained as we drank coffee at a restaurant near MIT. "They had relatives here and saw America as the land of opportunity for their children.

"I grew up in Conyers, Georgia. I lived there all my life and went to public school. My parents ran a small Chinese restaurant—which was the center of my universe until they sold it when I was sixteen. I remember doing my homework while sitting at one of the tables in the restaurant. I started working there when I was very young, helping out. For high school, I attended the Rockdale Magnet School for Science and Technology, which used classrooms in the Rockdale County High School. I took all my math and science classes in the magnet school and the rest of my classes in the high school.

"I initially resisted the idea of going to the school because I wanted to go to the high school where all of my friends were going, but my dad said, 'If you don't like it, you can always go back.'"

"So what made you stay?" I asked.

"The program was academically very challenging. Every class had a research component with a hands-on project. You choose your project, you choose the topic. I could say, 'I want to research brain cells,' and not have to worry about where the funding would come from. The school was also special because it had a partnership with Georgia Tech, so we would sometimes go there to sit in on classes."

Jodie's science project in ninth grade was to look at the effects of fiberglass and wood on geodesic domes. "I loved that first project because I would pile up all these weights to test the strength, and then the weights would come crashing down when the structure collapsed," she told me.

In tenth grade, her project was to test impeller designs for energy from dams. In eleventh grade, her project was to study the effect of radiation on brain cells.

"I really liked the eleventh-grade project because I thought the work could have big implications—saving lives. But I discovered I couldn't work with living cells. They'd die, and I wouldn't know why. Also, a lot of the results and research were contradictory. It was hard to know who was right.

"I also got into the science-fair world. For one of my projects, I was one of 250 Intel Science Fair semifinalists in the nation. And we had a math team. The coach, Chuck Garner, treated it like any other team experience. We had a logo, we would travel to compete with other teams, and we won championships. It was like a cool thing to do—instead of just being something for geeks. He also was the teacher who had the greatest impact on me in high school. He had a real love for math, and he brought in different perspectives—like the history of mathematics. And I could talk to him about anything."

Chuck Garner is a seventeen-year teaching veteran. I interviewed him about the math team and his recollection of Jodie.

"The team practices three hours a week, and we have thirteen tournaments a year, which are daylong events, and three of them require an overnight stay. Then there's American regions math week—they pay me an 875-dollars-a-year stipend to do all that."

"I guess you aren't in it for the money," I said, laughing. "What's the draw, then?"

"There are a couple of things about working with the team that appeal to me. I am able to present math to high-achieving kids—topics we all found interesting and which were not available in the curriculum. 'They'—whoever 'they' are—don't think it's stuff kids can understand. Plus these kids are fantastic people; I really enjoy getting to know them outside the classroom. We often have a one-hour ride to a tournament, and we pass the time in the bus just talking—they are witty, humorous, fun to be around. The chaperones who come with me are sometimes put off that I didn't talk to them. I'd rather be in the back of the bus talking to kids, teaching math on the fly. . . . It's amazing how little I know about math compared to these guys, and I have a PhD—the way their minds think, the way they solve problems."

"And Jodie?"

"She was one of the most organized students I may have ever taught. She was also just the kindest person—not a bad word about anyone. She tried hard not to show anger or frustration. It was refreshing. She was in a class of competitive and high-achieving people, and she wasn't at all like the guys who were loud and obnoxious. They hogged the attention. 'What's your GPA? What did you get on the test?'—she stayed away from all that."

Nevertheless, Jodie applied and was accepted at MIT, where she wanted to study mechanical engineering. I asked her about some of the highlights of her four years there.

"I had a freshman seminar that led to an internship at Parsons, a civil engineering firm. That gave me some business experience. In my second summer, I interned with a large, respected corporation. [Jodie preferred that the company not be named.] I was struck by the many inefficiencies: Some people working overtime while others with nothing to do were on Facebook. Three people doing the same job. The experience made me not want to be an engineer anymore. I didn't want to work for a company like that for thirty years and not have an impact. It's hard to see the impact of designing pipes between two systems. It wasn't fun."

A Transformative College Experience

"Everything changed when I took D-Lab, a sequence of courses that was developed by Amy Smith. She was in the Peace Corps in Botswana for three years and since then has always been interested in doing international development work and applying her engineering skills in a third-world context. At the time I went through the program, it was a sequence of three classes: D-Lab 1 was Development, D-Lab 2 was Design, and D-Lab 3 was Dissemination. What I loved about the course was that it integrated my wanting to make a difference in the world with my engineering skills—making devices that can have a huge impact in communities that don't have technologies."

I interviewed Amy about the origins and purpose of the D-Lab.[5] "It began as my effort to try to teach classes I wish I'd had when I was an undergrad at MIT. I began doing this work when I was a graduate student here in the nineties and started teaching this course eleven years ago. I spent a lot of time begging and got pieces of funding here and there. We are not an official center or lab, and we're not affiliated with an academic department—it's hard to define us in the structure of MIT."

"You're not tenured or tenure track, then?" I asked.

"Oh, no. They want me to apply to be a professor of practice—but that's not a tenure-track position, and I really don't have the time to do the application. I'd have to go back and document twelve years of work, and it would be a nightmare because I never thought I'd have to explain it to anyone. And I haven't published, even though lots of articles have been written about me and our work." (Amy was being modest, I later learned. In 2010, *Time* magazine named her one of the hundred most influential people in the world.)[6]

"So tell me more about the D-Lab."

"The D-Lab philosophy is very much experiential—real projects for real people and real feedback on your projects. Too often students don't get meaningful feedback on their work. In terms of design, our focus is on people who live on less than two dollars per day. We also believe in building the capacity of people we work with in the developing world—foster the belief that they are creators, designers—and that our students should value indigenous knowledge."

VIDEO CUE:

Smith and the D-Lab

Go to www.creatinginnovators.com
to watch the video.

"What about Jodie?" I asked.

"She is deceptively determined. She's always smiling, and she would talk in a way that you couldn't see and hear the drive underneath, but she thinks about what needs to be done and finds a way to do it. Would I have guessed from the first class that she'd be a poster child for what D-Lab stands for? No. She's not forceful or obnoxious, but she's dogged. She's another type of entrepreneur—she will just do it and doesn't need to announce to the world that she's going to make it happen."

From Engineering Student to CEO

Jodie described her transition from being a D-Lab student to starting a company in Tanzania:

"The most important part of Amy's class is that after learning about international development in the first semester, you go to a developing country in January. That was really appealing to me because I'd always wanted to go to a developing country and do something worthwhile. I went to Tanzania. That was an incredibly eye-opening experience. You go thinking, 'Oh, I'm going to change the world in three weeks—bring in this technology that's going to be groundbreaking and help all the people.'

"The first part of my trip was very frustrating—we never really got out of our American bubble, but in the last week I met up with Bernard Kiwia. I'd brought one of the machines Amy had introduced us to the first semester—a pedal-powered maize sheller that had been developed in Guatemala. He was a bicycle mechanic from Tanzania who had been a part of the first International Development Design Summit in 2007—another one of Amy's programs. Participants come from around the world to co-create and co-design new technologies for use in developing countries. Bernard showed me all of the technologies he'd developed after participating in the program—like turning the handle bars of a bike into a hacksaw frame, and a grinder that was pedal-powered. All these different inventions. I saw that development work can really have an impact, and I felt inspired to do what Amy had done.

"But I'd also realized that the maize-sheller technology I'd brought that I thought would save the world wouldn't work there. It was bulky and way too expensive. No one wanted to buy the machine. Using a cut-up bicycle, it was a frame with a shelling machine and a seat mounted on it. The machine itself was only twenty-five dollars, but with the bike that gets cut up for the parts, it becomes a two-hundred-dollar device. So I thought, 'What if we could just isolate that twenty-five-dollar technology and make it have all the attributes of a more expensive machine.' Then I realized, we should not cut up the bike, we should use the bike! It became the platform rather than the scrap part—and the bulk was gone. 'Now I have technology that I put on the back of a bicycle, and because it's on the bike, it's transportable. So communities can use it—it can be shared. And when it's not maize season, it can just be used as a bike.'

"So that was the design challenge that I pitched at the beginning of D-Lab 2. It was selected by students as one of the projects to work on, so I had a design team for the semester.

"That summer, I went back to Tanzania with a prototype of the new sheller design. It was a really raw design in its prototype stages, but it was still better than what they were using at the time. We started renting out bikes to shell maize, and it changed the value proposition. In Joost Bonsen's Development Ventures course in the fall, I pitched my idea for a business to other students. I explained how the sheller could pay for itself in the week through renting a bike. Joost Bonsen told me that I had to write a business plan—he really believed in the project."

VIDEO CUE:

Jodie Wu in Tanzania

Go to www.creatinginnovators.com
to watch the video.

Joost Bonsen is a lecturer in MIT's Media Lab, a program we will learn more about later in this book. He told me about the class of his that Jodie had taken:

"We created the Development Ventures class to figure out how to take the best ideas and get them out into the marketplace. Jodie had done this design for a pedal-powered corn shucker. Everyone pitches their ideas at the beginning of the class. I thought it was a great idea. Over the course of the next few weeks, we looked at the design in detail and thought about what other peripherals you could add to the bike."

Jodie continued, "Joost encouraged us to enter the $100K challenge, and my team won first prize in our category—twenty thousand dollars—and we were the only team in Joost's class without any MBAs or business skills.[7] One award led to another, and I walked away with thirty thousand dollars in awards.

"Through Joost, I met Semyon Dukach, an MIT alum who is an angel investor, the spring of my senior year. I'd just been accepted to the University of California at Berkeley. But Semyon got involved when he met my team, and he said, 'Just do it—you'll learn the most from being in the field.' Through Semyon, I got an investor who gave me fifty thousand dollars to start Global Cycle Solutions. I went to my father for advice, and he said I should do it. And he gave me an additional fifty thousand dollars matching investment, saying, 'It would be wrong for me not to invest in my daughter.' Later I learned that he had borrowed the money."

I asked Marshall Wu, Jodie's father, about his decision to invest in her venture.

"I think trying to do business in Tanzania is not a good idea—you have to do things their way, have to do some things under the table—it's dangerous. I asked her not to get involved in that part. But it's good for her to learn—she's young and learning things you can't learn in school. From this experience, she will learn what she needs for life. It will be good for her."

"Why did you decide to invest in her business?" I persisted.

"She needs support. She needs to know that her family is behind her—and that she's not alone. She's young, has to learn her own lessons."

"Do you think you will make your investment back?"

"I won't make any money," Marshall answered. "I didn't invest in her business to make money, just to support her. It's a Chinese tradition to help your kids, to support the positive. I don't need to invest in my retirement. I'm a handyman. I fix things—I can fix anything. I can do that when I'm old. I don't need a lot of money for my life." (After selling the family restaurant eight years ago, Jodie's father went to trade school to be trained in heating and air-conditioning repair.)

VIDEO CUE:

The Importance of Supportive Parents

Go to www.creatinginnovators.com
to watch the video.

After graduating from MIT in 2009, Jodie moved to Tanzania to launch her company. "I called myself a CEO in training. Semyon was my adviser—I had zero business experience."

Semyon Dukach is a serial entrepreneur and angel investor who serves as chairman of the board of Global Cycle Solutions. I asked him why he got involved.

"There is a movement to do cheap, practical stuff for the third world. It is not about the specific farm tools; it's about enabling entrepreneurship—it's the only way to grow the economies in Africa. But for me, angel investing is about the people, not the business—sharing the excitement, being helpful, being productive, having fun. You have to understand the needs of others, though—how to package, market, finance. I am more of an enabling catalyst."

"What did Jodie need help with?"

"The challenge for young entrepreneurs is to find the passion and just do one thing. Jodi needed help saying no, staying focused, hiring and firing."

In April 2011, Jodie and I Skyped to catch up. "The company has grown from five to fourteen, and we have sales reps in four regions of Tanzania," Jodie told me. "We also have a new product, a motorcycle-powered cell phone charger. We've sold six hundred shellers at sixty dollars each, twelve hundred bike chargers at eight dollars, and eight hundred motorcycle chargers for three dollars each (an invention of Bernard Kiwia—who is the company's chief engineer in charge of R&D). We've gone through $150,000 in two years. I'd hoped to be breaking even by now, but all the business aspects have been hard. Local manufacturing is always late—there's no pressure to move quickly anywhere here. The exchange rate changed fifteen percent in the last year and erased our profit margin. We lost power eight hours a day for two months and had no water for a month. We had to ration showers and water for dishes in the house where I live.

"We've redone the business model and raised additional capital. Now we are trying a mix of a bottom-up and a top-down strategy—trying to work with institutions like savings and credit cooperatives—and we're applying for grants, as well. I never thought we'd be talking to the minister of agriculture. We have traction, and now we're going for scale."

Some Differences and Many Similarities

Jodie's cultural background and circumstances growing up were very different from those of Kirk and Shanna. Nevertheless, the similarities of the influences that contributed to their development as innovators seem far more important than the differences. Like the others, Jodie had parents who believed in the importance of their children following their dreams versus worrying about a career, and they allowed—even encouraged—their children to take professional risks and to learn through trial and error. This principle was so important to Jodie's father that he was willing to take out a substantial loan to help his daughter establish her business, believing that he was unlikely to see a financial return on his investment.

Once again, we see the importance of an outlier teacher whose collaborative, project-based, interdisciplinary approach to learning had a profound effect on the development of a young person. I have to wonder about how different Kirk's, Shanna's, and Jodie's lives might have been had there been no Ed Carryer, Randy Pausch, or Amy Smith. Several other adults were an importance influence on Jodie as well: Chuck Garner, her high school math teacher; Joost Bonsen; and Semyon Dukach. She had a web of support.

In our conversations, Jodie had said comparatively little about her childhood play experiences, unlike Kirk and Shanna. So I wondered about the importance of play, passion, and purpose in the development of her intrinsic motivation and sent her an e-mail. Here is her reply:

> I would say that play to passion to purpose does indeed make sense—from *play*: when I used to build my Lego Village, K'Nex Roller Coaster, and constantly assemble and disassemble jigsaw puzzles—onwards to college where I fell in love with Mechanical Engineering (*passion*), going into the machine shop and creating things from nothing—to *purpose*: making things that help people.
>
> But the part that amazes me more is how my parents' habits live on in me—the fearlessness to start a business; the generosity, to always give more than take back; the loyalty you build in employees; their humility; their resilience; and then the care with money, to never waste it and spend every penny carefully. . . . Every year, I've grown and realized that I can do more in different contexts. I decided on engineering because I wanted to know how everything works. I decided to start Global Cycle Solutions because it was an application of my knowledge, but I also knew if I didn't do it, the idea and concept would disappear into oblivion.

Jodie's comments reflect how important it was that her parents, like those of Kirk and Shanna, communicated clear values to their children. Above all, the importance of "giving back" is an essential belief that all three families have in common. "Having fun" while innovating is a strong recurring theme in all three young people's lives. Innovation becomes a kind of adult play. But the more serious goal of making a difference in the world is at least as important. All three seek self-fulfillment while also helping others. The desire to be helpful—even more, to be enabling—is a fundamental value that the teachers whom we've met thus far share, as well.

Before turning to the question of how best to educate young innovators in science, technology, engineering, and math, let's consider the story of a young innovator who is a recent arrival to this country. At a time when America is restricting the numbers of immigrants who can work here, it is important to understand what some of the best and brightest from other countries have to offer.

David Sengeh

The youngest of five children, David Sengeh was born and raised in Sierra Leone, the son of Elizabeth, an administrative assistant in the Ministry of Education, and Paul, who works as a program evaluator for UNICEF. By the time David finished high school at the Red Cross United World College campus in Flekke, Norway, in 2006, he had already started his first NGO, called Global Minimum, along with three other students from the school. A year later, the organization pioneered new, more effective ways to distribute malaria nets in Sierra Leone.[8] As a sophomore at Harvard in 2007, David and four classmates started another social enterprise. Lebone Solutions explores ways to use microbial dirt to generate electricity and won a $200,000 prize in the 2008 World Bank Lighting Africa competition.[9] In the spring of 2010, a few months before he received his bachelor's degree in engineering sciences, David was chosen by Harvard president Drew Faust to introduce Bill Gates when he came to lecture at Harvard.

VIDEO CUE:

Meet David Sengeh

Go to www.creatinginnovators.com
to watch the video.

David and I first talked a few days before his Harvard commencement. I asked him about growing up in Sierra Leone.

"I used to pass by my father's office on the way home from school every day and would stop in because it was air-conditioned, and I could get something to eat. I was always reading. I remember reading about the Convention on the Rights of the Child and different UNICEF reports. When I was fourteen or fifteen, I joined something called the Children's Forum Network. We met every Sunday and talked about different topics like how to integrate former child soldiers into society. We went to visit a camp for former child soldiers, and on the Day of the African Child, we organized a huge march. I also helped to organize a children's version of the Truth and Reconciliation Commission, similar to one in South Africa, and we lobbied to pass a child rights act in parliament.

"My father subscribed to the BBC magazine. I was the first to open it every month. Of course, he wanted me to do well in school, but he gave me a lot of nonacademic things to read—like the UNICEF reports. He's a statistician and so I had access to the country's data, and I would be with him when he developed questionnaires and read reports. I learned about the problems of the country this way. He had friends and colleagues from work who were smart people, and he'd bring me to hang out with them. This gave me confidence, and I felt comfortable in front of powerful people.

"I knew I'd been given extra opportunities and that I could influence other people. I wanted to be a doctor for kids at the time."

Paul and Elizabeth Sengeh came to Cambridge for David's commencement, and we spoke over lunch.

"David has always had an inquiring mind," Paul told me. "He wasn't shy, and he asked a lot of questions. We enrolled David in the town library, and when he brought books home I would ask, 'Have you read that? Tell me about it.' He would seek out adults and ask them questions. They used to say to me, 'You have to know your stuff when you talk with David.'"

"What has made me who I am today didn't come from schoolwork or classes," David explained to me. "The greatest influence on me was going to the United World College for my last two years of high school. I chose their program in Norway because I knew it would be very different from anything I'd experienced. It's connected to the Red Cross headquarters there, and we would do some kind of volunteer work nearly every day. The essence of the UWC school in Norway is community service, participation, and international understanding.

"During my time there, I shared rooms with students from Uruguay, Kazakhstan, Bosnia, Albania, Ethiopia, Denmark, and Peru. We had human rights class with students from Israel and Palestine in the same class together—experiences like this change the way you view negotiation and academic discourse. We'd all work together after class to clean the school and tutor younger kids. While I was there, my roommate and I started Global Minimum, and our first project was to raise six hundred dollars for local school supplies in Sierra Leone." (Global Minimum's focus on distribution of malaria nets came later—when David was a college freshman.)

"If you go to UWC, you don't come back the same person. The kids who graduate from there all become social activists around the world. Everybody should go to a school like this."

"Tell me about your Harvard experiences."

"The summer I was admitted to Harvard, I had this idea about establishing a prosthetic bank, where people could come to exchange devices that no longer fit, instead of being on the street begging. I googled *Harvard* and *technology,* and the Technology and Entrepreneurship Center at Harvard showed up. I called the director, Paul Bottino, and we talked for twenty minutes. He listened and asked for a follow-up e-mail. The idea didn't go forward then for a lot of reasons, but I'm going to grad school for prosthesis design now.

"There are two people at Harvard I can link all my networks to, and Paul's one of them. From the moment I walked into his office the first week of school and we started talking, it was all about entrepreneurship and ideas. I could never just talk to him for five minutes—it was always at least half an hour, and he'd always ask questions and throw out ideas.

Talking with him changed everything. I wanted to become someone who did something, created things, developed ideas."

Paul Bottino described for me his goals as a mentor: "I try to take students as they come, show them that they are the authority by helping them create a query and explore an opportunity. More and more students are saying that education which is merely content delivery doesn't work, doesn't stick. For students like David, it's about applying what they know, in order to connect the dots."

VIDEO CUE:

Sengeh on the Value of Mentors

Go to www.creatinginnovators.com
to watch the video.

"Paul introduced me to David Edwards, a bioengineer who made his mark from aerosolized glucose and vaccines," David continued. "He created the Idea Translation Lab at Harvard and in Paris to start new organizations around innovations.[10] I started working in his lab my second week at Harvard. Just before I came to Harvard, I was working with my uncle Dr. Boima [a surgeon in Sierra Leone], and I saw a pregnant woman die because they didn't have a scanner—didn't even have lights that worked in the operating room. I brought a proposal to David Edwards to form a group to make health devices. He said, 'That sounds interesting, but I want you to work in my lab.' I got a grant that paid me to work there so I didn't have to get a job.

"The other person who I can link to all of the contacts I made at Harvard is Harry Lewis, a former dean of the college who has been a freshman adviser for many years. During orientation week, he led a group of us on a tour of the city, including Fenway Park. Then he invited me to go to a Red Sox baseball game with him and talked with me about how Harvard works—that it's decentralized, that you have to be active and go and get what you want."

"David has rare self-confidence, but he's not in any way self-promoting," Harry Lewis reflected. "He's deeply concerned about the welfare of his country. He's never bad-mouthed anyone."

Making a Difference in Africa: Malaria Nets and Electricity from Dirt

David described the evolution of his interest in malaria prevention in Sierra Leone.

"When I was in high school, I'd gone to visit my uncle in his village, and he'd given me the only malaria net he had to sleep under—but I couldn't sleep thinking about his giving me the only net. I talked with him the next day and began to see what a huge problem malaria is for the country. I knew the data, but it became much more clear after that experience. Freshman year, I took a class on global health challenges and wrote a paper about malaria. After I wrote the paper, I recruited two other guys from high school, and we fund-raised to buy fifteen hundred malaria nets. Two years later, we distributed forty-five hundred nets, and this summer we'll take eleven thousand to give away. Pricewaterhouse-Cooper gave us some money, and people will come from there to help the distribution.

"Before we distribute the nets in a village, we go to the chief and have town meetings, and all our volunteers try to learn Mende, the local dialect. Instead of just giving nets to pregnant women and infants, as UNICEF had done, we visit each house and leave enough nets for each separate sleeping area. We also do follow-up visits. Our success [usage] rate is ninety percent three years out. A consortium of other organizations organized a net campaign in 2006 and only had a forty percent success rate after six months."

"How did you get involved with starting another social enterprise?" I wondered.

"My second year at Harvard, I was working with Edwards in his Idea Translation Lab. We were given a seed idea to use biology to design lighting for the 2012 London Olympics. But three others in my group were from Africa, too, and we said why light London when we can light Africa, where hundreds of millions aren't on the electric grid. It was also personal. At that time, my sister had to have a cesarean when there was a power outage, and the operation had to be done in candlelight. The doctor mistakenly cut the baby on her forehead and back.

"We started with a bucket of dirt, then went to huge bowls of Tupperware. We went to Tanzania with the idea. Now we have pails of dirt that can power an LED to read by. All you need is dirt, and you just water it once a month—five years of power costs thirty-five to forty dollars. One of our teammates is in Namibia now launching this, and we'll announce the product at the World Science Festival next month. We were one of the Innovators of the Year for *Popular Mechanics.*"

"David and his group had this idea and applied to the World Bank Light Africa Competition in complete innocence," David Edwards told me. "Then they heard that they were in the finalist round and had to really learn what they were talking about. Students don't have to be blocked from dreaming by the fact that they haven't learned what they need to know to realize that dream. On the contrary, innovators are most interested in dreams that take them where they don't have learning. David was his own inspiration, and he discovered his own ability to learn by following his passion."

What David's College Classes *Didn't* Teach

A few days before his graduation, I asked David to reflect on his four years at Harvard.

"I've done everything I wanted to do. I've played soccer and football, learned guitar, traveled, had access to the brightest minds. I met Nicholas Negroponte—the man who started the Media Lab and the One Laptop per Child project at MIT. He's been my mentor, as well, and he gave me laptops to take to Sierra Leone."

"What about classes?" I asked.

"I don't remember anything I did in any of my classes—except for Spanish. I can speak Spanish. The advice that I wish I'd been given early on was to not worry about my GPA. In my junior year, I took four science classes and did terribly, but I stopped worrying after a while—I was a lot more worried about getting people ready to go to Sierra Leone that summer. The best thing Harvard has to offer is the out-of-school, out-of-class education. It's amazing—the resources, mentors, opportunities, friends."

VIDEO CUE:

Sengeh on Harvard

Go to www.creatinginnovators.com
to watch the video.

"What would have made your classes more relevant and useful?"

"There are some classes now that encourage people to go out and do things: the leadership class with Professor Ager, the Idea Translation Lab class, classes in human rights. There need to be more classes that matter to the world—courses that will translate into businesses, into social action."

Paul Sengeh talked about the arguments he and his son had about David's hair—he has dreadlocks down to his shoulders—and his declining grades. "His grades kept going down. Learning is more important than grades, but he'd always been a straight-A student. 'I don't want you to get a C,' I would tell him. But right after Harvard's Commencement last week, we went to MIT's open house, and we met Dr. Negroponte. David asked him if he would show us around, and he said, 'Gladly.' Later David said to me, 'I could have been magna cum laude if all I had done was study all day. But then, I would never have met Negroponte, and neither would you.' It's taken me two years to accept his lower grades, but I could not say, 'David, you're right.' We still have to advise our children."

I asked David how he saw his future.

"I'm going to study bioengineering at the Media Lab at MIT next year. It's the only grad school I would have gone to. There are no grades, no structured program, no required classes—you just create and build things that people need. That's what I want for my education—classes I want to take, skills I want to learn, instead of having to take silly classes that don't matter. I will be working on building better prosthetic sockets for amputees. I have other ideas of things to work on, as well. I want to make cool health technologies that matter to the world, that matter to Sierra Leone.

"I bought two acres of land in Sierra Leone a while ago. I was thinking I wanted to build a school—a place where kids come and don't think it's a school—a place you want to come every day, where your day is about feeling your presence in the world, knowing that you control who you are, that you can influence others, but at the same time you are not different or removed from everybody else.

"Last week, a friend said to me that we are like pebbles in a stream—with the tide and ripples moving us here and there." I instinctively said, "No, I'm not a pebble. I'm a stream." I know the flow. I am aware of the ripples, aware of some pebbles that fly away. But being a stream, you can influence the waves. This will be a school where everyone feels like a stream. You know what you represent, and you know that you can create change. You are not a helpless pebble being pulled or pushed around by a tide or waves. You are aware."

Play, Passion, and Purpose in Another World

There are some interesting differences between David's story and the others. David argued with his father about grades and his appearance, for example, while these were not issues with the three other sets of parents, so far as I know. And David told me that he sometimes felt his father was "too strict" when he was growing up. I think these differences can be attributed to David's father's being from a more traditional, patriarchal culture.

The similarities in the ways that David's parents—like the others in the four stories—encouraged him to pursue his passions and to explore and discover the world seem far more important than the differences. That Paul, David's father, took great pride in telling me about David's involvement with the Children's Forum Network and was constantly exposing David to ideas and to books—showing deep respect for David's initiative, intellect, and interests—is much more significant, I think, than their disagreements. David's parents—like the other parents whom we've met thus far—also instilled strong values in their children. Paul Sengeh told me, "I don't worry about David coming back and helping his country. He's already been back every year with more malaria nets."

Play, passion, and purpose intertwine in David's life and lie at the heart of his intrinsic motivation, but in a way that's somewhat different from that of our three other young innovators. Much of David's *play* growing up was the serious play of someone deeply aware of and concerned about the world around him. At an early age, he felt a strong *passion* about the plight of children in his country—probably because he grew up in the midst of a civil war with so many child soldiers killing one another. I have the impression that he didn't allow himself much time to play in the conventional sense until he got to college, where he relished learning a musical instrument for the first time and enjoyed playing soccer and football. From a young age, David has felt a strong sense of *purpose* about overcoming the suffering of his countrymen and others living in extreme poverty throughout Africa.

VIDEO CUE:

Sengeh on Sense of Purpose

Go to www.creatinginnovators.com
to watch the video.

By far the most striking similarity between David's school story and those of Kirk, Shanna, and Jodie is his experience learning in the collaborative, hands-on, interdisciplinary, problem-solving environment of the Idea Translation Lab and how he was challenged and supported by Paul Bottino's coaching—in the same ways that the three other young adults were by the mentors whom they named. Indeed, David is at his most eloquent in describing the kinds of courses he wished he'd had at Harvard—"classes that matter to the world, courses that will translate into businesses, into social action"—in his excitement about going to a graduate school focused on designing useful things—with no grades or required classes, and in his vision of creating a school where "you want to come every day, where your day is about feeling your presence in the world." Empowerment, in other words. Through the remarkable similarities in these four stories, we are beginning to better understand what kind of teaching and learning environments develop young people's capacity to innovate—how *expertise, creative thinking skills, and motivation* are best developed.

The final story in this chapter reveals some striking similarities, but also some interesting differences in what helps to shape another young STEM innovator and entrepreneur's development. Jamien Sills grew up in an economically disadvantaged community and has had to deal with significantly more setbacks than the four other young innovators whom you've met thus far.

Jamien Sills

Jamien is an African-American who was raised by his mother, Ernelle Sills, a schoolteacher in Memphis. When I first interviewed him in 2009, he'd just turned thirty. Here is his story as he told it to me then:

"When I was eight years old, I was watching Michael Jordan play basketball on TV. When he jumped up to make the shot that won the game, I saw his shoes, and I wanted a pair. I asked my mom, and she said if I got A's, I could have shoes like his.

"I began drawing shoes, and I collected new shoes as they came out. I was a fashion aficionado. It went from a passion to an obsession. I started working in a shoe store when I was fifteen so I could get the shoes early and at a discount. They let me cut up the defective shoes that were returned, so that I could see how they were made. I read the manufacturers' literature and talked to customers. I began designing shoes for my friends on paper, and they loved it. My mom got worried sometimes that I was too much into fashion, but I was a good kid and got good grades, so she was okay. My mom was a teacher, and it was never in my mind not to do well and go to college. But sometimes she'd ask, 'How many shoes are you going to buy?' And I'd say 'At least it's not drugs, Mom.'

VIDEO CUE:

Meet Jamien Sills

Go to www.creatinginnovators.com
to watch the video.

"But I had no idea that anyone could actually make a living doing this. I was in this health and engineering academy in a Memphis public high school, and the teachers were always pushing us toward being doctors or computer scientists. I was fortunate that I was given a mentor in tenth grade, from a program called Memphis Challenge that helps talented African-American students succeed. I learned how to interview, how to dress appropriately, and how to take the SATs. The program also provided us with internships in the summers. I applied to and was accepted at nineteen colleges and then narrowed it down to three: Emory, Notre Dame, and Washington University. My mentor was incredible: He got representatives from the three colleges on the phone at the same time and negotiated the best scholarship.

"My first year of college at Washington University, I was a computer science major and bored out of my mind. I decided to do a double major in graphic and advertising design—even though I had to make up a whole year of college. I was beginning to learn things about shoe design, but my design teachers weren't helpful. They would say, 'Are you really sure you want to be a shoe designer?' And they discouraged me from doing a double major. Sometimes I had the feeling that some of my design teachers wanted me to fail. But for my senior-year design project, I created an entire shoe company—product line, designs, company logo, everything. All of the students and parents who were in the audience for our presentations gave me a standing ovation. The teachers had no choice but to give me an A.

"For three summers while I was in college, I had a graphic design internship at AutoZone back in Memphis. A designer there, Kurt Meer, was my mentor and taught me web design, graphic design, and how to do research. It was fun for him, I think, and it was incredibly valuable for me. While I was in college, I talked on the phone to a guy at Nike whose work I admired, and he encouraged me to send him my portfolio. I didn't hear anything for six months, and when I finally reached him, he gave me the brush-off. But a year later, I saw one of my designs in the Nike catalog. . . .

"When I graduated, I had job offers in St. Louis, but I decided to accept the graphic design job offer back home at AutoZone. When I showed up there for my first day of work, they said, 'What job offer?' The entire design department had been laid off the Friday before I showed up.

"I had a lot of jobs after that—and a stack of rejection letters from shoe companies. I worked in the Nike warehouse for a while, then FedEx and Champs. I was offered management positions, but I was afraid I would be distracted. I spent all my free time drawing and entering online design competitions; we had a real community on the Internet. I'd stay up so late that sometimes I'd wake up at my drawing table in the morning with marker on my face.

"Then I met these two young black guys who wanted to start a shoe company, but they didn't have a designer. I showed them my work, and I was hired. It was my dream come true. But the head of the company had this street-hustler mentality. He wanted fame and glory, and he thought he was a big shoe mogul. His ego and lack of experience and focus killed us. I was in China at the shoe factory that was going to produce our shoes when I found out that the company had gone bankrupt.

"I didn't know what to do. My life dream was gone, and I wasn't sure that I could go on. So I decided to stay in China a little while longer, because I didn't know what else to do. The husband and wife who ran the shoe factory were like my family and let me watch and learn from them and try things. But when I was in the manufacturing area, I'd get a pounding headache, and I saw that people were working in the factory without masks—the fumes were killing these people! And there were big piles of waste, too. I began thinking that there must be a smarter way to do this—and have shoes last longer and not fall apart after two years.

"I fooled around for a couple of weeks and figured out how to make high-quality shoes without toxic fumes—a completely green tennis shoe that uses stitching instead of glue. The pattern uses materials more efficiently, too, so there is much less waste—plus the shoe is much more durable with stitching. Cheaper to make, too!

"I began to realize that I had learned about every aspect of the shoe business firsthand: retail, design, manufacturing, warehouse. I decided I could do it on my own. I began designing a line of eco-friendly tennis and work shoes. I partnered with one of the guys from the bankrupt shoe company and found some other partners and investors. We have six partners now. Three of them own their own businesses and are teaching us about all the aspects of running a start-up.

"My dream is to run one of the largest shoe companies and open up the first completely green shoe factory in the world. I also want to teach entrepreneurship and life skills to young African-Americans in the Memphis Challenge program that helped me. But I want to work more with at-risk kids. It's frightening how far behind they are—they can't read in tenth grade, can't do math. The foundation isn't there—not at home or at school. Everything at school is about discipline, not learning. These kids get labeled as dumb and shiftless, but they are actually brilliant."

The Importance of Persistence and Mentors

Now thirty-two, Jamien is several years older than the other innovators whom I've profiled in this book. He was also the first person whom I interviewed when I began this project in 2009, so I was interested to know how things had gone for him since we'd last spoken. When we talked again in the summer of 2011, he told me that he's continued to develop his business concept and potential products for his shoe company, while supporting himself with a variety of freelance design jobs and living at home. Jamien spent an entire year working on a revolutionary new design for a safety shoe, which is 75 percent lighter and better fitting because it uses a wire tightening system rather than laces. FedEx field-tested his new design, and it proved enormously popular, but each employee buys his own shoes, and so Jamien needs to raise $300,000 to have six thousand pairs of shoes—a minimum order—manufactured.

VIDEO CUE:

Sills on His Latest Invention

Go to www.creatinginnovators.com
to watch the video.

For the past three summers, Jamien had also worked as a counselor for the Memphis Youth Leadership Program, an eight-week series of courses for inner-city minority youth. "Teaching entrepreneurship and business skills changed me," he said. "I started taking my own advice about how to start a business. It also helped with my public speaking—a group of twenty fifteen-year-olds is the harshest crowd I've ever stood in front of. But seeing how they were transformed from the first day to the last was inspirational."

At the urging of a friend who was also affiliated with the Memphis Youth Leadership Program, Jamien got in touch was James Luvene, a business consultant and Methodist minister. James had served on the Mississippi State Board of Trustees of Mississippi's Institutions of Higher Learning for many years and was eager to help Jamien. He urged him to apply to an innovative MBA program at Mississippi State, sponsored by its university-wide Entrepreneurship Center. Jamien was accepted in 2011, and he's now working on an MBA degree tailored to the specific business skills he needs. The center provides him with professors and other MBA students who assist with market research, sales strategy, and developing a revised business plan, as well as office space for his company, in return for a 5 percent share in the company. James Luvene is also now one of Jamien's business partners.

In the summer of 2011, Jamien negotiated for the use of an abandoned textile plant and the surrounding fields for his company's warehouse and R&D center. He's now working with a consortium of three universities—Mississippi State, the University of Southern Mississippi, and Southern University in Baton Rouge—to develop new materials for manufacturing organic shoes, using kenaf (a tropical plant similar to jute), blended cotton, and bamboo. He also plans to perfect a new way to manufacture shoes, the concept for which came to him after watching a film about how Toyota revolutionized car manufacturing with a modular process that replaced the old piecemeal methods. "Shoe manufacturing in China is extremely labor-intensive," Jamien explained. "Thirty pairs of hands are used to make one shoe. But I've figured out a way where one person can make one shoe, using components, instead of many separate parts." Jamien is especially excited about this idea because it would enable him to sell affordable shoes that are manufactured in this country, instead of China. "Shoes for the everyday hero" is his company's new tagline.

I asked Jamien what were some of the most important lessons he's learned with the many ups and downs of his quest.

"Number one is patience. I used to be extremely impatient. Also to not stop believing and to stay focused—there's no time for pity parties. I've turned down all kinds of good-paying jobs, and people used to ask me why I worked sales in a sporting goods store when I had a college degree. And I'd say, 'Don't worry, I know what I'm doing.' It's hard to go back to school after all these years, but I'm glad I'm doing it. I'm learning the skills I need to be the CEO of a large company.

"It's so much easier now, though, because it's bigger than me. It's about employing Americans—bringing manufacturing back here—and helping the environment."

Ernelle Sills, Jamien's mother, had her hands full raising a son by herself while working a demanding full-time job. Nevertheless, like the other parents whom we've met, she played a critical role in encouraging her son's passions. She vividly remembers when he fell in love with Michael Jordan's shoes.

"My sister gave him a ball of clay when he was seven. He made animals and all kinds of things with clay. Then he said he wanted to make a shoe—a Michael Jordan shoe—but that he needed different colors of clay to make it look just right. I had to drive all around town to find that clay. But I found what he wanted and he made it—and it looked just like the shoes he'd seen on TV. I was floored. Then he told me he wanted to be a shoe designer. I said okay, but you don't just draw shoes—there are a lot of other things you'll need to learn. I thought it would be just a phase, but when I finally bought him the pair he wanted, he just sat and looked at those shoes for the longest time. Then he took an older pair of his apart to learn how they were made. That was in sixth grade, I believe. And he has not wavered from his dream.

VIDEO CUE:

Raising an Innovator

Go to www.creatinginnovators.com
to watch the video.

"I've tried to teach him to be an independent thinker, self-sufficient, and to embrace who he was and not give in to peer pressure. The hardest part was getting him to understand that just because his dad wasn't around, that did not make him less than who he was, and that he didn't have to be like the other kids.

"His college professors were not encouraging. It seemed like they were telling him, 'No, you won't make it as a shoe designer, you need to go into advertising.' I told him, 'Okay, maybe that's a skill worth learning, but if you want to design shoes, that that's what you will do.' His true passion was shoes."

I asked Ernelle why she thought it was important for Jamien to pursue his passion. "If you're not happy at work, then it's a job, not a career," she replied. "And it's not a path to happiness. My granddad had his own business in printing and was very creative. He was a minister, too, and he used to print his sermons. He wasn't rich, but he enjoyed what he did. That's so much more important than money. I've always encouraged Jamien to go for his own business. I knew it would be hard for him, that he'd fall down and have to get up and dust himself off, figure out what he needed to do to improve, and go try again. . . . It's taken a lot from my budget to keep him afloat, but I think it was the right thing to do."

VIDEO CUE:

"I'm Behind Him 100 Percent"

Go to www.creatinginnovators.com
to watch the video.

I asked Jamien if he could tell me the name of a high school or college teacher who had made a difference for him, and he said there were none in high school or in the graphics department where he majored. But Jamien did tell me that one of his advertising professors, Frank Oros, had made a real difference. "He saw that I was frustrated with the other teachers and brought me into his advertising design program, which was still a part of the graphic design program, but he was my main instructor. He encouraged my 'shoe addiction' and taking risks with my design work. He also really taught me how to 'think out' my design work before I ever picked up a pencil. It's a skill I still use to this day, and it allows me to design faster, smarter, and cheaper."

The person who had been most important in Jamien's development, though, was his mentor while he was interning at AutoZone. Kurt Meer—now a successful, full-time landscape painter—was a graphic designer for AutoZone's in-house publications when Jamien began the first of his three summer internships there after he graduated from high school. I asked Kurt what Jamien was like then.

"Initially, he was very shy," Kurt told me. "I started talking to him about his interests—this was the era of Michael Jordan—and I learned that he had hundreds of pairs of shoes. He'd really taken learning everything he could about shoes very seriously, but the environment he had been in [meaning his high school] had done nothing to foster his design interests.

"So I started showing him how to do things on the computer. I taught him how to design websites, how to integrate Java [a programming language]. Then he learned how to use Photoshop and 3-D computer illustration programs, and we'd discuss the aesthetics of shoes. But it was his imagination that really stood out. He'd take a theme like a Lamborghini sports car or a Disney character and explore what a shoe might look like, based on the theme. The things he'd come up with were almost bizarre. One was a Winnie-the-Pooh character where the shapes of the cartoon were overlaid onto the shape of a shoe—and the tongue of the shoe became an expression of the character. At first, I thought it was kind of silly—I had to stop myself from judging his design solutions—but I let him run with it. His juxtapositions were just so creative. Back then, I sometimes thought his approaches seemed 'naive,' but now look at how he's integrating biofibers into shoe design—state-of-the-art! So often in school, the what-if question is eliminated, but that's the source of true creativity and innovation."

Reflections

A number of things stand out for me in Jamien's story. First and foremost, I am struck by how both his mother and his mentor Kurt Meer actively nurtured Jamien's sense of play, passion, and purpose. Ernelle encouraged Jamien with his shoe design "play." When his play evolved into a passion, she continued to urge him to pursue his dream—even though his college teachers counseled differently. And now that his passion has blossomed into a driving sense of purpose—but one that has not yet borne fruit—she never says, 'So when are you going to earn some real money?' She continues to believe in him. Ernelle has also encouraged Jamien to be independent—to be true to himself. Finally, she taught him that it's okay to take risks and fail, and—most important—to persevere. These are incredibly important qualities for successful innovators and entrepreneurs. Kurt, too, has played an important role for Jamien. He taught him essential skills, of course, but perhaps most important, Kurt suspended judgment of Jamien's seemingly outlandish designs and encouraged him to keep at it.

Imagine, for a moment, if Ernelle had said, "No, I'm not going out to buy you different-colored clay. I've got better things to do with my time. Besides, making a shoe model out of clay is silly, and why would you want to be a shoe designer, anyway?" Or imagine if Kurt had laughed at Jamien's crazy ideas for shoe designs—had even made fun of him as others easily might have? As adults—parents, teachers, and mentors—it is sometimes too easy for us to treat the dreams and fantasies of someone like Jamien as peculiar or even ridiculous. Apparently, that's how Jamien's college teachers reacted to his aspirations. And it is precisely this kind of adult behavior that stifles curiosity, creativity, and imagination. Some of us respond in this way in the belief that we are being helpful and saving someone from wasting his or her time on "silly" ideas. I suspect Jamien's college teachers meant no harm; they were just being "realistic." Fortunately for Jamien, Ernelle and Kurt had a different view of his possibilities.

I am also struck that Jamien had to actively resist the pressures from both his high school and college teachers to go after a well-paying STEM career. Then he had to ignore his college teachers' advice in order to pursue a double major. He had the courage not to take a tried-and-true path to career success, and he knew better than to specialize—that he would need a variety of skills to succeed. The skills that he most valued were those that he learned from Kurt Meer. I wonder how many reluctant STEM college majors would actually produce more social and economic value and be happier by following their passions, rather than heeding the conventional advice of adults who say that a STEM career is the best way to a more lucrative future?

Finally, note that Jamien's mentors had made the greatest difference for him—not his teachers. These mentors have motivated him to "pay it forward" for other inner-city youth: First was the mentor from Memphis Challenge who taught Jamien some of the college and work skills he needed and brokered the best scholarship for him, then Kurt, and now James Luvene. Three of the eight innovators whom you will get to know in this book could not name a single teacher who had been truly helpful to them—perhaps because each of the three was in some way an unconventional student. It is far too easy for many teachers to overlook young people who don't fit the pattern of a "good student." Teachers like Ed Carryer, Randy Pausch, Jesse Schell, Amy Smith, Joost Bonsen, and Paul Bottino are rare.

All of the young innovators whom I interviewed while researching this book—including many whose stories I could not include—described a teacher or mentor who had made a significant difference in their lives. And when I then interviewed these teachers and mentors, I discovered that each of them is an outlier—an innovator—in his or her university, school, or work setting. Every one of them teaches and mentors in ways that are very similar to one another, but different from their peers. We will explore more of these important teaching and mentoring practices in chapter 5.

Jamien—like Kirk, Shanna, Jodie, and David—is committed to making a difference. This is a driving desire among many of the Millennials whom I have met in the last few years. They are ambitious—sometimes even appearing obsessed. But unlike some well-known older entrepreneurial innovators, they seem less ego-driven. I was struck by the lack of arrogance or pretense among these five highly accomplished young adults, as well as the three whom you will meet in the next chapter. Though all are quite self-aware and self-confident, which are vital qualities for innovators, none struck me as narcissistic or overly self-involved—attributes that some say characterize their generation. To the contrary, I enormously enjoyed spending time with each of them, which says a great deal, I think, about how they were raised.

Of course, the five young adults in these chapters, and the three in the next chapter, are all gifted. The point of this exploration, though, is not to admire their giftedness, but to better understand what the adults in their lives have done to help them realize and develop their gifts—and what we who parent, teach, or mentor young people can learn from their stories about nurturing the qualities of an innovator. As we discovered in the beginning of the book, babies are born with many of the qualities that make them potential innovators—qualities too rarely nurtured. Thus far we've seen how important it is for parents to encourage their children's intrinsic motivation—their curiosity, imagination, and concern for the world around them. We will explore what other parenting practices make the most difference in chapter 6.

To scale up innovations in science, technology, engineering, and math and to develop the skills of entrepreneurship, we need many more teachers and mentors like the ones whom you've met so far—and different kinds of courses. We will explore new approaches to teaching STEM-related courses and other innovations in learning in chapter 5.

But we don't just need innovators in the STEM fields. To maintain our standard of living and improve our world, every young person needs to become an innovator. Every young person can benefit from the very different approaches to teaching and learning that are suggested by the work of these teachers and mentors.

In the next chapter, we explore the stories of three social innovators and entrepreneurs whose interests and aspirations are somewhat different from those of the five young people whom you have already met. Yet, as we will see, the parenting, teaching, and mentoring that have enabled them to become innovators is consistent with what the adults in their lives have done for Kirk, Shanna, Jodie, David, and Jamien.

Chapter Four
Social Innovators

In the last two chapters, we explored the world of five STEM innovators—young people who came from a background of science, technology, engineering, or mathematics. But as I said in chapter 1, our world needs innovators and entrepreneurs in every domain of human activity. This chapter explores the development of three young people who are "social innovators."

In his important book *How to Change the World: Social Entrepreneurs and the Power of New Ideas,* David Bornstein describes social innovators as "people with new ideas to address major problems who are relentless in the pursuit of their visions, people who simply will not take 'no' for an answer, who will not give up until they have spread their ideas as far as they possibly can."[1] Bornstein observes that the communications revolution has given many more people a wider and deeper understanding of the world. Armed with new sources of information, young people grow up acutely conscious of environmental destruction, poverty, injustice, and so on. Those same communication technologies also armed people with powerful new tools for organizing and coordinating efforts. In the twenty-first century, it is no longer just the elites who are informed and empowered.

With their science and math background, STEM innovators are usually seen as differently motivated from social innovators, who frequently come from a liberal arts background. Certainly, the education, background, and aspirations of the three young people you are about to meet are quite different from those of the five individuals you have met in the last chapters and from one another. But what these two groups of innovators have in common is more important than their differences. Play, passion, and purpose have been every bit as important in their development, as was having parents who supported them in the pursuit of their passions and the influence of an outlier teacher or mentor who made a significant difference in their lives.

Laura White

STEM innovators want to *make things* that will change the world, and many people can readily understand that aspiration. Social innovators, on the other hand, want to *make change* and are, by nature, idealistic. They are often disruptors as well, and many may find these qualities harder to appreciate. So they need particular kinds of supports from the adults around them as the following story demonstrates. It will also show the important role nonprofit organizations play in strengthening social innovation and entrepreneurship, as well as the larger story of how a university is trying to reinvent itself, turning the crisis of a natural disaster into an opportunity to rethink its mission for the twenty-first century.

VIDEO CUE:

Meet Laura White

Go to www.creatinginnovators.com
to watch the video.

The eldest daughter of Don and Jane White, Laura grew up in the suburbs of Atlanta, Georgia, where Don teaches in the civil engineering program at Georgia Tech. At about age ten, Laura took up competitive swimming and became quite good—ranking sixth in the butterfly in the state by the time she was twelve. But when she was fourteen years old and a freshman in her local public high school, several things profoundly changed the future that Laura saw for herself.

The first event was becoming best friends with Tammy (not her real name). Laura would sit at the same table with her for lunch. Laura noticed that Tammy never brought any food and didn't go to any afterschool events. In time, Laura learned that Tammy was homeless, and so she began to share her lunch with her.

"Getting to know Tammy changed my sense of what my responsibility is in the world," Laura told me. "I began to feel that I needed to do something for others—not just the swimming for myself. I started volunteering on a regular basis. One afternoon, I was volunteering on a camping trip for inner-city kids from Atlanta and was asked to supervise them on a swimming trip to the lake. There was a near-drowning experience where I had to swim five kids out, which was really scary. I felt very strongly that they needed swimming lessons."

At about that time, Laura applied to and was accepted into the Youth Service Advisory Board of Hands On Atlanta, an area service organization. "We were asked to advise Hands On Atlanta on youth programs, we had guest speakers on service and social problems in Atlanta, and we did service projects. The big thing was that everyone had to plan a service project for National and Global Youth Service Day. I'd never been asked to do something like that before—it was superintimidating! But my swimming friends and I had skills that we might put to good use. So I organized a day where they could give swimming lessons to disadvantaged kids in Atlanta."

The summer after tenth grade, Laura got an internship with Hands On Atlanta. "My boss left after the first week, so I had a huge amount of responsibility for a sixteen-year-old intern. I was planning lots of service projects, managing volunteers, working late, weekends. While I was working there, another staff member told me about Youth Venture. I submitted an application to Youth Venture and received a thousand dollars to have the swimming lessons be ongoing. It was approved, and that's how Wild Water Swimming got started [later renamed Swim 4 Success]. Youth Venture is an amazing program—Ashoka started it after they realized their Fellows all had the experience of leading a project or venture when they were young. They saw that it was a critical step to creating a world with more social entrepreneurs and changemakers." (Ashoka was founded by Bill Drayton in 1980, and it is now the leading international organization promoting social entrepreneurship though support of Ashoka "Fellows" and numerous other programs.)[2]

Jane White, Laura's mother, talked about the ways she and Don have tried to support their daughter's budding interest in social entrepreneurship. "We've always encouraged our children to explore things they were interested in, but also to stop when they were no longer interested. By the time Laura was in high school, it was pretty clear that she was much more interested in community service projects than competitive swimming."

Don agreed, adding, "Laura's 'sport' was community service. Some of us thrive on competition, but the swimming competition stressed her. She did learn discipline, focus, and to manage her time through swimming, though."

"And when she had to compete to get funding for her swimming project, she threw herself into it," Jane observed. "Only fifteen finalists were going to get funded, and it was based on getting people to vote for your project. She was way ahead of the others with over ten thousand votes versus seventy-five hundred for the project that came in second. She put us all to work."

"She sent e-mails every day, with links reminding people to cast their vote online," Don added.

Jane contrasted what she and Don did with the focus of other parents. "Parents drive their kids all over the place for softball games and soccer games. We tried to put as much time and effort into supporting her projects. She'll tell you I whined about it a lot because I did not enjoy driving to those sketchy areas of Atlanta, but we did it anyway."

In fact, Laura never said anything about her mother's complaints. To the contrary she told me, "My parents were always very supportive. They valued my doing well in school, but they also understood that I'm my own person and had to figure things out for myself. They weren't too hands-on—when I started Swim 4 Success, they didn't tell me that I should do this or that.

"My parents also didn't schedule my time to the last minute. I had time to think and make up my own games. . . . Most kids' parents push them to excel in sports or get into a good college—they don't let kids explore—which makes a big difference developmentally."

When I first met Laura, she was nineteen and had just completed her freshman year at Tulane University. I asked her to reflect on her K–12 school experiences.

"In high school, I did work for good grades—not because of an interest in the classes, which were pretty boring, but more to prove I had drive and could sit down and get stuff done. But all the pressure from so many tests hurt my creative endeavors. Math was my least favorite subject—too abstract, and there was no creative way to apply what I was learning or mess around with ideas.

"I had one high school teacher, though, Ms. Pratt, who got me thinking about things in creative ways. I learned about boat propellers killing the manatees, and it got me and the whole class thinking about how to address problems like that."

"How was your first year of college?" I asked.

"I'm majoring in political economy, which is an interdisciplinary major—philosophy, economics, political science. I couldn't imagine doing a single discipline-based major.

"But there's lot of pressure to get all the work done and not enough time to explore things. It would be great if I could get course credit for my entrepreneurial work—like creating a company for an honors thesis."

"What about specific skills—skills you need that you wish you were learning in school?" I wanted to know.

"Problem identification" was her immediate reply. "It's just so important. I really didn't know the problem I needed most to work on when I started Swim 4 Success. After a couple of years, I realized it wasn't just about preventing drowning. Having volunteers who come from different backgrounds, having access to pools on college campuses, having an opportunity to get good at a sport and thus maybe have a chance for a scholarship—these were all ways that the program provided opportunities to disadvantaged youth. It would have been helpful if someone had taught me to think about problems systemically."

Laura and I have kept in touch since we first met two years ago. (In fact, she has been helping me with research for this book.) She is no longer involved with Swim 4 Success; several other Tulane students currently run the program. It is a smaller project and is now affiliated with Tulane, instead of being the large stand-alone nonprofit that she'd originally envisioned. Recently, she wrote me an e-mail about what she'd learned from the experience: "Two years ago, I would have thought it was a failure because it wasn't a big new organization. But now I realize that local solutions are okay. Sometimes, it's better to work through existing organizations because it's more sustainable. Being able to move between different methodologies is critical. What's important is being fluid and finding the best methods to make the change."

College: Challenges, Opportunities, and a Teacher Who Made a Difference

In July 2011, as Laura was about to start her senior year at Tulane, we talked about some of the projects she's been involved with there, what she's learned, and possible next steps for her. Our conversation made it clear that her social entrepreneurialism had blossomed. But it was equally clear that the challenge of meeting her school obligations while continuing her work as a social innovator had become more difficult.

VIDEO CUE:

White on Tulane University

Go to www.creatinginnovators.com
to watch the video.

"I've gotten very interested in the idea of creating learning experiences to develop the skills of social innovation. So I've been working with Carol Whelan, who teaches the Education in a Diverse Society class—which is the first one students take who want to get their teacher certification—to add a social-venture-leadership component to the class. This part of the class is taught by students and is meant to develop nonacademic skills like creativity and collaboration. The class was piloted last fall, and students came up with a number of different social change ideas, six of which are still going.

"One example was a Tulane music student who was working with a music teacher in one of the New Orleans public schools and learned the choir program was underfunded and needed volunteers. So his proposal was to have Tulane music students work with the students in the school to develop and give performances together to raise money for the program. Another student was working in a school that was totally focused on raising the test scores of the lowest-performing students and doing nothing for the kids who were succeeding. So she developed an after-school enrichment program for those kids.

"For the last year or so, I've been part of a group called Citizen Circles. The idea is to bring people together to work on a local problem, project, or need that they have defined—and that they then share what they learn in the process of making change. I've learned more from doing this work with my colleague Alan Webb than I have from most of my teachers at Tulane.

"I've also been helping Alan and another individual, Jeff Bordogna, on the idea of a digital 'living transcript' as a way people can document the work they have done as social innovators in a community and gather assessments from people with whom they have worked. We have been working with Tulane to develop an assessment tool for the university's social innovation programs as a part of this.

"I think I'm growing in my ability to design my own education. Tulane funded me for a study trip to Europe this past winter, which I researched and planned myself. I visited a number of schools that had outstanding models of social entrepreneurship learning programs. This was one of my best learning experiences so far in college.

"I just came back from the Ashoka Changemakers' Week in Paris, and it has become very clear to me that there is a real need to identify a framework and continuum for change-maker skills and competencies that schools, companies, and nonprofits can use. I want to explore this topic in depth as a part of my honors thesis next year. Deloitte France was one of the sponsors of the conference, and one of the managing partners took me to lunch. He said that Deloitte needs these competencies. He wants every employee to be a change maker.

"When I go back to Tulane in the fall, I will be continuing to work on getting more student-run courses going, as well as a social innovation major. I am also interested in working with the Peer 2 Peer University on creating a School for Social Innovation in partnership with Citizen Circles. It is an open-source, online community for organizing peer study groups on topics like conflict resolution and project management for social innovators.

"I feel stressed about next year and what happens after. It's hard to be a student and get the credits I need to graduate and do all these different projects. . . . I'd like to go to graduate school to study how to identify, teach, and assess the competencies to be a social innovator—but I don't know of any graduate programs that teach this."

Laura told me that two people at Tulane have been especially supportive of her work. Stephanie Barksdale is special assistant to the president for Social Entrepreneurship Initiatives and has worked with Laura on a number of projects. "I've basically given Laura 'permission' to do the projects she's passionate about," Stephanie told me. "She is sometimes a bit hesitant and I say, 'Sure, I think you should do that.' Give her permission and she blossoms. For example, she wanted to do a TEDx conference at Tulane. I didn't do anything to help her except say, 'Yeah, you could do that.' She found the funding, got the accreditation from TED, and put the program together." (TED is a nonprofit that sponsors conferences where speakers present "ideas worth spreading." TEDx are local, independently organized conferences that are authorized by TED to use their brand name.)[3]

"I see a lot of students who have a real fear of failure, which really limits them from even trying something," Stephanie added.

Laura's other mentor is Dr. John Howard, her faculty adviser. "He's totally supportive of what I want to learn," Laura told me, adding that if it were not for Dr. Howard, she would have transferred to another college.

VIDEO CUE:

White Talks About Her Mentor

Go to www.creatinginnovators.com
to watch the video.

John Howard earned his PhD in philosophy from Tulane and currently serves as associate director of their Murphy Institute, where he administers the undergraduate major in political economy. Independent of his work for the institute, he is engaged in a number of projects related to social innovation and entrepreneurship at the institute. In a response to the devastating effects of Hurricane Katrina on New Orleans, Tulane University president Scott Cowen instituted a community-service graduation requirement. John taught a course called Public Service and Civic Leadership, where students would collaboratively write an internal policy-analysis paper related to implementing and improving specific aspects of the service-learning requirement at the university for their final project.

"I believe very strongly in the idea of a student-directed curriculum," John told me. "But I think it has to be structured. So I give students the outcome—which in this case is a report to the administration related to improving the service-learning program, but the students determine how to do the research and what the content of what we call the Green Paper should be. It is extremely rare in a university setting for students to have an opportunity to work on a real project like this. My goal is to make students active participants in their learning—rather than consumers—by giving them power to make changes. For example, one group of students taking my class recommended that courses be built around specific service learning activities, rather than the students discovering after the course has started what the service learning is going to be. But unfortunately, the administration has largely ignored students' recommendations. The concern was that such a system would be too difficult to manage in the registration process."

More recently, John has become involved with Stephanie Barksdale's Office of Social Entrepreneurship Initiatives. Because she reports directly to the president of the university, "the chain of command is much more streamlined," John explained, "and our ideas are far more likely to be heard. So this semester, we have launched a new Social Innovation Fellows program for people like Laura who want to promote social entrepreneurship programs and opportunities for other students. It is not tainted by the resistance that the service-learning requirement has engendered among some of the faculty, and it has relevance to a broader range of students. And this time, we are involving students much more in designing the program as a part of something we're calling the Center for Engaged Teaching and Learning. Essentially, what we want to do is create undergraduate 'faculty.'"

I asked John about his work with Laura.

"I first met Laura three years ago when she declared political economy as her major. She has a very strong commitment to being competent in many different areas. She thought that to do her work she needed to understand political science, economics, philosophy, and history—which are the areas our political economy major encompasses. Our program also appeals to students like Laura who have strong quantitative skills and qualitative skills. Too often, because of the conventional system of university majors, we try to turn students into specialists very early in their college career—which may end up not being what they are most interested in.

"Last semester, she began taking education courses. By the third week of the semester, she was basically co-teaching the course. Carol Whelan, the professor, bravely acknowledged how much expertise Laura had. Laura gave her an example of a kind of student she'd never seen before. That's the way it should be—we should not be holding ourselves aloof from students' ideas and innovations.

"I recognized Laura's courage, openness, and ability to state her case almost immediately. But she's not an imposing person; she doesn't raise her voice or bluster. She's not hyperconfident. She's not going to convince you that she has a good idea by marketing or PR skills, but by the power of her ideas. Her commitment to social justice is very authentic. It's not lip service or résumé-building.

"Laura is in the best tradition of social democracy, where individual people take risks and achieve amazing things because of their ability to inspire other people. She is a tremendous student leader and asset to the university. She is someone who is going to make a difference in moral terms—rather than economic or political terms. We have a Heisman Trophy we give for the best college football player in this country. If there were a national Heisman Trophy for public service, Laura would be the winner. She never wants to hear that something can't be done, yet she is also a pragmatist who refuses to lower her standards."

"How do we develop and support more Laura Whites?" I asked John. His response helped me to better understand Stephanie Barksdale's comments that Laura and others of her generation sometimes need "permission" to pursue their passions.

"First, we have to be appreciative of the young people like Laura who are out there. There is a tendency among 'sophisticated' faculty to treat openness as naiveté—they see a belief in social justice as a lack of real-world experience. It is very damaging to treat students that way.

"Instead, we need to encourage students to give voice to their beliefs and to support their intrinsic empathy and commitment to justice. There are many students who could be like Laura, but they haven't been given the opportunity to grow in that direction because someone has told them that they are uninformed or overly sensitive. Many more students than we realize have a belief in the public good. I spend most of my time looking for glimmers of these qualities in students and then trying to encourage it to grow.

"One of the ways I try to act on this belief as a teacher is that, instead of giving tests, I have written 'conversations' with the students in my classes. Students write 750-to-1,000-word weekly essays, and then I write back to them an essay of equivalent length. I also set aside some class time each week for students to share their ideas and progress with each other with no interference from me. I believe that giving students this responsibility to be helpful to one another further develops their empathy."

"Are you tenured or tenure track?" I asked.

"I am staff here and will never be tenured. I am not a scholar or a researcher. I value those things, but that's not who I am. I am a teacher, and my job is to be in a classroom interacting with students. Anything that takes away from that is, for me, an imposition. But I do not recommend this as a career path for other people. I've struggled and went without a job for a long time. I'm very lucky to be in the position that I'm in.

"Tenure is based on 'teaching, research, and scholarship.' But these things are assessed in very conventional terms to make the process easier to manage. With respect to teaching, what if universities said, 'What we're looking for is evidence of successful innovation. Give us something that shows us your unique ability to inspire students.' If they want to play it safe with publications, okay, but don't play it safe in the classroom. Or perhaps we should have a research faculty that rarely interacts with students and a teaching faculty that doesn't have to worry about publications. It would cause trouble, it would be difficult, but I think students would be better served."

"Growing" a Social Innovator

Laura's parents encouraged her in more exploratory forms of *play* as a child. As she told me, "My parents didn't schedule my time to the last minute. I had time to think and make up my own games." Don and Jane White also defied suburban-parent conventions and strongly supported Laura's decision to quit competitive swimming and to focus on service. They encouraged her to pursue her *passions* related to social entrepreneurship, helping Laura fund-raise for her nonprofit and even taking some risks in driving her to the "sketchy" parts of Atlanta for various service projects throughout her four years of high school.

We also see how Laura's passion is evolving into a clear sense of *purpose* related to understanding the skills of a change maker and how these skills can best be taught and assessed. Her path toward this goal is unclear because the questions she's asking are comparatively new. She has to adapt or invent the education she wants and needs. The course that taught her the most about creativity and how to ask good questions, she told me, was playwriting.

In several respects, it is harder for Laura as a social innovator than it was for our young STEM innovators. First, as John Howard observed, people tend to view youthful idealism and a concern for injustice as naive. I believe the prevalence of these responses among adults in our society helps explain why Laura may sometimes have seemed initially hesitant about some of her ideas. Our education system does not encourage risk-taking and penalizes failure, and too many parents and teachers believe that a "safe" and lucrative career in business or law or medicine is what young people should strive for—rather than something to do with "changing the world."

Second, a problem-based, hands-on approach to learning has very few precedents in the liberal arts. In a recent e-mail, Laura wrote, "Besides the service learning classes, there are no project-based classes for liberal arts students as there are for students in engineering and architecture." Laura appreciates and wants to learn theory related to social innovation and change, but she believes it should be done in the context of a real project. At one of the schools she studied on her trip to Europe, KaosPilots, students start with real-world projects and then learn important theories related to their projects.

"I think all of college should be able to be shaped around students' experiences, work, and challenges," she explained. "It would probably be more demanding of professors' time and would require them to play a different role. The push for publication in order to get tenure is a big problem, as well. I don't think they're going to form their research agenda around the challenges students want to explore." For Laura, the independent-study courses she created with the help of John Howard were the only real opportunities she had to earn credit for her many projects and to have help in connecting change practice to theory, but the number of independent study courses students can undertake as a part of their degree is restricted to two.

John Howard's goal, like that of all of the other teachers whom we've met thus far, is to empower students. He strives to develop their individual voice and intrinsic motivation, while structuring projects so that students work collaboratively and use multiple disciplines to understand real-world problems. He is a highly innovative teacher, like all of the STEM teachers we met earlier. Unfortunately, John Howard is also the latest member of our "outliers who will never get tenure" club.

Coming Down from an Ivory Tower: A New "Moral Compass" for a University

We have seen over and over in our stories how the culture of academia and the traditional requirements for tenure are at odds with the development of the more hands-on and problem-based learning approaches that our young innovators need. The academic world sees its mission as creating and transmitting "pure" knowledge, divorced from any kind of application or the development of specific skills. It is not for nothing that universities are referred to as "ivory towers." However, under the visionary leadership of President Scott Cowen, Tulane is seeking new ways to serve the needs of both the New Orleans community and the students at the university.

"Katrina almost destroyed our city and our university," Scott told me. "In the aftermath, I began thinking about the future of the university, what I learned from the catastrophe of Katrina, and whether there should be a different moral compass for the university as we go forward—a reimagination of the mission of the institution.

"As a major research university, we have three components to our mission: research, education, and community engagement. But community engagement has been the stepchild to research and education. If you did community engagement, it was 'nice' and you might get an article written about you, but you wouldn't get any formal recognition in our system. And community engagement was not connected to either education or research outcomes. We concluded that we had to elevate the status of community engagement so that it was equivalent to research and education, and we had to find ways to link them together more powerfully. And we define this as our moral compass for the twenty-first century.

"We call the initiative Tulane Empowers. There are now seven pillars in our strategy. It started with the first two being public education and community health here in New Orleans. Both systems were destroyed by the hurricane. We began working with various organizations within the community to help develop new plans for the delivery of health care and public education—which are being enacted now.

"The third pillar of our initiative focuses on the next generation of engaged citizens and leaders. We wanted to instill a greater appreciation for public service and social innovation, so we became the first major research university in the country to integrate public service into the core curriculum."

Cowen then briefly described the four other pillars: disaster response and resilience; physical revitalization of the city and cultural arts; the Center for Engaged Teaching and Learning; and social innovation. "We want to reinforce in our students the idea that their role is to find solutions to difficult societal problems," Cowen explained.

I asked Scott what were some of the challenges in developing this new mission for the university.

"There were many. Initially, the faculty didn't embrace these ideas—in part because we made some of these decisions the semester the university was closed after the flood, so they couldn't play as large of a role in the decision-making process as they would under normal conditions. Over time, much of the resistance has dissipated. The second challenge was to incentivize faculty to get involved, and we found multiple ways—everything from planning grants for converting courses to service learning, to establishing professorships in social innovation.

"The third challenge was messaging around the things we were doing to all of our stakeholders, and this evolved over time. When I first began to talk about these ideas, some alums would give me a blank stare and say, 'What's the university now, the United Way? What's happened to research and education?' From these initial conversations, we learned how important it was to develop a compelling case for the work we were doing. It took us several years to find a way to explain how this new moral compass was strengthening the community, the university, and helping the next generation of young people to be more effective and engaged citizens."

"Are students who apply to Tulane today differently motivated?" I wondered.

"No question about it. Applications have more than doubled in the last four years, and when we read the essays of those who enroll, more than eighty percent say they applied because the message of community engagement resonates with them. This has improved retention and graduation rates, as well, because students are now coming here for the right reasons—instead of coming to the school mainly to 'enjoy' New Orleans. And another thing has happened which I didn't anticipate—very highly qualified faculty in increasing numbers are applying for positions here because of our new mission."

"What about student admissions criteria? I know that the ranking of a university is highly dependent on the average SAT or ACT scores of the students who enroll, but in my experience, these scores tell us nothing about students' abilities to contribute meaningfully to social innovation and community service. How are you dealing with this?"

"It bothers me every single day," Scott acknowledged. "I know that these test scores do not have great meaning, but that's one of the metrics that *US News and World Reports* uses, and so we can't ignore it. I have this constant dilemma about the testing and how we use it here, and I haven't found a solution yet."

"How do you see the future? Where do you want this initiative to be in five years?"

"We're working on the idea of a university-wide curriculum for undergraduates in social innovation—a secondary major. I expect that we will have this in place in the next two years. Last year, we established five professorships in social entrepreneurship. Over the next few years, I'd like to grow this to twenty-five appointments—individuals who can be role models for their colleagues across the university. Traditional academic research is still the currency that has the highest value in the system, but increasingly we are looking for evidence of innovation in teaching and community service as a part of the tenure review process. We also want to engage our colleagues in other highly selective universities in discussions about how to elevate the importance of community engagement."

Ashoka's Influence

Efforts to promote this vision of a more engaged university took a significant step forward in the fall of 2008, when Ashoka launched a new program called Ashoka U. The goal is "to link efforts across universities to improve teaching, research and engagement opportunities in social entrepreneurship—both on campus and in the local and global communities in which we work."[4] Tulane is one of ten "change maker" universities in the United States that have joined. The program brings faculty and student leaders from the ten campuses together for a variety of programs, and Laura was selected to be on the student team for implementing the Ashoka U/Tulane partnership when it was launched in 2009.

VIDEO CUE:

About Ashoka U & Laura's Leadership

Go to www.creatinginnovators.com
to watch the video.

According to Laura, "The Youth Venture program [sponsored by Ashoka] and Ashoka U have been the most important influences in shaping who I am today." I asked her to explain in what ways Ashoka has been helpful to her, and she wrote:

First was the vote of confidence in my ability to make change by investing money in Swim 4 Success and mentoring me for that project. Then they made me a Youth Venture Ambassador, which brought me to Washington, DC, for the first Youth Venture conference and allowed me to meet other Youth Venturers from all over the world.

The Ashoka U partnership has exposed me to social entrepreneurship education, which has really become my passion. I've been to both Ashoka U conferences where I've met amazing people in social entrepreneurship education, including Alan Webb, who started Citizen Circles with me. They've also given me a support network and access to best practices for Citizen Circles, my research, and anything else I do related to social entrepreneurship education.

The best thing about Ashoka is who they connect you with, and I've been connected to great people through them—for example, I met François Taddei, an Ashoka Fellow who is doing creativity and science education. He brought me to Beijing for another conference and invited me to join the education cluster at Changemakers Week in Paris last month.

Being invited to Paris was really important for me, too. Again, I was exposed to great people and given the opportunity to present on my and Alan's ideas. It was my presentation that got me connected to more people, including the executive from Deloitte.

Laura, no doubt, benefited greatly from the strong support of her parents. However, I think the encouragement that Laura has received from the two key individuals at Tulane, the chance to play a leadership role in a university that is trying to become a center of social innovation, and the opportunities for learning that Ashoka has provided have all been key in Laura's development. Fortunately, an increasing number of universities offer courses in social entrepreneurship, and the number of organizations that support social innovation and entrepreneurship has grown astoundingly in the last decade. Many of these organizations, both large and small, are playing a critical role in supporting young people like Laura, who want to be change makers. In the following stories, we will look at the support systems for two additional social entrepreneurs.

Syreeta Gates

In the 1960s, world-famous psychologist Abraham Maslow wrote extensively on his theory of the "hierarchy of needs." At the base of what he called "the pyramid of human needs" are requirements for food and water and sex. On the next level are the "safety needs" for security, order, and stability. Together, these represent the physical needs for survival. Only once these needs are met do human beings worry about their psychological needs, Maslow contends. And only after humans have satisfied their needs for love/belonging and self-esteem can they reach the pinnacle of the pyramid: self-actualization.

If Maslow's theory was true, we would expect to find young people from economically disadvantaged backgrounds to be far more worried about their physical survival rather than about how they are going to make a difference in the world. But as we learned from Jamien's story, and will see in the story of Syreeta Gates, it is not just the children of privileged families who want to make a difference in the world and who become innovators and social entrepreneurs. Like Jamien, Syreeta grew up in a family where a single parent struggled to provide.

A twenty-three-year-old African-American woman, Syreeta was born in Queens, New York. She is the only child of a single mother who recently retired from a career as a social worker in the city. In 2007, Syreeta founded an organization called The SWT (pronounced *sweet*) Life, which, according to Syreeta, "is dedicated to cultivating and maximizing young people's potential to succeed. The SWT Life provides entrepreneurial coaching, personal-development training, and exposure to professionals that are influential in guiding the Millennial Generation." Syreeta is currently enrolled in the City University of New York Baccalaureate for Unique and Interdisciplinary Studies, a program for students who want to design their own major and which awards some course credits for life experience. Syreeta's major is "urban youth culture," and she's taken courses in urban studies, social anthropology, introduction to hip-hop culture, and introduction to publishing. She also put together a portfolio that documents her community work experience, for which she received fifteen course credits.[5] Finally, Syreeta is editing a compilation of essays, entitled *Just BE Cause*, which is a guide to social entrepreneurship for the Millennial Generation and has more than thirty contributors. She plans to self-publish the book through Amazon.

VIDEO CUE:

Meet Syreeta Gates

Go to www.creatinginnovators.com
to watch the video.

Brenda Gates, Syreeta's mother, told me that Syreeta began "playing" at being an entrepreneur in elementary school. "I picked her up after school one day when she was in second grade," Brenda explained. "As we were leaving, the janitor said to her, 'Okay, sweetie, don't forget me.' I turned to my daughter and said, 'What is he talking about!' He saw and explained that Syreeta was selling popcorn at the school. She was charging four dollars for popcorn that I got at Costco for a dollar forty-eight.

"Later, she began making up bookmarks which I sold at work for a dollar. Then my aunt taught her how to make cakes, which I'd sell for her. In high school, she'd buy patches and sew them on clothes that she would sell to the other kids.

"But she's always been into helping others, too. One day, she asked about the men she saw just sitting out on benches, night and day. She wanted to know what she could do. I explained to her that some people are stuck, but you have to treat them with dignity and respect. And you have to pursue your own dreams and maybe be an example. You can't just daydream something. . . . And then she had a real 'aha' moment in high school, when she worked in a soup kitchen."

VIDEO CUE:

Brenda Gates on Raising Syreeta

Go to www.creatinginnovators.com
to watch the video.

"The soup kitchen was a cool experience," Syreeta told me. "I especially liked talking to the people there. I met homeless people as well as folks that were working who just needed a meal. One of the best parts of the soup kitchen was volunteering with my friends. From that, I realized service could be something fun and not boring."

That experience was the first spark of a passion for Syreeta, but the journey from her high school days to where she is now has been far from easy.

"I was a member of the two-thirty club in high school—meaning that I was out the door at two thirty," Syreeta told me. "I nearly flunked out. The only courses I liked in high school were business, business math, and communication.

"I graduated in '05 and went straight to City Technical College of New York. But after a year, I sort of dropped out and got kicked out at same time. I kept failing the math test."

Volunteering as a Path to Purpose

"As a parent, I tried to give Syreeta structure and let her find out what she was passionate about and to give her room to explore that," Brenda explained. "She found out that City Tech was nothing like high school. She came to me after the first year and said, 'I'm not ready.' I said 'Okay, but you have to do something.' That's when she started volunteering."

Syreeta continued. "It was when I began to do volunteer work that my life really started. I first worked for an organization called Team Revolution. Then I worked for Public Allies—an AmeriCorps program—for one year. In the beginning, I was a parent-community liaison for Project

Reach Youth—which was an AIDS awareness program—but I didn't like the position I was in, so I started going over to work at a teen program and loved it. I loved being in the space with teens. My first project was a young women's group. These were middle-school girls, and we were trying to help and guide them in their transition to high school.

VIDEO CUE:

Syreeta on Dream Managers

Go to www.creatinginnovators.com
to watch the video.

"The second project I led was a mural program for AIDS awareness. The program coordinator, Daniel Silber-Baker, was really great. He coached me and gave me the freedom to create the program."

When I asked Syreeta to name some teachers who had been especially helpful to her, she said there weren't any. But she did say that a number of people outside school had coached and mentored her in helpful ways, and Daniel Silber-Baker was one she named.

Syreeta's Mentors

VIDEO CUE:

Mentoring Syreeta

Go to www.creatinginnovators.com
to watch the video.

Daniel has a BA in American studies from the University of California at Santa Cruz and began working with youth when he was in eighth grade. "I stopped going to school for a while," Daniel told me, "and so my parents enrolled me in a counselor-in-training program at the YMCA. I fell in love with youth work from the very beginning." Now, at age twenty-seven, Daniel is director of Adolescent Health Education at Project Reach Youth, a program sponsored by Lutheran HealthCare, a hospital in Brooklyn. Daniel manages a series of programs aimed at creating a healthier and safer youth culture. He began working with Syreeta three years ago.

"I'm very protective of who works with our young people, but I quickly saw how good she was with adolescents. When her internship with Public Allies ended, I invented positions to keep her. And she's still involved with our programs. She gave the keynote address for our Project SAFE graduation a few months ago" (a program that "trains youth between the ages of 14 and 19 to provide life-saving information to their peers through workshops, performances, and community outreach").[6]

I asked Daniel to describe some of the ways he has tried to support Syreeta.

"Initially, I helped her find the space to realize her dreams. When she first started working with us, she came to me and said 'I want to do an HIV awareness mural with the kids.' Others in my organization thought that it would just be graffiti and didn't want to support the project. I said that I'd take the bureaucratic heat. So she organized a group of fourteen- to seventeen-year-old kids. They spent four weeks learning from a graffiti artist, and then they painted a mural on the side of a store. And it was obviously seen as valuable by the community because no one painted graffiti over it!

"In the last year or so, I've tried to support her decision to go back to college. I helped her put together the independent study for her major and choose classes. We've also worked on a number of projects together. One was World AIDS Day—her idea was to turn it into a campaign, not just a one-day event. Instead of 'fresh to death' [street slang for something really good], she came up with 'fresh to life.' She organized a campaign where kids used Facebook and Twitter to add to a list of one thing you can do each day to be safe, to protect yourself. There was a huge response.

"This past spring she organized a conference to partner Brooklyn kids with people in the community, and I was one of the people she recruited to be a coach."

Erica Ford was another important mentor of Syreeta's. "When I began working at Team Revolution, three years ago," Syreeta said, "Erica asked me what difference did I want to make in the world, what will be my legacy."

Erica is director of LIFE Camp (Love Ignites Freedom through Education), a nonprofit organization that, in Erica's words, "helps save and build lives by teaching young people to be entrepreneurs in music and fashion—as an alternative to gang life." Growing up in South Jamaica, Queens, at the height of the crack epidemic in the 1980s, Erica saw young people all around her being killed or jailed. She decided to work with youth to help them find other things to which they could dedicate their lives.

Erica knows how important it is to engage a young person around his or her passion, but she also understands the importance of teaching urban youth to push themselves.

"They've been trained not to think, not to go past their breaking point, to settle for mediocrity," Erica explained. "They are talented and intelligent, but lazy. And people accept that in the community. Syreeta would come with big words, like she knows stuff, but I told her, 'I'm going to push you.' I do that with all of the kids. You say you know how to play ball, I'll throw you a ball. You know how to rap, I'll give you a mic. You know how to design clothes, I'll find you a sewing machine. I've continued to push her. Last month, I had her go to a kids' settlement house in the Bronx and talk to them about her work and how they could get scholarships.

"Working with urban kids, you have to overcome their mind-set. We have to teach them that their economic condition does not have to define who they are. They need to understand that greatness is inside them, that if you are true to it, you can overcome barriers."

The Importance of Passion and Purpose in Syreeta's Life

According to the website Syreeta developed for the youth conference she created early in 2011, "THE SWT LIFE CONVO is a pilot program that will give 30 New York City teens (between 14–17) a clear understanding of how to have their passions, strengths, and purpose drive their success in school and life NOW. In 1-on-1 sessions with adolescent life coaches & astrologers, and workshops with millennial leaders across industries, teens will be introduced to a 30-day challenge designed to stretch their imaginations, skill sets and belief in themselves."[7]

When I asked Syreeta about why she thought "passions, strengths, and purpose" were important, she said, "In high school, they tell you to work hard at what you're bad at. But for me, it was so important to discover what I was good at and to find my passion—I couldn't go back to college until I knew what I was passionate about. It changes as you evolve and get older, but knowing your passion, you move with purpose, and when you move with purpose, everything makes sense."

Brenda Gates also talked about the importance to Syreeta of having found her passion. "She's passionate about what she's doing. She has a knack and confidence and skills to make a real impact on young people. My hope and dream is that she is passionate about whatever she does."

"Why do you think passion is so important?" I asked.

"When Syreeta is passionate about something—and when it's something she really enjoys doing—she gives it 110 percent, and she does it no matter what. If she's passionate, she's going to be successful—not necessarily making a lot of money, but because she's happy. So many people have all this money, but that's not happiness. It's not going to bring enjoyment in life."

Syreeta believes that young people must understand how youth culture shapes their values, beliefs, and behaviors. Not only are disadvantaged urban youth taught to settle for less, as Erica Ford observed, they come to think that it is the cool thing to do. It's not cool to study or take school seriously. It is more cool to skip school and hang out on the street. It is almost as though many young people who grow up in impoverished circumstances want to believe that the raw deal society has given them is something that they have freely chosen and prefer. Their schools are terrible, so it becomes more cool not to go at all, not to care.

VIDEO CUE:

Gates on Pop Culture

Go to www.creatinginnovators.com
to watch the video.

"She understands the power of cool better than anyone I've met," Daniel told me. "It is the driving force in youth culture and so is a key to understanding how we're going to engage young people. Syreeta is aware of how culture affects her and how she can affect it." He elaborated on this gift of Syreeta's in a recent e-mail:

> Following Syreeta's vision and understanding of how notions of "cool" so dominantly shape young people's lives and decisions, the SWT Life [the nonprofit organization that Syreeta started] serves as an engine and an umbrella, the driving force in bringing together key community members and organizations to create programs, conferences, mural projects, and community service activities which empower young people to make positive changes in their communities, all while re-shaping the boundaries of "cool." Syreeta's approach is a wildly imaginative and deeply practical one. It finds its base in the most concrete and urgent physical needs of our communities, and its solutions in the most beautiful and creative dreams of the people within those communities. Syreeta surrounds herself with the people most ignored, most silenced, carrying the biggest burdens, and she pulls from them the most effective movements for social change.

"Most people are taught that imagination has limits," Daniel later explained in conversation. "Syreeta refuses that logic—she honestly believes the way she imagines the world is the way it can be. She has the ability to dream of a more just, free, cool world."

Recently, Syreeta has gained some important recognition for her talents and achievements. She was honored as one of *Glamour* magazine's

"20 Amazing Young Women under 25" at the 2010 Glamour Women of the Year Awards. Syreeta was also named a StartingBloc Fellow, which enabled her to attend their four-day Institute for Social Innovation.[8] "I went to this business-plan-assistance workshop in Harlem, sponsored by StartingBloc and Goldman Sachs." Syreeta explained how she'd come to be in the program. "I started talking to this woman, Margaret Moore. I was reading Malcolm Gladwell's book *The Tipping Point*, and I just started telling her what I was doing. I later found out she'd been a StartingBloc Fellow and worked at Goldman. She helped me apply and paid for my application fee. I am truly grateful for the chance to be in that program. There were people from the nonprofit, corporate, government, and social-enterprise sectors. The network of young professionals is amazing."

This is not to say that Syreeta is home free, by any means. While she hopes to finish college in a year and a half, Syreeta told me that she struggles with the cost of school and often doesn't know how she will pay her next tuition bill. She lives at home to save money. Daniel, who helps Syreeta with schoolwork, worries that she can be impatient with the forms she has to fill out for financial aid and other bureaucratic aspects of school. "It's easy for her to say, 'Why bother?' But I think it's really important for her to finish."

Some Important Similarities and Differences

The similarities between Laura's and Syreeta's stories are striking. Both young women benefited greatly from parents who encouraged them to pursue their passion for making a difference in the world. Both found high school less than inspiring, and college for both of them has been a mixed bag. While both women have found or created courses that have interested them through interdisciplinary studies programs, they are more engaged by the work they're doing out of the classroom. Their goals are the same: to empower people and give them the tools they need to make change. In both women's lives, the support they have received from nonprofit organizations that work with young social entrepreneurs has been critical. Finally *play, passion,* and *purpose* have been equally important as motivators for Syreeta and Laura. "Knowing your passion, you move with purpose," Syreeta told me.

This comparison is not meant to diminish the significant differences in their lives, however. Growing up in a family that could barely stay afloat financially, Syreeta has had to scrape and struggle in ways that Laura has not. And while Syreeta did not say this, I think that Daniel and Erica are more than just intellectual mentors to Syreeta—they are role models. Both of them are doing the kind of work that Syreeta imagines for herself, and they are helping her to develop the discipline and persistence that she needs to succeed.

The role of passion and purpose in these two women's lives is different, as well, I think. For many middle-class young people growing up in a postindustrial society, discovering what they are passionate about gives their life deeper meaning, and having a sense of purpose drives them to work harder than they might otherwise and leads them to create important innovations. While this is equally true of urban youth, passion and purpose also play an even more important role in their lives. Discovering their passion enables them to have an alternative to street life and becomes essential to their very survival. Only by discovering what they most want and need to say yes to do, urban youth have the capacity to say "no" to the many things in their environment that drag them down and threaten to destroy them. In Syreeta's terms, *cool* goes from being "fresh to death" to "fresh to life."

Without a reason—without passion and purpose—many disadvantaged young people simply can't tolerate the tedium of school. Passion and purpose are what give them hope, a clear focus, and a reason to acquire the skills and the knowledge they will need to succeed.

However, not only minority students are "disadvantaged" in our education systems. Students who learn differently are disadvantaged in other ways, as we learn from Zander's story.

Zander Srodes

Twenty-one-year-old Zander Srodes has received international recognition for his work on behalf of endangered sea turtles. He's given presentations in hundreds of elementary schools in the United States and around the world, and he has been invited to lecture at conservation conferences in India and Japan. At the age of fourteen, Zander wrote a twenty-page activity book for elementary school children, called "Turtle Talks," which was illustrated by Linda Soderquist, an elementary school teacher and artist. Zander then recruited high school students to translate the book into Spanish and French. It was subsequently translated into three other languages, and to date 250,000 copies have been distributed free of charge in twenty countries.

Zander is currently working at a newly established sea turtle research and rescue station in the tiny village of La Baronna, located in the southernmost corner of Guatemala on the Pacific Ocean. The small group Zander has joined is pioneering a new approach by working with the poachers, educating them on the importance of donating 15 percent of the eggs they find to the station for rescue. The Akazul team asked Zander to join them because of his experience and interest in educating people about sea turtles. In addition to the exhausting duties of rescue and research in physically demanding circumstances, this station is teaching the kids about why saving turtles is good for them, their economy, and their ecology.

VIDEO CUE:

Meet Zander Srodes

Go to www.creatinginnovators.com
to watch the video.

This is how Zander explained the unlikely catalyst for his work in a talk he recently gave at a TEDx teen conference in New York:[9]

It started in 2001 when I was eleven years old. I was on the beach at night shooting off fireworks to impress my friends. And this old lady comes out and starts screaming at me about how the lights we're shining are messing with the sea turtles' vision of the moon so that they're not going to be able to get back down to the water. And being with my friends and a punk eleven-year-old kid, I said, "Get out of here, you old lady."

The next morning I wake up, and she's in my house, talking with my mom, and I know I'm in trouble. I come out after she's gone and my mom says, "You need to go down and talk to her. She's the state permit holder for protecting the sea turtles on this part of the beach." And I'm thinking, "Oh, great, she's someone important, so I'm really going to get in trouble."

So I go down to her house, expecting to get chewed out by this fifty-year-old lady who's just going to tell me about all these awful things I did. And she brings me inside, and she starts telling me about sea turtles. And she's not yelling at me. She's just educating me about these endangered animals. What I was doing with those fireworks was impeding a creature that's been on the earth for sixty-five million years, and they are integral parts of the coral system which they inhabit. And I don't know what happened, but something sort of snapped. I'd never cared about anything before. And all a sudden I was asking her, "What can I do to help protect these sea turtles?" And she said, "There aren't many youths doing anything to protect the sea turtles." After that day, there wasn't a day that went by where I didn't think about these animals.

Evolution of a Young Environmentalist

Zander told me the rest of his story in a conversation. "Linda and I came up with the idea to do school presentations. I'd read about a grants program for kids, wrote a proposal with my mom's and Linda's help, and received twelve hundred dollars from the Venice Foundation [now called the Gulf Coast Community Foundation]. I got a laptop to do PowerPoint presentations, borrowed the LCD projector from my dad's office. I made a costume for kids to put on that explained the anatomy of the sea turtle and used a sea-turtle-shaped sandbox that kids could use to bury mock eggs. I also had a full-sized model of the turtle.

"With Linda's help, I started calling teachers and going to schools near my home in Florida. When I first started the project, I never thought in a million years that teachers would want *me* to come in and talk to their classes because I wasn't the greatest student, and I never had a teacher who liked me. But teachers really liked my presentations—they liked the idea of an eleven-year-old coming in and talking to their kids. And I think it struck a chord with students because I was someone their own age talking to them.

"After I'd been doing presentations for three years—and I was doing more and more each year—Linda and I started talking about how to reach students I couldn't travel to present to, and that's where we came up with the idea for 'Turtle Talks,' which I wrote in the summer of 2004. Linda did the illustrations, while I fact-checked everything and started writing grants. The first printing was about five thousand books, and we began sending copies out to schools in Florida and then to Georgia and North Carolina, where they have sea turtle nesting populations.

"But sea turtles face even greater threats to extinction in the Caribbean countries, so we started sending books to Trinidad and the Bahamas. Then I worked with the Spanish Club at my high school to translate the book into Spanish. I started getting grant money to travel, as well. I went to Trinidad to do talks in schools, and we set up some sister-school programs, linking US schools with ones in Costa Rica, the Bahamas, and Panama. This year, I was invited to present at the International Sea Turtle Symposium, which was in India, and so now the book has been translated into two Indian dialects. I keep writing grants to produce more books and try to get them translated into more languages."

"How much money have you raised for the project so far?"

"About two hundred and fifty thousand dollars."

Zander didn't mention all of the youth achievement awards that he's been given for his work, including the Florida Wildlife Federation's Youth Conservationist Award and Earth Island Institute's Brower Youth Award in 2005; the Presidential Environmental Youth and Prudential Spirit of Community Awards in 2007; and the Volvo for Life Award in 2008. Zander donated the $25,000 he received for this award to the Florida Mote Marine Laboratory, whose scientists had helped him with research and materials for his first school presentations. Nor did he tell me that his picture and bio appeared on 25 million bags of Doritos chips, as a part of the Do Something Award in 2008. I learned all this from some of the numerous articles that have been written about him.

"So what's next?" I asked Zander.

"I've written two other activity books, one on the gopher tortoise and one on freshwater turtles. Because of the project, I've developed a lot of connections with people in the sea turtle conservation community. I'm an education intern for the Sea Turtle Conservancy—they're the oldest sea turtle conservation organization in the world. I'm also an intern for a group called SEE Turtles. They do eco-tourism and take kids from the US to Costa Rica, Mexico, and Trinidad to volunteer on sea turtle nesting sites. I led a trip last summer to Costa Rica, and this summer I'm leading another."

Brad Nahill is marketing director and co-founder of SEE Turtles, the group for whom Zander led his first eco-tourism trip. I asked him about how Zander's work for the organization evolved.

"I first connected with Zander at the 2007 meeting of the Sea Turtle Symposium in Myrtle Beach, South Carolina. He came to my attention through a colleague, Dr. Wallace Nichols, one of the leading turtle conservationists today. Dr. Nichols had Zander talk about his book and work to a group at one of the breakout sessions. He was only sixteen or seventeen at the time, and he had to get up in front of conservationists that'd been doing this work for a long time. But he was very eloquent, and he'd created a great book. I've seen a lot of materials, and his is one of the best. You don't see many young kids walking around these meetings, which usually consist of heavy scientific presentations. I recognized that he could be a real leader in the field.

"We kept in touch for the next year or so. As SEE Turtle began to develop a more intensive education program, I felt it was important to have a younger person's perspective and extended the offer of an internship to Zander two summers ago. He gave us feedback on curricula for teachers, which definitely helped improve them. Zander also helped me put together a database of college and high school environmental clubs. It's a valuable resource in getting more schools involved.

"We decided to offer a Costa Rica tour for college students that Zander would lead. He helped promote it and refined the itinerary. I wasn't sure about his leading the trip initially. He's one of the most motivated college-age students I've been around—but he's still a college student. But I was there and got to see him interacting with six students, most of whom were older than Zander. The feedback from the participants was outstanding. Several are hoping to go on the next trip that Zander will lead.

"What makes him effective?" I asked.

"It's his combination of personal charisma and unbridled enthusiasm. When he's at college and has a lot going on, he can be tentative and not confident. But out on the beach, he's on his turf and very confident. Zander doesn't claim to be an expert, but he's been in this long enough and has a strong knowledge base. He's also really good at making people feel comfortable. I've led trips, and there's always a spectrum of people—some are very enthusiastic, while others are intimidated, don't know much, and are worried they'll do something wrong. Zander has an ability to help them get over their initial hesitation, feel comfortable, and become part of the research and conservation work."

A Struggling Student and Schools That Didn't Help

Had it not been for the unwavering support of Linda Soderquist and Jean Srodes, Zander's mother, Zander's many talents might well have gone unnoticed and undeveloped, and none of these contributions to conservation would likely have come to pass. Unlike most of our other young innovators, who shone in school, Zander's accomplishments have come in spite of his struggles in the classroom. Jean Srodes explained this to me in an e-mail:

Zander has had many breaks and much support in pursuing his interests and passions. However, I would never say that the educational system was supportive.

I always say that everything he learned, he learned in kindergarten. His kindergarten teacher, who was also his 1st grade teacher, got him. She always said that she didn't believe all boys were cut from the same cloth. She was able to let Zander stand and do work, if he needed to, and move around. She made it easy for him to learn in school. But many teachers after that were so immersed in their style of teaching that his days spent in school were painful. The world of work sheets, busy work, and sitting quietly at a desk made school tough for our family.

Maybe we should have medicated him. We knew if he was tested he would qualify for ADD [attention deficit disorder] medications. But we didn't want to stifle his creative spirit.

During his time in high school [a public school in Englewood, Florida], not many teachers even recognized his conservation work. It was during this time that he received a number of awards. At the school's final awards presentation when he was a senior, they forgot to mention that he had received the Prudential Spirit of Community Award. They had never responded to the letter to pick up the plaque to present to him.

Linda Soderquist and Zander met when he was eleven. Linda never questioned that he would follow his vision, even though he was just a kid. She always took him seriously and has supported his interests. If it were not for her brilliant illustrations in the activity books that Zander has written, the project would never have happened. Linda has never asked or expected payment for her art work.

So I don't know the answer on the subject of schools as venues for creative students to thrive. I would have home schooled Zander, but he actually wanted to attend school for social reasons. He couldn't imagine staying at home while everyone else was at school. I actually thought school was a detriment to his learning.

I substitute teach in a public school system in West Virginia now. I see the same kind of teaching that my son received—flat, boring, rule-governed. I just spent a month working in a middle school special educa-

> tion class. I worked with five boys who were profiled as trouble makers, but if you dig below the surface, they all have talents. They have IEP's [Individual Education Plans], under a variety of diagnoses. But what if someone had let them find a passion or supported an interest? Not one of them should have had me following them from class to class to be sure they weren't disruptive. They all could do the work, but they were living up to their labels. Now I am moving to first grade to substitute, and I will really worry about those guys at the middle school.

Linda Soderquist retired in June 2010 after having taught elementary school for forty-two years. She, too, was eloquent and outspoken about the plight of students like Zander. "Most schools do not permit students who have ADD or behavior problems to be in gifted programs. I have the opposite view. Sometimes they are the most exciting kids to teach—they understand that I want them to think out of the box. Too many 'gifted' students just want to know the 'right answer,' but with many of the questions I posed, there was no right answer. A student like Zander would be standing up and walking around the room, coming up with all kinds of ideas. He's always got an idea he's jazzed about—gifted kids are like that. Too many teachers expect them to sit down and behave. I think teachers need to understand that just because a kid is a pain in the butt, it doesn't mean they don't have something very cool to offer. Teachers need to figure out a way to bring it out.

"I'm blessed that I've gotten out. In the school where I last taught, this year if it's a Tuesday, then everybody has to be on page twenty-one. It used to be that I had more flexibility when I was teaching gifted students. And so I made my units more relevant, more integrated, more interdisciplinary. And before every lesson, I'd explain what we were going to explore. I would also remind them that employers are looking for people with creative ideas, and the right answer isn't going to always be there. But now if it doesn't have something to do with the test, you aren't allowed to teach it. Some principals come right out and say, 'We're not going to teach science this semester because it's not being tested until fifth grade.' That's really scary."

VIDEO CUE:

Soderquist on the Future of Education

Go to www.creatinginnovators.com
to watch the video.

Zander wants to be a marine biologist, but after two attempts attending two different state universities, it is not clear to me that he will be able to earn the necessary degree. In high school, Zander could get by with little effort. "The best part of being an average student in a typical run-of-the-mill high school," he told me, "was that I could miss classes to go give presentations anytime, and no one cared. I always put my conservation work ahead of my classes. I had friends who were in advanced placement and International Baccalaureate classes, and they could never have done that." But college is a different story. "I need someone to give me an honorary degree," he told me, only half joking. "School is the biggest stumbling block in my life—it gets in the way of everything I want to do. I hate going to classes. I do well in classes that I care about and where I like the teacher—but if I don't, it's almost impossible to get out of bed."

I asked Jean Srodes how she saw Zander's future.

"At some point, he'll finish college. I don't worry about him. You can always go back to school, but can you always find your passion? Zander left school to go to Panama for a month when he was seventeen. A lot of people said to me, 'I can't believe you let him do that.' I felt it wouldn't be fair not to let him go. Maybe I should worry, but I see him living in his own skin, and it works."

"How does your husband feel about Zander's work?"

"He's very proud of him. But it's hard for my seventy-two-year-old husband who expects that when you do a job, it's for money—even though Zander thinks of his nonpaid internships as his 'work.'"

The Dangers of Labels and the Challenge of Credentials

Once again, we see a pattern that's now familiar in the development of a young innovator: parents who encourage their children to find and pursue their passions and an outlier teacher—in this case, an elementary teacher—who empowers his or her students to explore and discover in the classroom and does the same as a mentor outside of school.

For Zander, giving presentations at the age of eleven was initially a form of creative play that seemed to quickly grow into a passion. Zander's passion has evolved into a deeper sense of purpose. However, it's not clear how Zander will gain the credibility he will need to pursue his sense of purpose in the future. We live in a credentialed society—and especially so in the scientific community. Brad Nahill, Zander's mentor, compared his own struggle for credibility with Zander's. "With a degree in economics, rather than in biology, I found it hard initially to be taken seriously by scientists. With no degree at all, it would be a major challenge. Zander may be able to do it, but it will be much harder."

Many people are like Zander—especially among economically disadvantaged populations. The labels given them—hyperactive, ADD, ADHD, special needs, and so on—may describe certain symptoms, but all too often these "diagnoses" become a stigma, a mark on children's souls that tells us nothing about who they are, what they are capable of, and what they need to succeed. What is common to many that I have taught, however, is that they are not "book learners." They learn by doing. They are capable of making enormous contributions to society if given the right opportunities to learn and to develop—as we see with Zander.

VIDEO CUE:

Srodes on ADHD

Go to www.creatinginnovators.com
to watch the video.

Amy Smith, who was Jodie Wu's teacher at MIT, understands the problem in a personal way. "I'm pretty sure that if I were a student now, I'd be diagnosed with ADD," she told me. "There's a whole group of people who believe they have a disorder versus a different thinking style. And they are drugged because they are hard to control or harder to write lessons for. I was shy and so didn't get into much trouble, but I can't learn things through reading. I don't retain it. Words on a page don't go into my brain unless I can visualize or make real what it is I'm reading. But the people who become teachers learn in a particular way, and the whole premise of education is based on reading. Different creative-thinking styles get marginalized in schools. And so those kids don't end up in careers that allow that creativity to get fostered."

VIDEO CUE:

Smith on Learning Styles

Go to www.creatinginnovators.com
to watch the video.

I don't know what the answer is for Zander or how his story will turn out. I do not think that all students should go to a four-year college. As Amy said, we need to value different kinds of creativity and the many ways people can be highly innovative without four years of college. In Finland, which is one of the most innovative countries in the world, nearly half of all high school students choose to take more hands-on career and vocationally oriented programs and graduate from high school with offers for well-paying and innovative jobs. We will learn more about some of their other education innovations in the next chapter.

A Few Final Observations

Not all social innovators struggle with school as Syreeta and Zander have. Many of the most gifted students whom I have met in my research aspire to be social entrepreneurs and are good students—Laura White being one. Regardless of their socioeconomic backgrounds or degree of school success, what all young innovators have in common is the importance of play, passion, and purpose in their lives. These intrinsic motivations are what drive them to achieve and to persevere—and what gives their life texture and meaning. In the many conversations I've had with young people for this book, not once did any of them mention goals related to making money or finding fame. They want and need to make a difference—and of course they want a certain amount of recognition for this work. That's only human.

But passion and purpose are even more essential for young people from disadvantaged backgrounds who struggle against poverty and prejudice. For this group, having a strong sense of passion and purpose is what enables them to have the courage, discipline, and tenacity to transcend their circumstances and surroundings and to have hope and direction for their future. And mentors have played an even more important role in nurturing the passions and purposes of young people from disadvantaged backgrounds, as we've seen. Consider the many mentors who have helped Syreeta and Jamien in significant ways. You don't have to be a parent or a teacher to make a huge difference in a young person's life. But what you must do is listen carefully for—and then nurture—that vital spark of passion.

Some of our young innovators have done well in school, while others have not. But even those who were most successful in school derived the greatest benefit from only one or two teachers—and all of those teachers defied the conventions of their school or college in one way or another. The nonprofit and more informal networks our innovators became involved with seem to have been at least as important in their development as any high school or college classroom experience.

Fortunately, courageous educators everywhere are engaged in their own research and development to innovate learning at every grade level—pre-K–college. We have already met a number of these teachers through the profiles of the eight young innovators in this book. In the next chapter, we will explore in greater depth the kinds of educational changes most needed in order to "create" many more young people who are curious, creative, and committed to making a difference.

Chapter Five

Innovating Learning

The Challenges of Twenty-first-Century Teaching and Learning

Educational institutions are deeply and inherently conservative, especially at the high school and college level, for some important and valid reasons. Our education system is charged with an essentially "conserving" task—preserving and transferring our knowledge "capital" to the next generation. Such knowledge is essential for "cultural literacy"—a term coined by E. D. Hirsch—to be an educated adult, and it can be a source of enormous personal satisfaction, as well. Knowledge is also essential in order to innovate. You need foundational information to be able to discern what can and must be improved upon or changed.

One problem with this traditional approach to learning, however, is that the way in which academic content is taught is often stultifying: It is too often merely a process of transferring information through rote memorization, with few opportunities for students to ask questions or discover things on their own—the essential practices of innovation. As a result, students' inherent curiosity is often undermined—"schooled out" of them, as Sir Ken Robinson and others have written. Additionally, research has repeatedly shown that too many students graduate from even our most elite universities with little or no *conceptual* understanding of the science and math they have spent four years studying. They have learned the facts, but do not understand the ideas behind them.[1]

Another equally serious problem with the traditional model is the exponential growth of information. One cannot possibly cover all of the academic content in a given area. The more a teacher tries to do this, the more the curriculum becomes a kind of forced march through the material. The result is that far too many of our students graduate from high school and college knowing how to pass tests, but less motivated to learn and lacking essential skills.

Increasingly in the twenty-first century, what you know is far less important than what you can do with what you know. The interest in and ability to create new knowledge to solve new problems is the single most important skill that all students must master today. All successful innovators have mastered the ability to learn on their own "in the moment" and then apply that knowledge in new ways.

This chapter is devoted to an exploration of the many ways in which educators—both individually and working together in institutions—are exploring new solutions to these twenty-first-century learning challenges. We begin with profiles of two high school teachers—one working with at-risk students and the other with highly motivated science students. Both literally teach "out of the box" to motivate their students and develop their capabilities as innovators.

Scott Rosenberg

A filmmaker by training, Scott Rosenberg founded Art Start in 1991. It is a nonprofit whose purpose "is to nurture the voices, hearts and minds of at-risk New York City youth, providing the resources and outlet for them to change their own lives through the creative process."[2] Their tagline is "Art Saves Lives," and in the case of Chris "Kazi" Rolle, this is no exaggeration.

"I grew up in Virginia," Scott told me. "My first friends were sharecroppers living in a dirt-floor shack. So I never felt right indulging my artistic interests without trying to have a social impact. I came to New York to study filmmaking and later founded Art Start there. I began going to homeless shelters to see if I could help some of those kids. My goal was to bring their ideas, stories, and visions forth through art and give them the structure that allowed them to create. These kids were in last-chance schools or shelters—they had no homes, no consistency—nothing to tether them. They yearned to have a sense of connection and identity. I gave them a chance to explore their voice—what's important to you? What do you have to say.

"I started working on a curriculum related to the arts and media literacy. In 1994, I found a last chance high school [an alternative school for students who had dropped out or been expelled from other schools] that allowed me to come and teach a class [the Repertory Company High School]. We looked at films like *Menace II Society* [an award-winning 1993 film that graphically portrays life in the Los Angeles hood], and pieces of music from Biggie Smalls—a timeless icon in rap culture who was killed one week before his second album was released. I brought in the producer of *Philadelphia* (the first Hollywood movie to deal with HIV/AIDS), Scott Rudin, to have a conversation with the whole school and screen the film.

"I pushed the kids to think about what they saw and heard. What is the imagery here? Is that what you see or what you think? It was rigorous, inquiry-based. These kids were already experts at media consumption, but their understanding was not codified in a formal way. The kids were so motivated—they'd come in to talk about stuff after school.

"My approach was this: If I called a business meeting and I was unprepared and didn't take my partners seriously, then I wouldn't stay in business for long. So I approached these kids like colleagues or professionals, by going to where they were, respecting them, looking them right in the eye. I loved hearing what they had to say. I had kids study commercials, break them down, and they got very savvy about how they work. I gave them the goal to create their own public service announcement, but they had to do it as a team. So the kids had to pitch their idea for a PSA to everyone in class. I had kids go to an ad agency to find out what pitching is. Some said the PSA should be about child abuse, some said sexual abuse.

"My second year at the school, I noticed kids were rhyming and doing improv in the halls—always boasting. So I challenged them and said, 'Let's see what you can do with a mic and a beat.' We began meeting at lunch. It was amazing to see these kids come alive—Dominicans, African-Americans, all with different styles and approaches. This ended up being a ritual separate from my class, but Ellen [the school principal] said, 'We love you, but you can't do this in school. It's not art, and they're cursing other teachers. We can't allow it anymore.'

"The school couldn't let us stay and do this after classes because they didn't have the budget for a security guard. But these kids wanted to keep working. They were coming an hour each way to school and back, and there was no glee club or football team for them. So we held meetings in pizza places, or cafés, or in the park. They were working until six, seven, or eight at night. We moved the work into a part of my apartment for a while, until we found studio space. What amazed me was how they found ways to take their situations and express themselves with linguistic complexity, nuances, dexterity, and originality.

"I decided this work could become a new part of Art Start. We weren't just doing art in the shelters anymore. We now had a media works project—listening to music, looking at film, studying media imagery, deconstructing it, creating PSAs. And so what is now called the Hip Pop Project became the third leg of Art Start."

One of Art's students was Chris "Kazi" Rolle. Chris told me that he was homeless and hustling on the streets when he dropped into Art's class. Because of Art's extraordinary approach to teaching, Chris was motivated to stay in school, and he graduated from Repertory Company High School in 1996. After a brief stint in a community college, he began teaching in the Art Start media works project and then led the Hip Hop Project. "The Hip Hop Project helped me believe in my own creativity and develop my confidence, as well as my ideas," Chris explained. "I learned to be resilient, and to have a vision, as well as a focus. Now I want to pay it forward." Today Chris—Kazi as he is now called—continues to work with disadvantaged youth through a variety of projects and is pursuing a successful career as an actor and hip-hop performer. He also speaks to African-American adult audiences about the challenges of keeping families together. His life story is the focus of a feature-length documentary film, *The Hip Hop Project,* which was produced by Scott, and whose executive producers were Bruce Willis and Queen Latifah. The film was theatrically released nationwide in 2007 and has won numerous awards.

"These kids are utterly heroic," Scott said. "It is inconceivable to me that I could have endured what many of them have. And they are desperately thirsty for connection, to be taken seriously, and to be purposeful. I believe our job is to look for the threads, plant the seeds, and provide them with the tools and structures for purposefulness. Someone who has a purpose or a reason can endure a lot. This is where our education system is utterly lacking. Who wants to go through the crap of all that rote work and memorization for no reason?"

Leaving "No Child Behind": Having a Reason to Learn and a Voice

Scott's question is exactly the right one. He encouraged his students' development of passion and purpose in order to have a reason to learn. He began by observing them "play" in the halls and challenging them to take their play more seriously. He used their expressions of play—their love of music as well as their absorption in youth culture—as a starting point for learning through inquiry. Through his mentoring, many gradually developed the self-discipline they needed to succeed as their play became their passion, which, in turn, deepened over time, into a strong sense of purpose.

Syreeta would have benefited enormously from having had a teacher like Scott in high school—someone who took youth culture seriously and helped young people understand both the vibrancy of their culture and also the ways in which they were held back by it; someone who, like Scott, taught his or her students to use their experiences and insights to create their own culture. In the best tradition of the other highly innovative teachers whom we've met in this book, Scott also worked to create a learning environment that was hands-on, interdisciplinary, and collaborative, and one which enabled him to discover and cultivate students' intrinsic motivations for learning. And like the others, he was an outlier in his school and eventually had to take some of his most important work out of the classroom altogether.

Scott's successes with his students profoundly illustrate the importance of establishing relationships with young people based on a deep sense of respect. He didn't merely "look them in the eye," as he said. He listened long and hard. He sought to learn from them. Above all, Scott helped them give voice to their insights, ideas, and aspirations. When you give young people a real voice, some of what they have to say will be challenging—even disruptive, as Scott discovered. But if we are truly serious about "leaving no child behind" and enabling every young person to become an innovator, then these are risks we must take.

Amanda Alonzo

In his March 20, 2010, *New York Times* column, "America's Real Dream Team," Tom Friedman wrote about spending an evening with the forty finalists in the 2010 Intel Science Talent Search. It is the oldest and most prestigious precollegiate national science competition, in which more than sixteen hundred high school students enter original science projects and compete for college scholarships.[3] Friedman's column introduced me to Amanda Alonzo, then a thirty-year-old science teacher at Lynbrook High School in San Jose, California. She had taught *two* of the forty Intel finalists in 2010.

VIDEO CUE:

Alonzo on Science at Lynbrook High

Go to www.creatinginnovators.com
to watch the video.

Amanda grew up in Vacaville, a rural California town, and attended a public high school there. When I first interviewed her in June 2010, Amanda had just finished her eighth year of teaching. "I had no intention of studying science in college," Amanda told me. "I wanted to be a dance major, but my dad said he wouldn't pay for college if I majored in dance. My first science class in college was taught by a woman biologist, Meg Mathais, and she really inspired me to go on to major in science. I knew I wanted to teach, and because of Meg, I decided to focus on high school in order to introduce more women to science.

"I went to Stanford University for my master's in education and was fortunate in having Susan Schultz, a high school science teacher who was studying for her PhD at Stanford, as my curriculum and design instructor. [Most professors in schools of education have not had substantial K–12 school teaching experience.] We got to do a lot of hands-on, inquiry-based learning, which then informed my teaching. My first year of teaching at Lynbrook, I was asked to participate in the Intel Educators Academy, to get training to be a science-fair faculty adviser. Every other teacher at the school who had been asked had declined, but I felt I couldn't say no as a first-year teacher. I was very reluctant to go because my experiences with science fairs in the past weren't positive—what I'd seen wasn't really science, wasn't powerful learning, and parents were doing most of the work.

"I was blown away by the academy, though. About one hundred teachers came from around the world to learn how to get students more involved in science fairs. I went back and wrote a grant to start a program at our school, in conjunction with the middle school, and we received twenty thousand dollars from Intel. Initially, the idea was to run a summer program for incoming ninth graders, which would teach the scientific method, and at the end of the summer, each student would write a research proposal that they could work on in the fall. But I'm a scientist, and I observed after two summers' experience that many of the students in the program were not there by free will. Parents had forced them to go, and those students never followed through because science research involves a huge investment of time and energy and passion. I modified the program and now run a series of seminars throughout the school year, which meet at lunch and after school. The seminars are a general tutorial which introduces students to scientific processes in the fall, and beginning in January I meet with them individually to help them get started on their research.

"I worked with about forty students this year, and it is a huge time investment for me, but it is a labor of love. Whether they do well in the competitions or not, they learn a great deal, and I think they become better people. They see the world as a place with a lot of problems—it opens their eyes to what they are inheriting from our generation—but they also walk away feeling they can do something about these problems. For example, one of my students this year came up with a novel way of creating hydrogen fuel from algae. They are learning so much more in this work than they do in their science classrooms."

"What's different about what you are doing in these seminars, compared to the regular science classes?" I asked.

"In my classes, I have state standards that I have to teach, which are all about content knowledge. They have to know that mitochondria make energy. Whereas in the seminar, I am teaching them how to figure out that mitochondria make energy. Problem solving. Asking questions. Coming up with novel solutions. Unfortunately in my classroom, I don't feel that I have enough time to do these kinds of activities because I have all of these rigid content standards that I have to cover for the state tests."

"We have these state tests because policy makers believe we need more students to be scientifically literate so that they can go on to major in STEM-related fields," I observed. "But you are suggesting that this policy is having unintended consequences. What do you think we should do differently?"

"To be a successful science teacher, you have to make it fun, and for kids that means making it theirs—so that they have ownership over what they are learning. It's what motivates them. The other problem is that teachers think that, in order to cover the state standards, they have to give students all the answers, instead of having students discover the answers on their own. The most important thing is allowing students to ask questions and then give them the space to find the answers. They will actually retain more of the content by learning in this way."

VIDEO CUE:

Alonzo on Innovation, Passion, and Purpose

Go to www.creatinginnovators.com
to watch the video.

"What about advanced placement science courses?" I wondered. "Have you thought about teaching AP classes, and would they be any different?"

"I've resisted the pressures to teach AP classes for a couple of reasons," Amanda replied. "First, I like working with kids who have diverse interests, and I love teaching ninth graders [who do not take AP courses]. They're still curious, ask lots of questions, and they are willing to take more risks—think out of the box and not follow the rules. I also feel like AP courses drive the content down kids' throats. They memorize a vast amount of content for the tests and never get to apply what they have learned. There is a lot of pressure on kids, as well. It takes the love out of science. And ultimately, the courses are not good preparation for college. I've seen kids who have gotten fives on their AP tests [the highest score possible] and not have to take an introductory biology course in college, but then they struggle with the next-level course. Their brains were not developed enough to be able to apply what they've learned at the level required in the advanced classes."

VIDEO CUE:

Alonzo on the Value of Failure

Go to www.creatinginnovators.com
to watch the video.

"You are clearly teaching in a very different way. Has that been difficult for you at the school?"

"It's been hard. I've felt quite alone. At the end of the school year for my first four years, I was going to quit. The school has traditionally gotten excellent test results, and so there was enormous resistance to doing anything differently. I didn't feel supported—and that my creativity wasn't valued. But the kids have made it worthwhile for me—despite the huge time commitment."

I pressed Amanda for details and learned that teaching her noncredit seminars in the fall takes about six hours a week. But when students begin working on their individual projects in January, she spends an average of four hours a day working with students after school! She does this work on top of her regular full-time teaching load. Amanda is paid a stipend of $1,800 a year for this additional work.

I recently checked in with Amanda via e-mail and asked how her students had done in the 2011 Intel science competition. None of her students were among the forty finalists this year, she told me, but she had *four* out of the two hundred and fifty semifinalists—two of whom were young women, her first female students to win recognition in the competition. She was especially pleased with this result.

I also asked if there were any new developments in her teaching, and she wrote that she was now experimenting with "inverted teaching." In 2004, Salman Khan began making videos, which he posted on YouTube, to aid his cousin in learning math concepts. The idea caught on, and the Khan Academy has now produced more than twenty-seven hundred short (ten- to-twenty-minute) instructional videos on every conceivable topic related to math, science, finance, and history. According to Khan, more than 1 million students a month watch between one to two hundred thousand videos a day—for free![4] Amanda is assigning students the appropriate video lectures as homework so that class time can then be used for projects and tutorials that help students apply what they've learned and understand the content more deeply.

"Race to the Top" versus Accountability 2.0

Amanda Alonzo is, without question, one of the most innovative and effective science teachers whom I have ever met. The best judge of her effectiveness as a teacher is not her students' scores on California's standardized tests, however. It is not how many science facts they have learned, but rather it is what her students can *do* with what they know that makes her such a remarkable teacher. Amanda's students don't just know how to define the scientific method; they know how to *use* it. They know how to ask and keep refining their inquiry questions, design and perform experiments, and analyze the results. They know how to *be* scientists, and the work they produce is the best evidence of this. Amanda motivates her students with what is now a familiar formula for the readers of this book: She makes science fun, and she empowers her students to pursue projects that deeply interest them. Her success has been achieved by putting *play, passion,* and *purpose* at the center of her teaching. She refuses to teach advanced placement science classes because they "take the love" out of learning science.

The Obama administration's education initiative, Race to the Top, has received strong bipartisan support. One of the central elements of the plan calls for states to design programs for evaluating teachers based on how well their students score on standardized tests. Even if the federal government's role in education is diminished in the future, as now seems likely, the idea of evaluating teachers' effectiveness based on students' test scores has become popular and will likely persist. I agree that teacher evaluation programs in most school districts are totally ineffectual, but the answer is not to judge teachers by scores on standardized tests, which tell us nothing about what students can do with what they know. We must look at the work that students actually produce in order to assess the effectiveness of the teaching—and not just in science. We can look at what a student wrote for an English or history class in September and then in June and evaluate progress in both understanding and communication.

Race to the Top is a race to mediocrity. We need Accountability 2.0: an accountability system that incents the kind of teaching that Amanda does for her science club students and that relies on human judgment, rather than computer scores, to assess the quality of students' work and teachers' effectiveness. I believe all students should maintain a digital portfolio, beginning in first grade, that follows them through school and contains their best work, and that students should have to periodically demonstrate what they know. Progress from one school division to the next—say from middle school to high school—should be based on evidence of proficiency in students' oral and written work. Think of this as the "merit badge" approach to learning and to accountability. We need clear evidence of students' progressive mastery over time of the skills that matter most—which multiple choice tests can't give us. How many corporations make important hiring or promotion decisions based on a computer-scored test? If human judgment is good enough for business, then it can and must, with diligent work, become good enough for education.

Amanda does her best teaching in a world that she has created that lies completely outside the boundaries of the conventional classroom and science curriculum—much as Scott Rosenberg did with the Hip Hop Project. They are both teaching out of the box. Thus far, Amanda has maintained the freedom to do this because of her extraordinary Intel competition success and her willingness to work many long hours, for which she is paid a pittance. But with the increased pressures that the current test-based accountability system is placing on teachers, I fear that the most innovative and committed teachers like Amanda and Scott will be driven out of the profession. Who would want to teach in a system that measures your worth as an educator by how much your students can regurgitate on a two-hour multiple-choice test and that has reduced much of the curriculum to tedious test-prep exercises?

The Race to the Top initiative may have another serious unintended consequence, as well. According to a February 4, 2011, *New York Times* article, participation in high school science fairs—like the ones Amanda's students participate in—is declining. The reason? According to the *Times* article, "Many science teachers say the problem is . . . the Obama administration's own education policy, which holds schools accountable for math and reading scores at the expense of the kind of creative, independent exploration that science fair projects require."[5]

Rethinking College

What keeps the Amanda Alonzos of the high school world from innovating in their classrooms is not just the most recent reform du jour, however. The challenge to change lies in the origins of the high school curriculum and the kind of teaching that predominates. The overwhelming majority of high school students in our country take courses and learn in ways largely dictated by the practices and perceived demands of colleges. Content for state tests—such as the ones for which Amanda must prepare her students—is also substantially determined by the perceptions of what students will need to get into college. What subjects are taught in high schools, as well as the teaching methods themselves, are profoundly influenced by the now near universal mandate that all high school graduates should be "college-ready," meaning that they have taken and passed all the academic subjects required for admission into college. In *The Global Achievement Gap*, I profiled three schools that represent a significant rethinking of the traditional high school experience. High Tech High, in particular, and the New Tech High network of schools are outstanding examples of how best to educate all students to develop their innovation abilities at the secondary level. But such schools are still very rare.

The organization of academic subjects in high school—called the Carnegie Unit system—dates back to the late nineteenth century, when the president of Harvard University at the time, Charles W. Eliot, led efforts to standardize the secondary school curriculum. Now, more than a hundred years later, almost all high schools in America organize their curriculum according to this system that is largely unchanged. Likewise, many high school teachers' instructional techniques continue to be based on the lecture method of covering academic content, which was also pioneered at Harvard under Eliot's tenure. Finally, parents and teachers have come to believe that high school students must take as many advanced placement courses as possible, to be admitted to places like Harvard, despite the fact that such courses do not teach the skills needed to be an innovator or even to succeed in a selective college, as I show in *The Global Achievement Gap*.

So if we are to transform high schools in America to better educate young people for an innovation-driven economy, we will need to start by rethinking college—the curriculum, the teaching methods, and the admission requirements.

The evolution of the university has a long history, whose retelling is not essential for this book. The simplest way to understand the university is to see that its ultimate purpose is to create and transmit knowledge. Research is the primary means for the creation of knowledge, and courses exist to transmit knowledge and to recruit promising new scholars who will go on to do graduate work and generate new knowledge.

The modern university, however, has drifted quite far from this vision. In an influential *New York Times* commentary entitled "End of the University as We Know It," Mark C. Taylor, chairman of the religion department at Columbia University, wrote, "Graduate education is the Detroit of higher learning. Most graduate programs in American universities produce a product for which there is no market (candidates for teaching positions that do not exist) and develop skills for which there is diminishing demand (research in subfields within subfields and publication in journals read by no one other than a few like-minded colleagues), all at a rapidly rising cost (sometimes well over $100,000 in student loans)."[6]

Even worse, new research suggests that many students are incurring enormous debt to go to college and aren't learning much in their undergraduate courses. College debt now exceeds credit card debit in America, with the average college graduate owing nearly $30,000.[7] A recent book, *Academically Adrift*, reports on a study demonstrating that, after two years of college, nearly half of all students showed no improvement in their complex-reasoning, critical-thinking, or writing skills.[8] *We're Losing Our Minds: Rethinking American Higher Education*, a new book authored by Richard Hersh, former president of Hobart and Smith and

Trinity Colleges, and Richard Keeling, is another powerful critique of our nation's colleges and universities. In a recent conversation, Dick Hersh told me that college has increasingly become merely "a sorting and credentialing mechanism. What you get out of college is largely a function of accident: You manage to get into the right program or you have the right professors or you take initiative on your own. It's unconscionable that so much is left to chance when we know what is powerful learning and good teaching. It's a very inefficient way of giving people an education, and it is a very costly endeavor."

With the rapid evolution of many different kinds of wikis and other forms of crowd-sourcing, we now have new ways to create knowledge and have it shared far more widely. As one example, for more than a century the US Army relied on veteran soldier-scholars to write various manuals on how to conduct war. Today, these manuals are written as wikis, with soldiers from every rank—from privates to generals—contributing and reviewing "just-in-time" learning from the field. The *New York Times* reports that a growing number of scholars within universities are challenging "the monopoly that peer review has on admission to career-making journals and, as a consequence, to the charmed circle of tenured academe. They argue that in an era of digital media there is a better way to assess the quality of work. Instead of relying on a few experts selected by leading publications, they advocate using the Internet to expose scholarly thinking to the swift collective judgment of a much broader interested audience."[9] Dan Cohen, director of the Center for History and New Media at George Mason University, observes, "Serious scholars are asking whether the institutions of the academy—as they have existed for decades, even centuries—aren't becoming obsolete."[10]

Finally, the pressure to rethink the purpose of the university also arises because, in the world of the Internet, how knowledge is transmitted is changing rapidly. Much of the knowledge high schools and colleges are organized to teach students is now available free. As we learned from Amanda Alonzo's story, the Khan Academy offers at no charge more than twenty-seven hundred video lessons online for many of the advanced subjects taught in high schools. As one science teacher at an elite private school said to me, "Why should I have students listen to my chemistry lecture when they can watch a better one on their computers whenever they want?" MIT has led the way with universities by making all of its course content freely available online.

Paul Bottino, David Sengeh's mentor at the Technology and Entrepreneurship Center at Harvard, puts the new challenge to universities quite succinctly. "The value of explicit information is rapidly dropping to zero," he told me. "Today the real added value is what you can *do* with what you know. And it is really in the *doing*—in the probing of the universe, the pursuit of a query—that the real learning takes place."

VIDEO CUE:

Bottino on the Value of Doing

Go to www.creatinginnovators.com
to watch the video.

Paul also pointed out that the complexity of most economic, environmental, or social problems now requires a different kind of education. "The kind of preparation students are getting is very specialized, but when they try to apply their knowledge into a problem space, they need to think and see much more broadly." Google's director of talent, Judy Gilbert, said something similar when I asked her what universities must do to better prepare students for work in innovative companies: "We need to eliminate the bright lines between subjects. A more interdisciplinary approach to learning will better prepare people for the kind of problems they'll be confronting. Students also need more experience with collaborative problem-solving."

So what might a college look like that was designed to address these new challenges and prepare all young people to be innovators? A college that sought to develop collaboration skills and encourage an interdisciplinary understanding of problems through learning by doing, rather than listening to lectures; a program that sought to encourage intellectual risk-taking and intrinsic motivation? In research for this book, I discovered just such a place: a brand-new school called the Franklin W. Olin College of Engineering.

Olin College

Olin is a small undergraduate engineering school in Needham, Massachusetts, with a total enrollment of 350 students, 45 percent of whom are women. Dr. Richard Miller, Olin's founding and current president, described the history of the college's formation in a recent conversation. "Beginning in the late 1980s, there was a growing unhappiness about how engineers were being educated. The Olin Foundation was committed to addressing the problem. They'd given funds for eighty new buildings on fifty campuses over a fifty-year period and were disappointed by the lack of effect. They started thinking about starting a new engineering school in an existing college that didn't have one. But if you do that, you inherit the culture that exists—the same metrics and expectations. The only alternative was to start over. They chose the site for the college because it was adjacent to Babson College, which had established a very highly regarded entrepreneurship program. The challenge was to create a skill set and mind-set for engineers who are capable of entrepreneurial thinking."

The foundation launched the college in 1997 with a $460 million commitment, one of the largest grants in the history of American higher education. During the 2001–02 academic year, while its campus was being built, the college's newly hired faculty "worked with thirty student 'partners' to create and test an innovative curriculum that infused a rigorous engineering education with business and entrepreneurship as well as the arts, humanities and social sciences. They developed a hands-on, interdisciplinary approach that better reflects actual engineering practice."[11] The first class was admitted in the fall of 2002; Olin has graduated about 350 students since then. Today, Olin aspires to "redefine engineering as a profession of innovation encompassing (1) the consideration of human and societal needs; (2) the creative design of engineering systems; and (3) the creation of value through entrepreneurial effort and philanthropy."[12]

VIDEO CUE:

Miller on the Origin of Olin College

Go to www.creatinginnovators.com
to watch the video.

Rick Miller explained Olin's unique approach to me. "The engineering profession is about creating new things and doing whatever it takes to make it happen. So our students have to start and run a business in teams as a requirement for graduation. Olin also embraces creativity. Another requirement is a hands-on course called Design Thinking, where students have to work in groups to create a new product or service based on customer research.

"We're trying to teach students to take initiative—to transmit attitudes, motivations, and behaviors versus mere knowledge," Miller continued. "Today, it's not what you know, it's having the right questions. I see three stages in the evolution of learning: The first is the memorization-based, multiple-choice approach, which is still widely prevalent; then there's project-based learning where the problem is already determined; finally, there's design-based learning where you have to define the problem. That way of learning is part of every class here. We are trying to teach students how to frame problems versus repeat the answers."

VIDEO CUE:

Miller on Olin's Approach and Motivation

Go to www.creatinginnovators.com
to watch the video.

"Is there a tenure system here?" I asked.

"Faculty are hired with a three-year contract and, after a review process, can then be given a six-year contract. [I later learned that potential faculty must, among other things, teach a class and be interviewed by students.] We do not have a tenure system, but there is an expectation that faculty will contribute to the 'intellectual vitality' of their field. Ben Linder's work is a good example. He's passionate about sustainability and cofounded the International Development Design Summit with Amy Smith [Jodie Wu's teacher at MIT]. His work might not have been recognized as research by MIT, but it's valued here because his work impacts people's lives."

Miller discussed the mismatch between what is important in the larger world and to students versus what academia has traditionally valued. "The criteria for admission to the National Academy of Engineering [a highly prestigious award for the most accomplished engineers] aren't the number of research papers you've published or what your PhD students have done. It is about how you have changed the field of engineering.

"Faculty in the old mold have primary loyalty to their research community outside the university. But teaching is inherently local and inwardly focused. One reason why teaching isn't valued in the same way as research is that it is something that doesn't have transferability.

"The draw of doing research and writing academic papers is also the potential to influence your chosen field for generations to come. But that's not the only way you can influence people and change the course of history now. You can also do it with ideas and relationships, and the importance of those kinds of influences is growing with the impact that social media now enables—versus publications in journals that are only read by a few academics."

After my initial conversation with Rick, I spent the morning observing classes at Olin.

I sat in on Foundations of Business and Entrepreneurship, taught by Steve Gold, a physician. He told me that the class used to be more of a business course, but now his focus is on teaching entrepreneurial behavior and life skills, specifically (1) strategic thinking; (2) resourcefulness;

(3) effective communication. Of the thirty students in the class, about half were women. The students have to work in teams to start a business, with start-up money provided by the school. This morning, teams of students offered short presentations to persuade others of an idea. They were, in a lighthearted way, practicing the skills of salesmanship that they would later apply to a real business that they would create.

The first presentation enticed the audience to try the new sport of "extreme ironing." The group's tagline was "the thrill of the dangers of iron boarding with the satisfaction of the well-pressed shirt." They offered a PowerPoint of photoshopped pictures of peers and experts ironing in extreme places—on cliffs, the wings of planes, and so on. The next presentation, about "embracing Apple goodness," was selling the idea of putting apple juice on Apple Jacks cereal. Their real-life demonstration concluded with a question for the audience: "Why would you ever just put milk on your cereal?"

History of Technology, taught by Robert Martello, was next. He began the class by asking students, What are some good analytic messages from the Three Mile Island nuclear power plant disaster? It was a discussion of readings that students had done for homework. Some of the answers students gave included:

- interface between user and machine
- theme of cracks that turn into bigger problems
- safety was number two
- competing priorities: the technology, the public, safety
- need to design systems for failure as well as success
- costs of redundancy
- deadlines drove staff to fail
- companies need to make a profit
- deadlines are arbitrary
- essence of technology is a race

The discussion made it clear that there was no one right answer. Next, a team of students made a presentation on two of the additional readings for the day, which were case studies about the *Challenger* disaster and the explosion of the rigid airship R101 on its maiden voyage from Britain to France in 1930. The class watched two video clips that the students had chosen. Students then asked the class, who was to blame for each disaster? What were the ethical issues?

Lynn Andrea Stein and Shannon Bator were the co-teachers of the next class I observed: Human Interface and Design. Teams of students had been researching different kinds of human problems, including how a busy family coordinates their complicated schedules; how different kinds of people take unique types of notes for different purposes; and how to make the mass-transit informational kiosk more useful. After defining a problem, the teams had to create a persona for an archetypical user of their service or product as a means of being able to test the usefulness of the various designs they will develop later in the course. Lynn and Shannon went around the room checking in with different teams and asking them to describe their persona in great detail, while the teams continued to work on their project.

Lynn and I talked later about some of the challenges of teaching "the Olin way." She had previously taught at MIT, where she was a highly regarded teacher, she told me, but at Olin she considers herself to be "in the middle of the pack."

She explained, "You need to have a different notion of yourself and your role here. Being the 'sage on the stage' is problematic when you are trying to encourage intrinsic motivation and encourage students to have ownership of their learning. One thing that distinguishes entrepreneurs is the belief that 'I am master of my fate, and that I can make decisions that will make a difference,' but that's not what the education environment has fostered in the past. It's hard to make the shift to being the 'guide on the side,' though. Giving up control is a huge issue for many teachers who are used to the old way."

The last class I observed was Failure Analysis and Prevention, taught by Jon Stolk, who is one of the founding professors of the college. Groups of four students talked about different parts of an article that had been assigned as reading. Their task, outlined by the teacher at the beginning of the class, was to extract "nuggets of wisdom" from the portion of the article they were assigned and then briefly summarize for the rest of the class what they thought were the most salient points. After all the groups had completed their brief presentations, the students discussed a case study about the death of a woman on a toboggan run. First, teams of students were asked to analyze the cause of the failure and to propose solutions. Then one student from each group got up and presented their analysis and proposed solutions—which ranged from redesigning the toboggan run, to improving the brake systems in the toboggans, to changing how people are belted into the toboggans. The teacher ended the class with a brief explanation of a new project, where students will have to choose an example of a failure, analyze it on their own, and present it to the class.

Jon Stolk and I spoke after the class. Jon has a doctorate in materials science and engineering from the University of Texas at Austin, extensive industry experience, and taught at Bucknell University before coming to Olin. I asked him why he applied for the job at Olin. "Bucknell was a great place, but I got a little bored. The engineering curriculum was traditional and much like what is taught in Research One universities: lecture and lab. It was the same course over and over. Students loved the class, and I had good course evaluations—maybe because I had a lot of stories to tell from my work in industry. But I was in control, setting content, asking all the questions. The labs were the same: I knew the answers, the problems, the questions students would ask.

"I was a little overwhelmed when I began at Olin. For the first time, I was working with faculty who were knowledgeable about education and who wanted to collaborate, and the charge was to create something innovative, bold, new—something that would have an impact on engineering education. Sixteen of us were handed this enormous task. At the time, I felt I was a bad hire because I didn't know much."

"How did you get beyond feeling overwhelmed?" I wondered.

"I've tried to be very intentional. I used to do research in the field of materials science. Now my research is in education. I am interested in the problem of how to develop intrinsic motivation, self-direction, and lifelong learning. Traditional classrooms are all about instructor control.

You tell students what's important to learn and why and then you evaluate them. I've come to realize a lot of responsibility and choices can and should be turned over to the learner. In the Failure and Analysis class you observed, students are pretty self-directed. They choose topics, ask and answer questions, develop hypotheses. I don't give letter grades as an evaluation. Instead, I provide a narrative evaluation by competency area. [In the Failure Analysis and Prevention course, the four competency areas are communication, quantitative analysis, qualitative analysis, and diagnosis.][13] I also require a lot of self-reflection and self-evaluation, and individuals in teams give feedback to one another as a part of the evaluation process.

"When I first started presenting in engineering education conferences, I'd get attacked for saying things like 'intrinsic motivation is important, as is letting students ask their own questions.' Faculties over the ages have based their sense of competence on what they know versus how they facilitate learning. It's a huge shift. It took me many years to focus on how I design learning experiences and co-create with students."

Stolk and his colleagues are attacked less frequently these days when they do presentations at conferences. Instead, interest is growing in Olin's approach to learning because of the quality of its graduates, as we will see.

Alyssa Levitz, an Olin student in the class of 2011, gave me a brief tour of the campus and took me over to the cafeteria for lunch. We talked along the way.

"Why did you decide to come here?" I asked.

"I was pretty sure I didn't want to go to an engineering school. I was afraid I would have to give up my interest in social studies and the humanities, but Olin changed my mind. I came for the women's open-house admissions weekend, and I was hooked. I loved the team project where we had to connect a series of foam slabs to create something that would move water. All of the teachers, students, alums whom I met were smart, interesting, and passionate about what they do. I also got a sense of Olin community—how people would help each other. The sense of community is what tipped the scale—plus I can still pursue my interests in social studies and humanities."

Alyssa is a musician, and she was also excited to learn that the college had what it calls a conductorless orchestra. ("Not even," goes the campus joke, "a semiconductor.") She was also impressed that the college requires all students to take at least twenty-eight credits and complete a senior Capstone Project in the humanities and arts. Olin College students can take courses at Babson College in business or at Wellesley College in the humanities, or courses at Brandeis University as well, but few students do that because it's farther away.

I asked Alyssa to describe her favorite course. It was a required design studio class, where the idea was to take inspiration from nature for designs. "In the first half of the class, teams of students had to design something that hopped. The second team-based project was to build a swimming toy based on an animal in water. The projects were graded by a jury of fourth-grade students."

Alyssa has created her own major in environmental engineering. Students are encouraged to create their own majors, and at least a third of the students do. The college has also created a number of new interdisciplinary concentrations, such as bioengineering, which are increasingly popular with students.

"What are you doing for your SCOPE project?" (The Senior Capstone Project in Engineering is a required yearlong project in which students work in teams on a real engineering problem supplied by one of the college's corporate partners.)[14]

"Six of us are working with Lexmark International. We're trying to help them reconfigure printing systems. Companies buy printers as they need them in individual departments versus looking at needs across the company. We are creating an automated system to look at what printers are currently in place—their location and type—versus what should be there. The idea is to reduce waste."

I also asked Alyssa to describe her required arts and humanities Senior Capstone Project. "I've taken a lot of classes at Wellesley in environmental policy, history, and economics, and I am writing a senior thesis at Wellesley on the sustainability of international cities. I'm exploring different factors as they relate to sustainability. I'm the first Olin student to do a thesis at Wellesley, and my teachers here have been excited and helpful in encouraging me to do this."

During her upcoming January break, Alyssa was going to India to study water quality and policies. She would be working with a local NGO and using sophisticated software to track outbreaks of diseases related to poor water quality, and sources of environmental pollution in relation to areas of poverty. "It's an opportunity to experience a different culture, values, problems, and to better understand how problems vary across countries and populations. So many problems elsewhere can't be solved by just taking US solutions and dropping them in. I believe the experience will open my eyes," she told me.

"What about after college?"

"Perhaps I will go back and study environmental law and policy, but I want a job in an environmental consulting firm first. I want to make a difference in how we interact with the environment and how that could impact human health and climate change."

"In what ways do you feel most and least well prepared?"

"My classes at Olin have taught me how to think. They've also given us a breadth of knowledge, as well as some depth. I know how to think about problems from different perspectives. I've learned how to learn new things on my own, teach myself."

Alyssa could not think of something the college might have done to better prepare her for the career she imagines, but she was worried about how her background and résumé will be perceived by people doing the hiring for companies. "My interdisciplinary concentration has given me many different ways to look at pollution problems. But the people in HR departments look for keywords in résumés. I'm not an environmental engineer; I didn't major in government. I don't neatly fall into a bucket in the real world. But I'm happy with my choice. I wouldn't give this up just because of a hard job search." Alyssa also told me that she worried about women being such a small minority in the engineering profession—only 10 percent—versus at Olin, where women comprise 45 percent of the student body.

Over lunch, I chatted with four students, whose table I joined. I asked why they'd chosen to come to Olin. Neil was drawn by the SCOPE project and working in partnership with a company. Scott really liked that almost all learning is project-based and with a hands-on emphasis. Jenny liked the focus on working with people and collaboration. "It's not as cutthroat as MIT," she added. "You don't have to compete to get a teacher's attention, and there is a real emphasis on undergraduate research."

"I liked the idea that I didn't have to take boring classes before I got to do the fun stuff here," Andy added, and then explained how his Olin experience had influenced his thinking about a career. "I want to be in a job that allows me to create new things versus just having a task to do for eight hours and then go home. We are all doers here. And we like doing things that require us to take on multiple tasks and interact with other people."

"What have you liked most about the experience here?" I then asked the group.

"The collective excitement! Everyone is excited."

"The chance to work with other people. My understanding of teamwork has changed completely since high school."

"The responsiveness of faculty to feedback. Most come here because they want to teach."

"And like least?"

"Sometimes the workload and the idea that we're stuck here. We have our weekends free for adventure, but then people think it's okay to have a Friday-night meeting, which cuts into weekend time."

"The small size of the school can be a problem, too. When things go wrong socially, it's really bad!"

"One thing you'd like to see changed?"

"More arts and humanities classes."

"Better transportation to the city."

I talked briefly with Rick Miller and Lynn Andrea Stein about efforts the college was making to evaluate the effectiveness of Olin's unconventional approach.

"We've only five graduated classes—three hundred fifty kids," Rick answered. "So there isn't a lot of data yet. Our scores on the National Survey of Student Engagement, which we give in freshman and senior year, are off the charts. Olin data is over ninety percent in all ten metrics." (The survey is a widely used assessment of students' perceptions of the quality of their learning in four-year colleges.)[15]

"The area where our graduates are most likely to have trouble with is acceptance into engineering PhD programs in traditional schools. Despite that, more than a third of our students have gone on to graduate school. Of that group, more than twenty percent have gone to Harvard, Stanford, or MIT, and seventeen percent have won National Science Foundation fellowships.

"We also send surveys to the managers of companies who have hired our graduates, and they report that our students behave as if they've been in the field for three to five years, and that our graduates have exactly the skills they need."

"It may be hard for the first Olin graduate to get in the door and past HR," Lynn added. "But it's never hard for the second student. Microsoft hired three of our first-year graduates; the next year, they hired seven, and the year after, it was ten."

I returned to Olin in May 2011 for a colloquium on educating for innovation. Rick Miller, who had written and circulated an interesting white paper for the day, began by explaining that the goal of the presentations and subsequent discussions was to better understand how much to recognize and cultivate potential innovators. Next came a report on how money from the special Innovation Fund was spent. Established in 2010 to promote curricular innovations at Olin, the fund has supported the development or improvement of a number of interdisciplinary courses.[16] Jon Stolk and Rob Martello briefly explained the evolution of the Stuff of History—a course that focuses on the intersection of the history of technology and materials science.

"This course is taught by a historian and a materials scientist," Stolk told the audience of trustees, students, teachers, Advisory Committee members, and invited guests. "Beyond teaching students about the history of technology and the nature of materials, our goal is to develop students' intrinsic motivation for lifelong learning, as well as their collaboration and communication skills. All work is done in teams. Students must complete three projects related to materials used in different periods of history.

"For the last part of the course, with support from the Innovation Fund, we developed additional readings and conceived of a new final project. We asked students to explore the concept of ethics as design and consider the ethical and environmental impacts of materials and technologies as they created a new product out of currently available materials."

Stolk and Martello explained that the impact of the new course goes far beyond the students who take it. They showed a slide indicating the numbers of people from across the country and around the world that have come to the college to learn more about its innovative education practices.

The next part of the program, entitled "Innovation in Action," was an opportunity for current students and recent graduates to share some of their work. Maia Bittner, class of 2011, and her five teammates described the project they had just completed for SCOPE—the Senior Capstone Program in Engineering. This group had worked for Autodesk, which is a world leader in 3-D design, engineering, and entertainment software (and where Shanna Tellerman now works). Their goal was to redesign the software learning experience for both students and professionals. Tom Cecil, Olin class of '06 and an associate at the law firm of Nelson Bumgardner Casto in Fort Worth, Texas, talked about how he's applying the innovation skills he learned at Olin to the practice of intellectual-property law. Susan Fredholm Murphy, also from Olin's class of '06, was the final presenter. She is a senior consultant at PE Americas, a firm that specializes in software solutions and extensive services in the field of sustainability. She took some time to describe to the audience the evolution over several years of her remarkable innovation:

"I've always been interested in sustainability. The summer after my junior year at Olin, I found an internship at SolidWorks. They produce a 3-D CAD software tool to model different products, which I'd been learning to use at Olin. As an intern, my responsibility was to make software demonstrations for their resellers to use with potential buyers.

"I had a great mentor at SolidWorks, Kishore Boyalakuntla, who was in charge of managing the tech sales team. He encouraged me to bring my personal interests into the examples I was creating. I'd just taken the Sustainable Design class at Olin with Professor Ben Linder, who taught us about life-cycle assessment: how to think about the entire life cycle of a product—what materials are used in a product, how they are mined from the earth, how they are processed into a product, how the product is used, and how it's disposed of. So I played around with the idea of adding a software module to the SolidWorks program that would enable a user to assess the environmental impact of the materials they propose to use in the design as it was being developed.

"I went to MIT for a master's in technology and policy program in engineering and learned more about life-cycle assessment. Kishore kept in touch. He'd call every six months or so to see how things were going. He likes to know what former interns are doing—he's a really great mentor.

"In the summer of 2008, after graduating from MIT, I joined PE Americas—I wanted to do more in sustainability. I liked the idea of a small environment. PE Americas had a small, start-up feel—there were only five people when I joined—but it felt less risky because it had two established firms as start-up sponsors: PE International and Five Winds.

"My role was as a life-cycle assessment consultant—I performed life-cycle assessments on products for a variety of companies. About a month after I started, Kishore called again. He said SolidWorks was getting interested in life-cycle assessment. I introduced him to folks at PE Americas. At a meeting with directors from both SolidWorks and PE Americas later in the fall, we started brainstorming what a collaboration between the two companies could look like.

"Critical decisions are made early in the life of a product. Our goal was to give guidance to designers at a very early stage. We knew this group didn't want another task—and weren't necessarily interested in the environment. So we had to make it easy and intuitive for them to do a life-cycle assessment of a potential design. The information had to live right inside of the SolidWorks design software—a dashboard on the right side of the screen that would automatically update how a product's environmental footprint is getting better or worse, as the design changed.

"The companies agreed to collaborate to add this capability into the SolidWorks software, and I was the connection between them as new software was developed by both. The new product was released in the fall of 2009. A 'lite' version of the life-cycle assessment part of the program now ships with every copy of SolidWorks Express, and companies have the option to upgrade to the full version.

"The software has gotten a number of awards, including the Golden Mousetrap Award for Best New Product in 2010 and the Green Awards Winner," Susan concluded.

The morning ended with the students and alums responding to questions from the audience in a panel discussion.

"What was important about the Olin experience for what you are doing now?" a member of the audience asked the two alums on the panel.

The lawyer, Tom Cecil, answered. "Being able to design my own major was hugely important. I was able to integrate different content from very diverse courses. I also learned to think about problems from multiple perspectives."

"The culture of Olin is critical," Susan added. "Almost all of my courses had a project component where you were encouraged to pick something of interest; you could build off an idea you'd started in one class and now look at another aspect in a different class. There were also a lot of interdisciplinary projects and courses—opportunities to take things you are interested in and examine them in different ways. You're always being challenged to think about what's interesting to you, and how you can pull different things together. There were also lots of leadership opportunities—space to be creative and to try new things. At Olin, I learned to not be afraid to try something new."

"Jon Stolk and Rob Martello talked about the importance of developing students' intrinsic motivation. What were your motivations for getting involved with the projects you've described?" another member of the audience asked.

A member of the team who worked at Autodesk replied, "The project we did was a lot of fun. But I also felt I was riding the wave of a paradigm shift, being a part of something big. Rethinking how people learn best."

"I think it was important that each person on the team had different skills, and each of us was motivated to make a unique contribution," another member of the team explained.

Susan Murphy described her experience. "When I began working on the sustainability software, I was doing it on my own time after I completed work that was part of my internship. I worked a lot of extra hours, but I had a mentor who supported me—who believed in what I was doing. It was really exciting. The project was a lot of fun, but it was also something I was passionate about."

VIDEO CUE:

An Alum's View of Olin

Go to www.creatinginnovators.com
to watch the video.

I came away from the morning at Olin impressed by the consistency of values among the leadership of the college, the faculty, and the students. All appeared to deeply appreciate the process of innovation and what it can produce. A sense of pride, purpose, and excitement permeated the presentations by the faculty, students, and alumni. Clearly, Olin is a very different kind of teaching and learning experience.

As we learned earlier in this chapter, Olin College was designed to develop the capacities of young people to become innovators. Returning to Teresa Amabile's diagram, we see clear evidence that students are gaining expertise in their content areas through their classes, while also acquiring creative-thinking skills—including many of the Seven Survival Skills, which I described in *The Global Achievement Gap*. But it is the third area of Amabile's scheme—motivation—as well as the academic culture of the school that I think warrant a closer look. The culture of Olin is radically different from the culture of most high schools and colleges in five fundamental respects.

Individual Achievement versus Collaboration

The culture of schooling in America celebrates and rewards individual achievement, while offering few meaningful opportunities for genuine collaboration. Students are ranked and sorted according to their levels of achievement, as measured by tests and grades. Even in so-called group work, which can occasionally be found in some high school classes, one or two students often do most of the work, while the rest of the group sit passively. Serious and sustained collaboration is not a real expectation, either for students or faculty.

Not so at Olin, where the understanding is that collaboration and the resultant integration of different perspectives is essential for innovation. The emphasis on collaboration begins with the admissions process, where students must do a group project as a part of their weekend interview on campus. Every class requires forms of teamwork and collaboration, and as we learned from students, learning how to collaborate is one of the educational outcomes they value most highly—along with the sense of community that frequent collaboration helps to create. When I asked students sitting at my lunch table what they most valued about their college experience, they singled out collaboration. Faculty also work far more collaboratively with other faculty than in most academic settings, often developing new courses together.

Specialization versus Multidisciplinary Learning

To be clear, there is and will always be an important role for specialists and specialization. I'm glad I had a highly trained orthopedic surgeon for my several surgeries, rather than a general practitioner, and I certainly want the pilot I fly with and the plumber who fixes my leaks to have real expertise. Innovators need enough expertise in a given field to understand the possibilities for innovation. Some degree of content expertise and specialization, then, is necessary but not sufficient for innovation.

Throughout this book, we have heard college teachers talk about the dangers of students being pressured to specialize too soon—often before they know what their real interests are. More important, Paul Bottino and Judy Gilbert, as well as numerous other interviewees, have all described the importance of developing the skills for understanding problems from multiple perspectives. Problems in today's world are simply too complex to be solved using only the intellectual tools of a single academic discipline. Yet few college graduates have had experience in analyzing a problem from multiple disciplinary perspectives.

In most colleges, the expectation is that students will begin to specialize early in their academic career, and interdisciplinary courses are the rare exception. The system for organizing knowledge, as well as promotion, tenure, funding for research, and professional recognition—all create, incent, and reward specialization in academia. Olin, with its absence of tenure and a mission to develop better ways to prepare engineers who can innovate, has created a radically different incentive structure. Courses at Olin aim to create better problem-solvers, first and foremost, and this is one of the skills its graduates value most highly. As Tom Cecil, the lawyer, said, "I learned to think about problems from multiple perspectives." Alyssa Levitz said much the same: "My interdisciplinary concentration has given me many different ways to look at pollution problems."

Risk Avoidance versus Trial and Error

With its promise of a job for life, many timeworn traditions, and long-established bureaucratic institutions, the education sector tends to attract individuals who are risk-averse, and much of the training of young scholars underscores the importance of a deliberate and cautious approach to one's work. Students' risk aversion in conventional classes takes a particular form. To get an A, students learn to discern what their teachers want—the "right" kinds of answers or papers for each class—and give it to them. While education performs a necessary conserving role in society and so shouldn't be subject to every fad that comes along, the question remains: How can established educational institutions encourage the trial and error and intellectual risk-taking that are the hallmarks of innovators?

Perhaps because its mission is to develop innovators, and it is still a start-up, the culture at Olin encourages teachers to take risks and try new approaches in their classes. Many at Olin are constantly reinventing their courses and reshaping the curriculum, as we learned in the interview with Jon Stolk and in the description of the Stuff of History course that he continues to refine with Rob Martello.

The most innovative companies celebrate failure. The design firm IDEO's motto is "Fail early and often," and they encourage what they call "rapid prototyping" as a way to learn from failure—meaning that they create models or simulations of a product early in its design to test the viability of the design concept. But it is the rare class that genuinely encourages students to take intellectual risks, and that encourages learning from—rather than penalizing—failure. Olin students, on the other hand, have been taught to view trial and error—or failure—as an integral part of problem solving. As one student told me, "I don't even think about 'failure' here. It's not a word we use. Instead, we talk about 'iteration.'"

Consuming versus Creating

In most conventional education settings, learning is overwhelmingly passive. In high school and college, students in most courses just listen to lectures. Students consume knowledge, which they all too often experience as disconnected bits of random information. Students must then recall the knowledge they have consumed for tests or the occasional paper. Not having had to use the knowledge they've acquired and frequently not even having a real-world context for understanding what they've been asked to learn, it comes as no surprise that many students forget much of what they have been required to memorize as soon as the test is over and so seem poorly prepared for the next phase of their education or career.

In classes at Olin, the primary goal is not the acquisition of knowledge. The goal is to develop a set of skills—or, in Jon Stolk's terms, competencies—by solving a problem, creating a product, or generating a new understanding. Knowledge is important, but it is acquired on an "as needed" basis. It is a means to an end. Traditional academics often criticize this approach for being too utilitarian and lacking an appreciation of learning for its own sake, but the evidence is that Olin students are very well prepared for graduate school and better prepared for work, with managers who have been surveyed by the college reporting that Olin students who've just graduated act as if they've had three to five years of experience. Learning research shows that students understand and retain much more of what they learn when they have studied and used the knowledge in an applied context.

Beyond being better prepared for graduate school and work, Olin students experience themselves as creators, rather than consumers. They are empowered in multiple ways. First, they are encouraged to create their own majors—an option that exists in some colleges such as Harvard, but one that's rarely chosen by students due to the bureaucratic hurdles involved. Second, most Olin courses are hands-on and require students to create a final product and to actively think about how their work in one class relates to work they've done in other classes. Third, teachers at Olin strive to relinquish a good deal of control in classes to make them more student-led, and they place considerable emphasis on self and team evaluations versus the grade given by the teacher (though the college does have a conventional grading system after freshman year, when all courses are pass-fail). Finally, all students must complete two in-depth Capstone projects in their senior year—one in engineering, in which they are asked to solve a real problem in a corporate setting as a part of a team, and one in arts and humanities, which provides them with a significant opportunity to create something new.

Extrinsic versus Intrinsic Motivation: Play, Passion, and Purpose

Conventional academic classes rely on extrinsic incentives as motivators for learning. You learn in order to get a good grade on the test so that you can have a good GPA. While professors may tout the value of learning for its own sake, they nevertheless make liberal use of the traditional carrots and sticks to ensure that students come to class and learn the material. One has to wonder how many students would show up for their classes if no grade was involved.

Olin's founders and teachers understand that the desire to innovate is not primarily driven by extrinsic incentives. Teachers at Olin have an explicit goal of strengthening students' intrinsic motivations to be lifelong learners, to be the architects of their own learning, their own careers, to bring into being that which they desire. So courses at Olin provide numerous and varied intrinsic incentives for learning—which can be viewed through the lenses of play, passion, and purpose that we have used throughout this book.

Many aspects of the classes I observed had a strong element of *play.* The first class, where students were trying to persuade their classmates of the value of outrageous activities—such as "extreme iron boarding" and pouring apple juice on your Apple Jacks cereal—brings to mind Ed Carryer's use of "whimsy" in the Stanford class assignments he gave students. The Human Interface and Design class also had a great deal of play and laughter, with students making up archetypal users for the products they were developing. Then there was Alyssa's description of her design studio class, where their final projects were juried by fourth graders! But there was also ample evidence in every class of more serious forms of adult play, as well, the sense of play that comes from being so deeply engrossed in a project that you lose all sense of time; the sense of play that is an integral element in any creative endeavor.

The *passion* that students had for many of the projects in their classes and for their Capstone projects was apparent. Both the senior who worked with a team at Autodesk and Susan Murphy described their projects as having been "a lot of fun." But what I found most persuasive was

Susan's description of her overall experience in courses. She said, "Almost all of my courses had a project component where you were encouraged to pick something of interest; you could build off an idea you'd started in one class and now look at another aspect in a different class. There were also a lot of interdisciplinary projects and courses—opportunities to take things you are interested in and examine them in different ways." Opportunities for students to pursue their own interests and to discover their passions and so move toward a deeper sense of purpose were the driving forces for learning in most Olin classes.

This deeper sense of *purpose*—a mission, if you will—came through strongly in my conversation with Alyssa and in the work of everyone who spoke at the colloquium. Alyssa's and Susan Murphy's sense of purpose in wanting to make a contribution toward a more sustainable planet was clear. The Autodesk team was hoping to contribute to the development of a new paradigm of learning. And while Tom Cecil sees himself as putting in the necessary time at his law firm, he nevertheless has a clear purpose in mind: He wants to do work that will contribute to the protection of the intellectual property of emerging entrepreneurs and innovators.

STEM versus Liberal Arts Education for Innovation—Olin's Answer

Bill Gates advocates that students take many more courses in STEM-related fields to have the best chance for a decent job. On February 28, 2011, he gave a speech before the National Governors Association in which he seemed to strongly suggest that only those college departments that produce jobs should be subsidized.[17] Just three days later, at the introduction of the iPad 2, Steve Jobs said, "It's in Apple's DNA that technology alone is not enough—it's technology married with liberal arts, married with the humanities, that yields us the result that makes our heart sing, and nowhere is that more true than in these post-PC devices."[18] When it comes to educating young innovators, who is right? Do we need students to take more STEM classes or more arts and humanities classes?

Steve Jobs's biographer, Walter Isaacson, contrasted the intelligences of the two men in a recent *New York Times* Commentary. "Bill Gates is super-smart, but Steve Jobs was super-ingenious. The primary distinction, I think, is the ability to apply creativity and aesthetic sensibilities to a challenge. In the world of invention and innovation, that means combining an appreciation of the humanities with an understanding of science —connecting artistry to technology, poetry to processors. This was Mr. Jobs's specialty. 'I always thought of myself as a humanities person as a kid, but I liked electronics,' he said. 'Then I read something that one of my heroes, Edwin Land of Polaroid, said about the importance of people who could stand at the intersection of humanities and sciences, and I decided that's what I wanted to do.'"[19]

Vivek Wadhwa is a technology entrepreneur turned academic. He and his research team from Duke and Harvard surveyed 652 US-born chief executive officers and heads of product engineering at 502 technology companies and found that "92 percent held bachelor's degrees, and 47 percent held higher degrees. But only 37 percent held degrees in engineering or computer technology, and just 2 percent held them in mathematics. The rest have degrees in fields as diverse as business, accounting, finance, health care, arts and the humanities."[20]

Wadhwa concludes, "Even though I believe that engineering is one of the most important professions, I have learned that the liberal arts are equally important. It takes artists, musicians, and psychologists working side by side with engineers to build products as elegant as the iPad. And anyone—with education in any field—can achieve success in Silicon Valley. . . . My advice to my students—and to my own children—is to study what interests them the most; to excel in fields in which they have the most passion and ability; to change the world in their own way and on their own terms.[21]

Semyon Dukach, Jodie Wu's mentor and chairman of her board, has a master's in computer science from MIT and has had a successful career as a high-tech entrepreneur. Despite his technical background, Semyon is passionate about the importance of a liberal arts education for young innovators. "Humanities seminars where people form ideas and argue about them foster creativity and innovation in engineering. To innovate, you have to question the status quo—rebel in a sense. Humanities, at their best, teach you to question everything, and they foster a belief in argument and logic. For example, when you come up with a new interpretation of a piece of literature, that experience empowers you to question and to use your mind creatively in other endeavors."

One of the final important lessons from the Olin story is how the college actively encourages students to pursue *both* engineering and liberal and fine arts classes; they don't have to choose one over the other. Indeed, Olin requires its graduates to take at least one-fifth of their classes in the arts and humanities and to complete senior Capstone projects in both arts and humanities and engineering. A number of students commented on how they had come to a deeper understanding of engineering problems because of their humanities studies.

None of this description is to suggest that Olin is an educational utopia. It is still very much a work in progress. In a focus group I conducted with some faculty, several worried that the criteria for contract renewal was vague and even beginning to look too much like the criteria for tenure in a conventional academic setting. Jon Stolk and Alyssa Levitz both expressed the concern that Olin may lose its innovative edge, and several students said they wanted *more* arts and humanities classes to be offered by the college.

It is hard to be ahead of the crowd in any setting—and especially so in education. The pressures to conform to the norm—or in this case to revert to the established ways of doing things—must not be underestimated. Nevertheless, I think that Olin College has succeeded in giving us a thoughtful and largely successful model of a college that is designed to graduate young people who are capable of innovating in many different fields. Just like the best charter schools in public education, Olin has been—and continues to be—a laboratory for educational R&D, and their diligent work shows us what it means, in practice, to completely rethink learning and teaching in college.

Now imagine what a high school would need to do to prepare students for Olin. In fact, several High Tech High graduates have come to Olin and done exceedingly well. If you consult my description of High Tech High in *The Global Achievement Gap* (pp. 207–28), you will see remarkable similarities in teaching and learning between the two schools. Taken together, I think High Tech High and Olin provide an outline of what eight years of educating for innovation can and must look like.

VIDEO CUE:

What Is High Tech High?

Go to www.creatinginnovators.com
to watch the video.

Innovation in Other Colleges and Universities

Olin is not the only example of an effort to create a postsecondary experience designed to develop the capabilities of innovators and entrepreneurs. Some of our young innovators' choices for graduate school point to other fascinating examples of new ways to organize learning. Shanna Tellerman, you'll recall, earned her master's degree in entertainment technology at the Entertainment Technology Center at Carnegie Mellon University, a new independent program sponsored by its College of Fine Arts and School of Computer Science.[22] The explicit goal of the program is to promote innovation and entrepreneurship—something it did well for Shanna, as we learned. She spent three of her four semesters there working on one project, which became her start-up business. And David Sengeh chose MIT's Media Lab for his graduate work. "It is the only place I would have gone to," he told me, "because there are no required classes or grades, and you have opportunities to build things that people need."

The MIT Media Lab

Now in its twenty-fifth year, the Media Lab was the brainchild of MIT professor Nicholas Negroponte and former MIT president Jerome Wiesner. The goal was to create an entirely new multidisciplinary degree-granting research laboratory that "focused on inventing a better future through creative applications of innovative digital technologies."[23] Its areas of exploration have evolved as new challenges and opportunities are identified. Currently, much of the lab's work is around the topic of "human adaptability"—work ranging from initiatives to treat conditions such as Alzheimer's disease and depression, to sociable robots that can monitor the health of children or the elderly, to the development of smart prostheses that can mimic—or even exceed—the capabilities of our biological limbs."[24]

VIDEO CUE:

The MIT Media Lab

Go to www.creatinginnovators.com
to watch the video.

The Media Lab is organized around a series of research topics, each of which is led by a faculty member. There are currently more than twenty different areas of inquiry—everything from synthetic neurobiology to civic media to personal robots.[25] In their application (which does not require any kind of standardized test) prospective students list their top three areas of interest. Once accepted, students' tuition is covered in full, and they are also paid a stipend—which is made possible by corporate partners who sponsor much of the research being done. The courses students take depend on their area of concentration; there is no required core curriculum.

But it is not just *what* the Media Lab does that makes it such an innovation in education. It is also *how* learning happens there. I came to understand more about the Media Lab's approach to teaching and learning from my conversation with Mitchel Resnick, who is a professor of learning research and head of academic programs at the lab. He has taught there since 1992.

"The key to success in the future is not what you know, but whether you are able to think and act creatively," Mitch said. "Here at the lab, we take our inspiration from the ways people learn in kindergarten, where kids have opportunities to create, design, and build collaboratively. The best way to develop creativity is to design and create things in collaboration with one another. We also find that people do their best work when they are working on things that they care deeply about—when it's their passion. Finally, the work here almost invariably leads our students to cross academic boundaries, just like in kindergarten where finger painting is also about learning how colors mix, which is science, and often the kids will write a story about their painting as well.

"The challenge is to set up systems that allow students to follow their interests. People tend to dichotomize approaches in education: The teacher is either telling students what to do, or standing back and letting them figure it out. I think that's a false choice: The issue is not structure versus no structure, but rather creating a different structure. Students need to be exposed to new ideas and learn how to persist. They also need support."

David Sengeh's concentration is in a field called biomechatronics, which is addressing issues related to how technology can be used to enhance human physical capability. The research group's web page explains, "Permanent assistive devices are viewed by the physically challenged as separate, lifeless mechanisms and not intimate extensions of the human body—structurally, neurologically, and dynamically. The Biomechatronics group seeks to advance technologies that promise to accelerate the merging of body and machine, including device architectures that resemble the body's own musculoskeletal design, actuator technologies that behave like muscle, and control methodologies that exploit principles of biological movement."[26]

In January 2011, I visited David at the Media Lab, and we talked about his first semester in the program.

"The Media Lab allows me to work on many different projects at the same time. Some of the things I've been working on include optimizing the microbe-eating energy cell that we'd explored back in the lab at Harvard; a survey on usage rates for the malaria nets we've distributed in Sierra Leone; a program for giving microfinance loans for people who want to start new small businesses in Africa. Then I am working on a couple of medical devices for use in third-world countries. One of them is a tamponlike device to stem the bleeding of women who've just given birth.

"My main project is working on how to connect machines to man—prosthetics. Here in the lab, we can do rapid prototyping to figure out what kinds of materials you need for more comfort—like for people with sclerosis who won't wear their brace because it's too uncomfortable. I am also working with postdoctoral students to write a cell phone application with a 3-D image of a limb and a prosthetic socket, where you can zoom in to create a pain map that you can send to the doctor or person fitting your device."

Knowing how critical he had been of his Harvard classes, I asked David about the classes he's taken so far at the lab.

"It's all been good. I took a class called How to Make (Almost) Anything, and it was really important—stuff everybody should know, like how to do rapid prototyping. The Development Ventures class gave me an opportunity to form something we're calling the African Initiative, which is to connect technology from the Media Lab to Africa more directly and also get talent from the continent to attend the Media Lab. And then there was the Design for Empowerment class, where we learned how to create different kinds of tool kits for people who are not interested in technology that would enable them to make or fix things, as well as how we can create stuff with the end user in mind.

"What I like best is the freedom to do whatever I want to do," David said. "Frank Moss, the head of the lab [who has since stepped down after five years in the position], always says, 'Push the envelope, use the creative freedom you've been given.' We have access to all the tools we need, and we have the support we need. A friend of mine made an electric cello, and another guy made a flute using a 3-D printer—things other people would think are crazy or stupid. Plus I still play soccer on the MIT graduate-student team, I coached the men's club soccer team at Harvard, and I taught a class in Creole there, too. I'm not sure I'd have this freedom anywhere else."

The "freedom" that David prizes so highly is not the absence of structure but rather a different structure for learning, as Mitch Resnick reminds us. And the structure and culture that have been created at the Media Lab are stunningly similar to Olin's and radically different from those at most conventional graduate schools. Here again, we see a strong emphasis on collaboration (versus individual achievement); multidisciplinary learning (versus specialization); an emphasis on creating things and student empowerment (versus passively consuming knowledge); encouragement of intellectual risk-taking and trial and error (versus risk avoidance); and, finally, a strong emphasis on intrinsic (versus extrinsic) motivation, with the absence of grades and the faculty's focus on encouraging students to pursue their passions.

Understanding Obstacles to Innovating Learning

The successes of Olin and the Media Lab may give the impression that it is easy to innovate learning, when, in fact, the work is difficult for a number of reasons. Olin, the Entertainment Technology Center at Carnegie Mellon University, and the MIT Media Lab were "start-ups," founded by education visionaries, who set out to create a new kind of school. It is far easier to create a very different kind of learning culture for both faculty and students in a start-up. However, the opportunities and resources to create entirely new colleges and graduate schools are comparatively rare, and so we need to better understand the challenges of working within existing academic institutions. The story of the Institute of Design at Stanford and our conversation with its founder, David Kelley, reveal some of the aspects of traditional academic culture that make innovation especially difficult.

David Kelley is the Donald W. Whittier professor of mechanical engineering at Stanford University, where he has taught since 1978. He became a tenured professor there in 1991. In 1978, David co-founded a design firm which he merged with several other companies to form IDEO in 1991. IDEO is ranked as one of the ten most innovative companies in the world. David then founded the Hasso Plattner Institute of Design at Stanford in 2005—more commonly known as the d.school.

VIDEO CUE:

Kelley on Stanford's d.school

Go to www.creatinginnovators.com
to watch the video.

The d.school is actually not a school at all in the conventional sense. It does not admit its own students, hire its faculty, or grant degrees. Rather, the school sponsors classes and projects that attract students and faculty from every school in the university. The goal of the d.school is to teach the skills of innovation while addressing some of the world's most challenging problems related to sustainability, third-world development, education, and so on. Recent classes have included Lab: Design for Service Innovation; Designing for Sustainable Abundance; Design for Change: Poverty in America; d.Media: Designing Media That Matters; and d.medical: Design Thinking for Better Health. One course is titled From Play to Innovation and "is a class focused on enhancing the innovation process with playfulness. We will investigate the human state of play to reach an understanding of its principal attributes and how important it is to creative thinking. We will explore play behavior, its development, and its biological basis. We will then apply those principles through design thinking to promote innovation in the corporate world. Students will work with real-world partners on design projects with widespread application."[27]

The process of learning at the d.school looks remarkably similar to Olin's, where faculty and students work together to understand a particular problem and co-create possible solutions. Learning and teaching in both schools have been profoundly influenced by the "design thinking" philosophy and innovation methods pioneered by IDEO and described by Tom Kelley (David Kelley's brother and managing director of IDEO) in several books and by Tim Brown, IDEO's CEO, whose article I quoted from in chapter 1. Here is how the d.school describes its approach:

> At the d.school, we learn by doing. We don't just ask our students to solve a problem, we ask them to define what the problem is. Students start in the field, where they develop empathy for people they design for, uncovering real human needs they want to address. They then iterate to develop an unexpected range of possible solutions, and create rough prototypes to take back out into the field and test with real people. Our bias is toward action, followed by reflection on personal discoveries about process. Experience is measured by iteration: students run through as many cycles as they possibly can on any project. Each cycle brings stronger insights and more unexpected solutions.[28]

A February 2009 article in *Fast Company* featured an extended profile of David Kelley, in which he described his goal in starting the d.school to reporter Linda Tischler. "I really do believe I was put on the planet to help people have creative confidence. I don't have twenty-seven agendas. I'm not the sustainability guy, or the developing-world guy. My contribution is to teach as many people as I can to use both sides of their brain, so that for every problem, every decision in their lives, they consider creative as well as analytical solutions."[29]

The article goes on to describe the founding of the d.school. "When David was making the case for the d.school at Stanford," says Tom Kelley, "he went to [university president John] Hennessy and said, 'Look, we're good at "deep." We have Nobel laureates drilling down into esoteric topics. But what if there are problems that aren't solved by deep, but broad? We should have a side bet in broad.'" In that climate, Kelley's notion finally began to find an audience. By 2005, he had persuaded Hasso Plattner, a founder of the software giant SAP, to pony up $35 million to the d.school. The new 42,500-square-foot home of the Hasso Plattner Institute of Design, smack in the middle of the Stanford campus, will open this fall.[30]

The article suggests that the d.school's founding was merely a matter of a little persuasion and some fund-raising. However, my conversation with David revealed how much of a struggle it has been to launch and sustain a radically different model of learning in a conventional academic context.

VIDEO CUE:

Kelley on d.school Struggles

Go to www.creatinginnovators.com
to watch the video.

"Many of the problems we've faced are related to the culture of academia," David told me. "Sometimes it can be quite subtle. The professors' vested interest is to try to find people to be in their research group—people they can turn into PhDs and do work for them. Everybody else who is 'merely' a master's student and is not going on for a PhD is not of interest, and students acquire that self-image—that they're not as cool as the students going off for PhDs. It's hard to find professors who will value the guys who are going out to start Google and other innovative enterprises.

"Some of the greatest problems I had getting started relate to the fact that, on the one hand, faculty who have done applied work in industry—work which is much closer to the kind of work students want to do—don't have the same status as the tenure-track faculty. But on the other hand, the regular faculty had no interest in our approach, which emphasizes breadth over depth. The university couldn't handle the idea of an institute that wasn't populated by regular faculty. I could be a catalyst because I had all the credentials of regular faculty, but I'm not actually regular faculty, which has allowed me to value this approach more than someone who'd gone through the system. Hasso Plattner's gift is actually what got us in. Money is still one of the most important catalysts at the university."

"What are you finding most difficult now in sustaining the work of the d.school?" I asked.

"The problem is that I can only use either tenured faculty or adjunct faculty. I can't use the young, exciting tenure-track faculty because we're not seen as serious. Being involved with the d.school is viewed as a distraction from research and probably will affect your tenure case negatively. Most of our faculty are adjunct, who are often at the cutting edge of innovation and who, because they have just one course to teach, can take much more time to prepare. They do a fantastic job. But I need tenured regular faculty because you have to have academic clout to get things to happen in the university. I have a few—some of my buddies who realized the importance of this approach a long time ago—but I'm dead in the water if I can't find successors when they retire.

"When I started, I didn't realize how important it would be to have tenured faculty for influence and institutional status. Yet I worry that too many faculty who have achieved tenure have been ruined as design thinkers. They will have established their reputation in the world for their pure analytic research and will be reluctant to give that up in order to work with us.

"The good news is that once you're over the hurdle, the work is self-sustaining because it's so gratifying. People see that when they are in multidisciplinary teams, they are coming up with much more interesting, novel innovations and better problem-solving. They never want to go back to their silo after experiencing the difference."

VIDEO CUE:

The Good News . . .

Go to www.creatinginnovators.com
to watch the video.

Stanford's academic culture and the difficulties it presents for innovating learning are hardly unique. You'll recall the resistance Tulane's president, Scott Cowen, faced in trying to promote service and interdisciplinary social entrepreneurship programs and courses on his campus. I also spoke at length (on the condition that his name not be used) to a professor whose course on social entrepreneurship is one of the most popular offerings at his Ivy League college. His classes are always oversubscribed, but he is scorned by members of his department and thinks it highly unlikely that he will receive tenure. "They have no respect for anything that is not part of traditional academic research," he told me. "And even worse, having to teach their classes and meet with students are seen as annoying distractions from their research."

Aside from the learning culture, which I have already critiqued, another obstacle to educating innovators in universities is the lack of respect for interdisciplinary inquiry, practical knowledge, and applied learning. Discipline-based, in-depth knowledge is important, and basic research makes significant contributions to innovation. It is essential to our future that we continue to support this kind of inquiry, but this cannot—and must not—be the only kind of knowledge that is valued by our universities and our society.

Dean Kamen is one of America's most successful and highly regarded inventors and high-tech entrepreneurs. He is also a passionate advocate for STEM education and the founder of US FIRST Robotics—an afterschool program for budding engineers and scientists. "On the one hand, education should be its own reward, and that's fine. Curiosity-based research is important, too," he told me. "But if we want to invest taxpayer and corporate dollars in our ability to solve problems, then that's a different goal. People jumble all of that together and think the universities do both, but they don't." Dean, like so many other famous innovators, was a college dropout.

At its best, the charter school movement in the United States has sometimes offered a serious alternative to traditional public education and acted as a catalyst for real innovation in conventional schools. We need to support the development of "charterlike" programs in our universities as a way to incent innovation in the postsecondary world. We need many more d.schools and Media Labs on existing university campuses—laboratory schools where professors and students can choose to work on real-world problems and create new products and services, as well as new knowledge. And these should not just be engineering-based schools; we need innovators in the liberal arts and social science fields as well. And the teachers in all these programs should have the same salary and status as the professors who do more conventional research.

The other serious problem in colleges and universities is the poor quality of instruction in far too many courses. "Publish or perish" is the near universal dictum of the postsecondary world—meaning that, to get tenure, you have to publish articles and books based on your research. Teaching ability is rarely considered as important a qualification in most universities' promotion and tenure policies, and few places exist where college instructors can get help to improve their teaching. Not only must we support more applied, hands-on R&D, we must also value excellent teaching as essential in the development of innovators.

We have seen how remarkable educators had a life-changing influence on some of the young innovators in this book. Teachers and mentors such as Ed Carryer, Amy Smith, Paul Bottino, John Howard, and the Olin professors whose classes we visited didn't just take their teaching craft seriously. They also taught differently, as we saw. Most of us teach in the ways we have been taught. It takes a conscious effort and a good deal of trial and error to alter this pattern, as Jon Stolk told us. The next story is about two new graduate schools of education that have been established to disrupt conventional teaching models and to create better approaches to the preparation of teachers. Their story also illustrates some of the problems external accreditation agencies can pose for existing institutions when they try to create innovative programs.

High Tech High Graduate School of Education and the Upper Valley Educators Institute

High Tech High (HTH) was launched in 2000 as a single charter high school by a coalition of San Diego business leaders and educators. Today, High Tech High is a network of nine schools—spanning K–12—with thirty-five hundred students. While its student body is predominantly minority and representative of the demographics of its area, the schools' graduates nevertheless have a 100 percent acceptance rate to college, with 80 percent going to four-year schools.[31]

HTH initiated its master's of education programs in 2007 and currently offers a Teacher Leader degree for experienced teachers who want to deepen their practice and a School Leader degree for individuals who are heading—or plan to head—a small innovative school. The Graduate School of Education also offers a variety of teacher certification and professional development options for teachers, as well as training and support for teams working in the same school or district.

High Tech High's certification and degree programs were developed for several reasons. Dr. Robert Riordan, president of the Graduate School of Education, explained, "Because we were a charter school, we could hire people who were in the process of getting their teacher certification. One of our early teachers was a mechanical engineer who'd worked at Boeing. He took a big pay cut to come work with us, then he had to pay to take courses in the evenings to get certified. The problem was that he was learning to teach in ways we didn't like. [In fact, graduates of even the most prestigious schools of education rarely have the teaching skills that HTH wants for its classrooms.] So we applied to the state to create an alternative certification program and were approved in 2004."

The Upper Valley Educators Institute (formerly called the Upper Valley Teacher's Institute), located in Lebanon, New Hampshire, has more than a forty-year history as an alternative certification program for teachers. Recently, under the leadership of Dr. Robert Fried, the UVEI has developed a principal certification program and is now establishing a master's of arts in teaching program.

The master's programs that both schools offer are highly innovative and influenced by similar educational philosophies, which emphasize the importance of student teachers as creators and collaborators who must show what they know through portfolios, projects, and exhibitions of mastery. Students in both schools also spend the majority of their time working with a mentor in a school setting—similar to the idea of a residency for medical students—rather than spending most of their time in classes learning education theory and history, as is the case with conventional schools of education.

This is not to say that students do not learn theory and education history in these graduate programs. Theory is learned at HTH as a part of an extensive "action research" project—an inquiry into a particular learning problem that each graduate student identifies in his classroom context and studies intensively during the second year of the program. Results of this research are summarized in a required master's thesis. UVEI students must demonstrate mastery of ten essential competencies in oral presentations and in their e-portfolios. One requires students to "identify major terms, concepts, and movements of educational practice in the 20th and 21st century and to discuss them in relation to current challenges in student learning."[32] All UVEI programs are now "competency-based," meaning that students have to show that they are proficient in the skills and background knowledge that have been identified as essential for each area of certification.[33] Think of this as the scout merit-badge approach to learning, where badges are earned by showing evidence of mastery of specific proficiencies.

Both schools also regularly videotape their student teachers to help them assess and develop their skillfulness as teachers. Collaborative discussion of these tapes and of the student work that is produced in classes makes the work of teachers transparent and is the best way to continually improve instruction. Yet these practices are exceedingly rare in most schools and teacher preparation programs. Beyond the specific innovations, both schools are also developing teachers' skills to work collaboratively, to create interdisciplinary courses where students construct new knowledge, and to more actively engage students in their learning and the pursuit of their passions. In other words, they are preparing teachers who can develop the essential skills and dispositions of innovators that we have explored throughout this book.

There is growing alarm in this country about the inadequate preparation of teachers and school administrators, and these two new master's programs represent significant efforts to completely rethink the preparation of future educators. Both programs are being offered by organizations that have strong track records for other education programs they've developed. Based on the idea of student teachers apprenticing themselves to master teachers for one to two years, these programs resemble Finland's outstanding teacher preparation programs, which are largely responsible for their stunning results on international education assessments. However, as of this writing, neither High Tech High nor the UVEI program has received accreditation from its respective regional accrediting agency. The battle to gain these seals of approval has consumed an inordinate amount of time of both leaders.

Rob Riordan, who has been struggling with gaining accreditation from the Western Association of Schools and Colleges for several years, told me, "There are real tensions between innovation, which people may applaud, and becoming a peer in the university community. For example, we don't grant tenure at HTH. WASC [the Western Association of Schools and Colleges] wants us to find comparables as a part of our application process—but there aren't any!

"At one level, the association is excited by the model of a teacher preparation program being so completely embedded in a K–12 system of schools. They were in town for their annual conference and brought a group over to see High Tech High. But then in our most recent accreditation visit, the Review Committee for Educational Effectiveness said we have to have a full-time CEO. Larry Rosenstock [the founder and CEO of the High Tech High organization] had been the part-time head of the graduate school of education, and there was no problem, but now suddenly there was. So Larry said, 'Okay, we'll make Rob the full-time president, and I'll be dean.' We did a phone meeting of our board and approved the change before they left.

"We keep getting mixed messages from WASC about our assessment processes. One person said we were doing fine, but then another committee told us that our program objectives were institutional objectives and had to be rewritten. And then the chair of the Visiting Committee told us that our program was visionary and went way beyond the National Council for Accreditation of Teacher Education's recommendations for teacher-education reform. But her comment was nowhere in the final written report.

"The whole process seems to be checklist-driven, with little attention and perhaps some aversion to innovative approaches," Rob concluded.

I sent Rob Fried an e-mail inquiring about some of the accreditation issues the Upper Valley Educators Institute has faced, and he replied:

> UVEI has faced challenges of its own when it comes to accreditation. Initially warmly received by state and regional accreditors as a small "alternative" route to certification, the climate has changed as the feds have increased pressures for "accountability," especially with respect to institutions receiving federal student loans. Ironically, while the new focus on "results" or "outcomes" would seem to favor such competency-based initiatives as UVEI, the emphasis on "clock hours" [meant to rein in the more egregious of for-profit institutions] has forced UVEI to defend its competency-based assessment processes to nervous bureaucrats.

The full story of UVEI's recent quest for recertification reads like something Franz Kafka would have written. The Commission of Career and Technical Institutions, a division of the New England Association of Schools and Colleges (NEASC), was the longtime certifying agency for UVEI, but it recently decided to merge its accreditations with the Elementary and Secondary Schools division of NEASC, which left UVEI without an accrediting agency. Rob petitioned NEASC's Commission on Institutions of Higher Education to be included under their umbrella, but he has been told that UVEI must start over with their accreditation application—a process that will take at least three to four years to complete. So UVEI has had to seek and be granted accreditation from the Accrediting Council for Continuing Education and Training. "That's the agency that certifies everything from truck-driving schools to training for hairstylists," Rob told me, only half-joking. So while UVEI certification programs are now covered, its new master's degree programs in education are not, which means it is unable to offer federally backed loans to any of its students.

Teaching Innovation in Business Schools

Our final story reveals some of the challenges in preparing future business leaders to be innovators. Joel Podolny, who works at Apple, and Annmarie Neal and Robert Kovach at Cisco Systems, describe how our country's most prestigious business schools have developed a "status quo" learning loop, where true innovative thinking is seen as an unnecessary risk by students and perhaps too unconventional for their teachers.

Joel Podolny is vice president of human resources at Apple and dean of Apple University. Joel earned a PhD in sociology from Harvard, and he has taught in both Harvard and Stanford's business schools. Prior to joining Apple in 2008, Joel was dean of the Yale School of Management. "Based on what I saw when I was a business school dean and professor, it was clear that there was a lot in the world of traditional business schools that undercuts creativity and innovation," Joel told me. "Let's start with the business school application process, as seen from the vantage point of a college student attending an elite liberal arts college. They are essentially told that if they want to maximize their chances of getting into a top-five business school, they need to start building a résumé based on recommendations from the more established and traditional banks or consulting firms because this is the background of the model admit to one of those top programs, and I think it is safe to say that almost without exception, these established firms aren't looking for innovation and creativity from new college graduates."

"So you're saying the incentive structure to get into the 'best' business schools in the country is to be conventional?" I asked.

"Yes, and I spoke with a number of students who were terrified that this was true. Even though I had the good fortune to know many MBAs who were quite creative, I knew too many who looked at what they did to get into a business school and felt that it had squelched their ability to be creative and innovative. They felt that they had learned to play a game where innovation wasn't allowed by the rules."

Moving from the topic of who gets into the top business schools, Joel turned to the question of what gets taught in the courses. "Having taught strategy, you can be a viable ongoing economic enterprise either because you are very good at value creation or you're really good at capturing the value that others create," Joel explained. "Capture is how you squeeze more juice out of the orange. It's not about how you grow a great orange. In business schools, we really teach people how to squeeze oranges—how to manage for greater efficiency and economies of scale—not how to grow new and better oranges, which requires a different kind of thinking. Business schools may offer a few selective courses in innovation, but they foster a mind-set that promotes way more obsession with how to make money than how to create a truly great, innovative product, and that obsession will suck the life out of the organizational pursuit of innovation."

Annmarie Neal, who is chief talent officer and vice president of Cisco Systems's Center for Collaborative Leadership (about which we will learn more in chapter 6), told me that when she and her colleagues were establishing Cisco's new executive-education program, they could not find a single established business school that had the expertise they needed. "We've combed the world, talked to every business school, and went through a list of who's who among the business school professors. None were ready to do the work that's in front of us. They are too focused on managing and controlling and learning from the past, versus understanding the new challenges of the future."

VIDEO CUE:

Neal on US Business Schools

Go to www.creatinginnovators.com
to watch the video.

Robert Kovach, director of the Cisco Center for Collaborative Leadership, framed the problem as a question of where real expertise resides. "Professors at universities are considered the true experts in the US. I asked a professor who is the author of one of the most popular textbooks on management about speaking with managers in highly innovative companies, and he said, 'What do they know?' I think that captures the whole problem of priests on high who think they know what is best for business. They go out and teach it to managers, who learn it and then replicate it—and that's all they know how to do."

Joel Podolny described one of the ways in which the Yale School of Management tried to "disrupt" conventional business school thinking and to develop the capacities of students to approach problems in more innovative ways. "Managing an innovative organization requires much more than a generic set of business skills," he told me. "You have to understand the business you are in. So at Yale, we created more than forty joint degree programs with the schools of medicine, law, theater management, forestry, and so on. Joint-degree students graduate with something to hang their business skills on [*expertise*, as we've been saying in this book]. For example, in forestry, you need to move to local sourcing for your wood products, and so the important question is how to do that. Having a content background enables you to pose the right problem."

The Finland Phenomenon

A new business school in Finland, Team Academy, has taken a radical approach to innovating learning and preparing future business leaders.

Founded in 1993 by Johannes Partanen and operating as a part of JAMK (Jyväskylän) University of Applied Sciences, Team Academy is a fully accredited program, leading to a BA in business. But it has no classes, classrooms, or teachers. Instead, students (about two hundred per year) are admitted as teams, and all teams operate as independent cooperative companies engaged in real-life projects for the three to five years of their time at the school. Teams are coached by entrepreneurs and innovators from the business world as they work on establishing their own new company or on projects that have been given to them by existing corporations.

The results of this extraordinarily innovative program speak for themselves:

- total revenue of team companies has surpassed €1.5. million
- 91 percent of Team students are employed within six months of graduation
- 37 percent of Team students launch their own business within six months of graduation
- 47 percent of Team students are still entrepreneurs two years after graduation
- 150 projects have been completed for various companies [34]

Finland does not wait until students are in college to prepare them to be innovators and entrepreneurs. I was invited to consult to their National Board of Education in 2010, and Bob Compton and I both spent time studying their education system and then collaborated on making a documentary film about what we saw.[35] At one high school where we visited a number of classes, we observed an after-school program that was teaching the skills of entrepreneurship through immersion. Teams of students spent thirty consecutive hours together (with adult mentors) at the school working to create a new business. They were obviously having fun, but it was also clear that they were deeply engaged in the challenge of starting a business. When I asked one of the young organizers of the event what he expected students to learn in such a compressed time frame, he told me, "You learn to cooperate, to form a team, and you realize that you cannot innovate alone."

VIDEO CUE:

Teaching Entrepreneurship in Finland

Go to www.creatinginnovators.com
to watch the video.

Forty years ago, Finland was a comparatively poor country with an agrarian economy and an underperforming education system. Their leaders knew that their economic survival required them to radically transform their entire education system and develop the capacities of their young people to be innovators and entrepreneurs. Today, Finnish students start school one year later, do less homework, and have a shorter school day and year than students in most developed countries, and the country does not administer *any* tests for accountability. Yet Finland has consistently been at, or very near, the top on every international assessment given by the Organisation for Economic Co-operation and Development since the OECD testing program began in 2000. (By contrast, in the most recent OECD assessment, the United States ranked fifteenth in reading, twenty-fourth in science, and thirty-second in math, out of the sixty countries and five education systems that participated.)[36] Finland is also ranked as one of the five most innovative countries in the world—ahead of the United States.[37]

The full story of how the Finns have transformed their education system is beyond the scope of this book. Nevertheless, I think it is worth sharing a few highlights: (1) They have transformed the teaching profession through a radical overhaul of their teacher preparation programs. (2) They've pared down the curriculum to a few concepts that are deeply understood, in sharp contrast to the bloated, fact- and test-based curriculum that burdens many of our high schools and colleges. (3) They place a high value on career and technical education in their upper secondary schools (grades ten to twelve) and postsecondary program offerings (45 percent of all high school students choose a technical career versus an academic track). (4) They emphasize students learning independently and making choices about what they study. And (5) they have embraced innovations in teaching and learning at every level.

VIDEO CUE:

Finland Phenomenon Trailer

Go to www.creatinginnovators.com
to watch the video.

Reflections

All of these are changes that we can—and must—pursue in our high schools and colleges. I believe that the Seven Survival Skills I wrote about in *The Global Achievement Gap* and reviewed in chapter 1 are essential for every young person today to master. But I have learned in working on this book that Finland's reforms and the new skills I describe, while absolutely necessary, are not sufficient for the development of young people's capabilities to innovate. The culture of schools and classrooms must also be transformed.

You'll recall that, earlier in the chapter, I contrasted the learning culture at Olin with the conventional learning cultures one finds in most classrooms. As we've seen, the learning culture in all of the schools and programs profiled in this chapter have similar characteristics. They all are organized around the values of:

- collaboration
- multidisciplinary learning
- thoughtful risk-taking, trial and error
- creating
- intrinsic motivation: play, passion, and purpose

In everyday life, the contrasts that I have drawn between the conventional culture of schooling versus the culture in these programs are less stark, of course. It is perhaps not so much a matter of "either/or" as it is "both/and." Both individual and team achievements should be valued in the classroom, as should specialization and multidisciplinary learning. Information must often be "consumed" before you can create, and risk-avoidance and risk-taking can both be prudent actions, depending on circumstances. Finally, most of us act out of a combination of intrinsic and extrinsic motivations. The essential point is that education for innovation must be constructed consciously and needs to cultivate the capabilities for collaboration, multidisciplinary inquiry, trial and error, and the creation of new ideas, products, and services. It must also incorporate the intrinsic motivations of play, passion, and purpose in learning.

From all of the examples in this chapter, we see that it *is* possible to innovate learning and teaching in postsecondary education. I have tremendous admiration for the educators whose work we've explored in this chapter, as I think that they are all doing important research and development for postsecondary learning and teaching in the twenty-first century. But we've also come to better understand the formidable challenges in this work. Whether it's the system of tenure or accreditation, the motivations of some students, or the problem of challenging elitist or status quo thinking, the institutional forces that oppose change in education remain formidable obstacles to innovation.

No sense of urgency exists yet for change in higher education—especially in the most prestigious schools. While the deficiencies in our public education are widely acknowledged (though poorly understood), our system of higher education is still seen as one of America's great strengths. When people talk about creating a more innovation-driven economy, they almost always argue for more education for all students. But what I have learned is that merely giving students more of the same education will not create students who can innovate. For students to become innovators in the twenty-first century, they need a *different* education, not merely *more* education.

Chapter Six

The Future of Innovation

Transforming the classroom experience at every level is essential to develop the capacities of young people to become innovators. However, the experiences of young people before they even enter first grade and then later in the workplace also profoundly influence the development of their capacities to innovate. What parents do—what and how they teach their children, as well as what they value—matters greatly in the growth of young innovators. We've had a glimpse of how parents have raised the young people whom you've met in this book. In the following section, we will explore in greater depth the parenting practices and preschool experiences that are most important for future innovators. We will then explore some key challenges for employers in attracting, retaining, and developing young innovators. Teachers, parents, mentors, and employers all play essential roles in shaping the future of innovation in America and the world.

Parenting Young Innovators

A vast number of books offer advice on how to be a good parent, and I do not intend mine to be one of them. My interest is much more modest and more focused. I set out to answer a few questions: How do parents encourage the development of the intrinsic motivations that drive successful innovators—the spirit of play, passion, and purpose that are the wellsprings for creative work? Also, how do young innovators learn that it is okay to take risks and even to fail? "Tiger moms" such as Amy Chua (author of *Battle Hymn of the Tiger Mom*) don't believe in play and won't allow their children to fail. Helicopter parents, on the other hand, tend to indulge and insulate their children from failure at all costs. Neither kind of parenting is likely to produce innovators or entrepreneurs. So what parenting practices do contribute to the development of young people capable of being both?

I interviewed scores of parents for this study and conducted a focus group. My criteria for selecting whom to interview was simple: One group consisted of the parents of young innovators—those that I profiled in this book, as well as the parents of young innovators whom I had to leave out for space reasons; the other group of parents I interviewed were individuals who had jobs that required a high degree of innovation or entrepreneurship, or both. As a whole, the group spanned several generations, ranging in age from their late thirties to over sixty, and they were quite geographically dispersed as well.

I also spent the morning at one of the most innovative preschools in the country, located on the campus of Stanford University. The Bing Nursery School is a laboratory school that opened in 1966 with a grant from the National Science Foundation and a gift from Dr. Peter S. Bing, a recent undergraduate at the time, and his mother, Mrs. Anna Bing Arnold. The school provides a place where undergraduates at Stanford can learn firsthand about child development, and where faculty members and graduate students can conduct research in child development.[1] What intrigued me about Bing was that its entire faculty had recently spent a professional day with faculty at David Kelley's d.school and so had done a good deal of thinking about how to begin preparing young children to be innovators. The education philosophy and learning experience at Bing is also quite consistent with that of many Montessori schools, which, as we learned in chapter 1, have been responsible for producing an inordinately high number of innovators.

Play

All kids play. Certainly most parents encourage their children's play. However, I learned that *how* children are encouraged to play and *what* they play with matters greatly to all of the people whom I interviewed—and that there were clear discernible patterns to the kinds of play these parents and educators encouraged.

Opportunities and Time to Experiment

With a PhD in child psychology, Annmarie is also a passionate, and highly informed, advocate for developing young people's capacities as innovators at an early age. She told me that much of the executive education she does for Cisco (about which we will learn more later) is about helping executives to unlearn many of the bad habits that school had taught them.

VIDEO CUE:

Neal on Parenting Her Young Innovator

Go to www.creatinginnovators.com
to watch the video.

For her son Tucker, who is now six, she has only two rules, Annmarie explained, safety and character: Tucker can experiment and explore to his heart's content, so long as he is careful (comparatively) and caring—meaning that he is a good person. Everything else is up for grabs—sometimes literally. "So when he was little, he understood that if he pulled the Christmas tree down, someone may get hurt," Annmarie explained. "But when he wanted to take all the ornaments off the tree, line them up, and put them back the way he wanted, I let him. He was experimenting with his version of what a Christmas tree should look like. The same goes for dessert. He only gets it once a day, but if he wants it at breakfast, that's fine. We have to suspend judgments about how things are supposed to be if we're going to develop the capacities of children to be innovators as adults."

Malcolm Campbell, a professor of biology who is director of the James G. Martin Genomics Program at Davidson College and father of two teenagers, said something similar. "I've learned how important it is to indulge your kids' interests. If they want to wear polka dots and stripes together, that's fine. If they want to paint with food, that's fine, too—so long as they help with the cleanup afterwards."

Semyon Dukach—a serial entrepreneur, angel investor, and chairman of Global Cycle Solutions, Jodie Wu's company—talked about negotiating the boundaries between basic rules and letting his five children between the ages of three and seventeen "rebel." "As a parent, what is most important is to respect your children and to listen, but not to be too free. There have to be limits, boundaries, structure. But too much of this—of teaching them to be obedient—can kill the creative impulse. The challenge is to balance respect for authority with constructive engagement and constructive rebellion—teaching your kids to be strong, but giving them the walls to push against. You can't separate innovation from disobedience. But you can't be an innovator and rob banks."

VIDEO CUE:

Kids Still Need Limits

Go to www.creatinginnovators.com
to watch the video.

Many of the parents whom I interviewed mentioned the importance of not over-programming their children's time, ensuring that they had plenty of unstructured time for play and discovery. While all of these parents enjoy spending time and doing activities with their children, they were clear about the importance of not being "helicopter" parents.

Susan Lynch, one of the participants in my parent focus group, is a partner with Sankaty Advisors, an affiliate of Bain Capital. She is a highly successful and innovative investment manager and the mother of three children, ranging in age from eleven to fifteen. "We hire young adults coming out of the best schools," she told me. "With some who do not succeed, I think it's often because of how structured their lives have been—the constant pursuit of the A, of the thing that will get them to the next level. They didn't have enough time to pursue their interests on their own or be creative."

Christine Saunders, a research associate professor of pharmacology at Vanderbilt University, agreed with Susan, saying, "I see graduate students here at Vanderbilt who have gone to Brown or other good schools, and they have worked very hard to get in. But they're really not sure what they want. It shocks me the number of young people who have no idea what they are interested in because they have been pushed to achieve versus pushed to explore. I want my daughters to have more time to breathe and think and use their imagination. But I really feel like I am in the minority and swimming against the tide, compared to how other parents arrange their children's lives."

You'll recall that Lea Phelps, Kirk Phelps's mother, chose not to fill up her children's out-of-school time with additional classes and lessons, preferring that they have more unsupervised time playing outside. "A child has to get bored before he can figure out how to get himself out of boredom," she told me.

Brad Harkavy, a serial CEO for entrepreneurs' high-tech start-up companies, and Zen Chu, the founder of Accelerated Medical Ventures, which assists start-up medical companies, are fathers of children in their early teens. In separate interviews, they both stressed the importance of parents' not hovering. "Too many parents today are hyperinvolved in their children's lives," Brad said. "That kind of hovering doesn't produce innovators—people who can think for themselves." Zen observed, "Kids are naturally curious. They will experiment and explore on their own, given the right environment—and no helicopter parents."

Less Is More

These parents were unanimous: Fewer toys, and toys that encouraged imagination and invention, were seen as essential. You'll recall that both Kurt Phelps and Jodie Wu talked about how important building with LEGO blocks was for them. This kind of toy, with which young people can construct anything they can imagine and do it differently each time, encourages creativity and imagination. But sometimes the best toys can be even simpler.

Susan Lynch recalled that one of her children's most favorite toys when they were young was a scarf. "They'd dress the dog up in the scarf or use it as a superhero cape. Then it became the costume for their play based on the story of Gilgamesh, which we'd been reading together."

Leslie Lee is the mother of Mac Cowell, a brilliant young innovator who is developing do-it-yourself biology kits that enable people to do sophisticated science experiments without a laboratory or expensive equipment.[2] Mac's mother described some of the "toys" she gave Mac that he enjoyed most. "There were LEGOs, of course. But one of his favorite toys was something I gave him for his fifth birthday: a large cardboard box and two sticks—one six feet and the other four feet—and two lengths of rope. That was it. But he played with those same things for years. For another birthday, I took Mac to a hardware store, gave him twenty-five dollars, let him pick out his own presents. He was like a kid in a candy store. As I recall, he bought a length of chain and some pulleys; he found some clear tubing and valves, as well."

For many parents, peer pressure can make the decision of what to buy, or not buy, quite difficult. Christine Saunders said, "I'm concerned about the problem of consumption with kids today, and I feel surrounded by parents who have a different view. Lots of girls my daughters' ages have entire collections of American Girl dolls. [More than fifty different varieties of these eighteen-inch dolls have been marketed since their introduction in 1986, along with every conceivable accessory.] But our daughters only have one. I also encourage them to play with toys from my childhood—to play with what they have and use their imagination."

Screen Time

The "less is more" philosophy was also reflected in these parents' views on technology and screen time. As a group, they resisted buying their children electronic toys and limited screen time—both television and computer. Most of the children in these families did not have a computer in their own room until they were older.

Brad Harkavy and his wife, Ann Marie Mador, who is COO of the Neocure Group, which helps medical-technology innovators bring their products to market, have three children between the ages of seven and thirteen. I spent the morning talking with them about innovation and parenting in their kitchen, which, I noticed, had a computer readily available. I asked about their views on children and technology.

"Our children ask us questions constantly, and rather than answer them, we say, 'Why don't you look it up?' So they are always going to the computer to find out something," Ann Marie told me. "It encourages them to be curious."

Brad and Ann Marie are selective in what they allow their children to do on the computer, though. Because they are concerned about privacy issues with Facebook, at the time I interviewed them none of their children had yet established an account. But their oldest was recently given a cell phone—with an interesting consequence. According to Ann Marie, "Sometimes she will say way more in a text—like 'I love you, Mom'—than in person."

Brad explained how they were careful to limit screen time. "The computer is right here in the family space, so we can limit how much time they spend on it. And being a Jewish family, we honor Shabbat [the Jewish Sabbath]. So after sundown on Fridays, there's no phone or e-mail, but we will watch a movie together, and baseball on the radio is okay. We limit TV time."

You may recall that the Phelps family, while limiting screen time, also enjoyed movies and occasional TV programs together as well. The idea of sharing the screen time as a family—whatever the program may be—turns the experience from something solitary into a social event.

The Bing Nursery School philosophy on toys and technology for their children, ages two to five, also strongly emphasizes the idea of less being more and encourages the social element in all forms of play. The school buildings are surrounded by a large, fenced-in outdoor space for play. It is equipped with a variety of simple climbing and play spaces, including wood structures that can be anything a child imagines, from a fire engine to a fort, but nothing as complex or engineered as one finds in many public playgrounds in suburbia. Light and airy classrooms all open out to the play area, and children move easily between the rooms and the outside play spaces, where they are most often engaged in activities in small groups of two or three—sometimes with a teacher and sometimes not. The classrooms, themselves, are alive with colors and textures, many of which were the children's works of art.

Beth Wise, assistant director of the school, explained what she believed to be the most important "toys" children needed to develop their imagination and creativity: "Sand, water, clay, paint, and blocks. Once they can use these materials, they can create anything."

The school does have a few computers and digital cameras for the children's use, and they are increasingly popular for making photo albums, but the children must use these technologies together as a group so that they learn both the use of these tools as well as how to share and solve social problems. "One of the things we took away from our day at the d.school," Beverley Hartman, head teacher at Bing, told me, "is the idea of rapid prototyping in the social domain. We want children to learn to observe what a particular conflict is about and think about other solutions and try different ones until they find what works best."

VIDEO CUE:

A Visit to the Bing Nursery School

Go to www.creatinginnovators.com
to watch the video.

Intentionality

While the play at Bing may seem spontaneous and random, what the teachers are doing is quite intentional. "We are here to help children bring their ideas to life," Beth told me. "We want to guide and promote exploration. Design materials and art are used to teach problem solving with materials. We also teach how to solve problems socially with one another. Children have a natural drive to excel—to become much more independent and creative in their work when they know adults are there to help. The challenge for teachers is knowing when to intervene."

Beverley explained further, "It is a competency model, we build on what they can do – on what is self-directed, and self-selecting. The teacher brings attention to the students' task—to help them go further and articulate what they are doing. Teachers must be alert to what interests the students. Their powers of observation are critical."

I ask what they most wanted Bing students to learn from their play.

"To observe, problem solve, be able to take perspectives, have empathy, use multiple strategies for problem solving, have a love of learning and a capacity for design thinking" was Beth's immediate answer. Learning to read and to count weren't on her list of essential outcomes.

"What about parents? What do you hope to teach them?" I wondered.

"To build on their children's strengths, to nurture and respect what we see beginning to develop," Beverley replied. "To help them be observers of their own children and know who their child is, not just what he or she can achieve. Also, to be advocates for their children, and to have and use judgment about what's appropriate for their child and what they want as a family." In a word, they want parents to be as intentional as the teachers are in observing and extending their children's play.

Reading as Play

While learning to read and count are not the most important things children learn at Bing, the school nevertheless has a rich literacy environment, with many different kinds of books available for the children to peruse. Teachers also frequently read to the children, who will then often enact dramas based on the stories they have heard. Books, then, are another expression of play for children.

I found this approach to literacy, and the importance of literacy, to be another common thread in my conversations with many parents. Nearly all read to their children frequently. Books that encouraged imagination, as well as books that helped young children understand the world, were both considered important. For example, Ernelle Sills, Jamien's mother, told me: "I read to him beginning at a very early age, maybe four or five times a week. All of Dr. Seuss, Amelia Bedelia—we were always reading together. That's my passion." Many parents mentioned the value of the Richard Scarry series of books about Busytown, which illustrate how mechanical devices work and how adults—who are almost always anthropomorphic animals—performed different kinds of jobs.

Continuing to encourage children to read on their own as they get older is essential as well. Lea Phelps told me that their hour of enforced free reading a day—material that had nothing to do with any schoolwork—was something her grown kids have told her they will do with their children as well. And Cord Phelps explained why he and his wife persisted with this rule: "We wanted to create an alternative to the pressures of school where teachers were always saying memorize that, do these problems. It's different when you can pick something up that you've chosen and move at your own pace." My own observation is that the discipline of reading develops the muscles of concentration as well as the habit of self-motivated learning.

Passion

All of the parents whom I interviewed were adamant that one of their most important jobs is to encourage their children to find and pursue their passions. The importance of finding your passion came up in nearly every single parent interview. Recall that Cord Phelps, Kirk's father, talked about putting as diverse a buffet as possible in front of his children so they could learn what truly interested them—and then adapting, based on what he observed. With additional interviews on this topic, I gained some valuable insights about parents' struggles with what to do—and not to do—to encourage their younger children's pursuit of their passions. Challenges related to sports and musical instruments—how hard to push and what decisions to allow their children to make—were recurring themes.

Katie Rae, former product director at Microsoft Labs and a founder of Project 11, a firm that invests in and assists early-stage start-ups, is Zen Chu's wife and mother of two children ages seven and twelve. When we were discussing the importance of intrinsic motivation for innovators and entrepreneurs, she said, "We struggle with how much do you push your kids so that they master something versus letting the kids figure out what they actually like. I think it's a balance, and we've been wrong a bunch of times. Our kids are very good at the piano, but there's been at least two or three times when they've said they want to quit, and we've said no. We think that they probably have benefited from not quitting piano, but we probably should have encouraged our son to quit soccer several years ago and find another sport. He doesn't like soccer, but he loves hiking—he's never more motivated than when he is on a hike—so now we're sending him to camps where hiking is the focus. We've tried to listen for what they really care about."

Susan Lynch also talked about struggling with decisions related to her children's participation in sports. "Megan is a great soccer athlete, but she doesn't want to play every weekend. Other parents and the coaches have told us that if she is really going to be good, we had to take her to all the away games, soccer camps, and so on. I agree that nothing is fun until you are good at it—and I've had to remind Brian [her youngest] that he can't expect to walk on the field and be great—but so many parents think of their children as trophy possessions. It's not about their kids loving the sport. It's the 'tiger mom' mentality. It makes me sick to my stomach. So many kids are so programmed to succeed that they have no chance to explore things.

"We've tried hard to be supportive of their choices," Susan continued. "Megan played the piano and clarinet, but she wasn't really interested in either instrument. Then we took the kids to a holiday brass concert, and she fell in love with the tuba—of all instruments! The girl is passionate about her tuba playing."

François Barrault, the former CEO of BT Global Services, described a unique approach to helping his children choose a musical instrument. "When my children were nine and eleven, I took them to a store and let them try different instruments. I tried to watch their body language as they played each one to see what fit each child. I think every child needs to find the right tools that will allow him to express himself creatively."

Erik J. Andresen is president of Polytech Filtration Systems, a company that he started in 1987. Erik's wife, Leslie Andresen, is chief technology officer for a division of General Dynamics Corporation and one of the world's leading authorities in cybersecurity. The Andresens—like the Phelpses—have tried to expose their children to a wide variety of activities, including scouting, a number of different sports, and a variety of musical instruments. Erik explained that their two children studied piano for years—and their oldest became quite good—but they both decided to quit. "I'm criticized by some of my friends for letting my kids 'dabble' with different instruments and sports," Leslie said. Quitting something "doesn't have to mean a lack of discipline," Erik observed. "Parents can create the expectations. 'If you want to pursue an instrument, then we expect you to practice a certain amount of time every day.'"

Apple's Joel Podolny was adamant about not giving false praise to one's children. "It's important to support them in what they want to do, but also keep them honest in terms of how they are really doing. I don't think kids should be pushed to play cello [as an example], but parents shouldn't say it sounds great when it doesn't. Excellence matters. Not everyone can or should get a trophy. At some point, you need to experience the satisfaction of doing something really well."

David Sengeh's mentor at Harvard, Paul Bottino, told me an amusing story about how he helped his daughter "self-assess" her musical performance. "She found a flute in the attic," he explained. "So she went out on the street and started trying to play for money. She stayed out there all day and finally came in with just two dimes. I asked her why she thought she'd earned so little—and she got the idea on her own that it's the quality of the music that people pay for."

Pulitzer Prize–winning author and journalist Thomas Friedman told me, "Whatever my kids come up with, I'm for it. One of my daughters has an idea for a fashion website, and I'm going to help her fund it."

"What if the chances of success are only two percent?" I asked.

"I don't care, because I know that she will learn from the experience. I also know about the serendipity of life."

However, it can sometimes be hard to support your children's passions when they make what may seem to you, at the time, to be the wrong choices. Tom told me a story about his daughter that illustrates the point. "When she graduated from Yale, she was offered a scholarship to Cambridge and was also accepted into Teach For America. She asked my advice, and I had to bite my tongue because I didn't want my idea of what I thought was the right decision to always be in the back of her mind." (Friedman deeply values his experience at Oxford, where he'd studied on a Marshall Scholarship.) "So she chose Teach For America and went through the program for two years, which was an extremely difficult experience. At one point, she wondered if she'd made the wrong decision, but I'd come full circle because she had succeeded under very difficult experiences, gotten her master's degree, and she is now a fourth-grade teacher in the DC public schools. The experience has made her stronger.

"CQ [curiosity] plus PQ [passion] is greater than IQ," Tom observed.

VIDEO CUE:

Friedman on Parenting

Go to www.creatinginnovators.com
to watch the video.

Purpose

We have already learned from our young innovators what they aspire to. They all have a sense of purpose, as well as a passion. All of them want to make some kind of difference in the world. Our three social innovators—Laura, Syreeta, and Zander—see their explicit purpose in life as being change makers. Our five STEM innovators have a larger sense of purpose, as well. Kirk, who loves learning and managing complex technology projects, is excited about creating an affordable way to harness solar energy. While Jamien's passion is designing shoes, he, too, wants to create a greener manufacturing process, as well as jobs for Americans. About her new job at Autodesk, Shanna said, "I'm not just impacting the digital world, I'm impacting the real world: how to design buildings and factories that are sustainable, efficient, with less waste and huge cost savings." David's mission is to develop new technologies that can help alleviate poverty and suffering in Africa, as is Jodie's.

I think the larger sense of purpose that these young people feel is partly because they have been exposed to so much information about the threats to our future, especially climate change and global poverty. But information is one thing, and values are another. More information doesn't necessarily create the desire to do something. In fact, too much information can cause a kind of paralysis.

Values must be "caught" as well as taught. In one way or another, the parents of the eight young innovators whom you've met all have communicated—and demonstrated—the importance of giving back. I wondered what the parents in my focus group, who all have younger kids, wanted for their children—what they saw as most important.

Susan Lynch replied, "I hope they find someone they're happy with, that they enjoy their work, and that they are making a difference."

Leslie Andresen agreed, saying, "I want them to care about what they do, whatever it is. People who innovate care about what they do, care enough to take a chance, spend extra time, care about people they are working with. I also want them to feel that what they're doing makes a difference. I've tried to model this in charity work—it can be doing something small."

Leslie Lee, Mac Cowell's mother, reflected on what her son gained by going to school in rural Michigan. "To me, the most important thing he learned attending a small-town high school was a set of values: You don't treat people differently because of what they do or wear, or that they have mud on their jeans. People with humble jobs are sometimes the smartest people."

I also spoke with several other senior business leaders who are parents. They, too, talked about the importance of focusing on something larger than oneself.

Ellen Kumata is managing director and partner at Cambria Consulting, a firm that consults to Fortune 100 companies. "Business leaders talk a lot about passion. Passion is actually not quite enough. As you get older, you think about 'what am I spending all this time for?' There has to be something bigger, besides just liking to do something."

The recently retired CEO of Best Buy, Brad Anderson, has two children, twenty-eight and thirty. He told me, "There isn't anyone that doesn't need to be a creative problem-solver. Creative problem-solving comes from being engaged with what you are doing. What I want most for my kids is that they care about and are engaged in something that matters to them—that their life is authentic. As they get closer to this, I can see that they are happier. But I can't transfer my life. They have to find it on their own. I can coach them, but I have to do it gently and leave a large amount of space for them to be the individuals they are."

Dov Seidman is the founder and CEO of LRN, a company that helps businesses develop ethical corporate cultures. He is also the author of *HOW: Why HOW We Do Anything Means Everything.* He told me about what his son's name means and why it is important. "We believe we gave our son a good name, Lev Tov, which means 'lionhearted' and 'good-hearted.' But it is not enough to *have* a good name. He needs to spend the rest of his life *earning* it, and my job is to help him become that person. It's about values, it's about character, and it's about the strength to be resilient and keep your feet on the ground when unthinkable things happen—not every twenty years, but every twenty days. And it's about the ability to relate to the world. Most of all, I want to inspire hope in my son. The most fundamental value is hope, because when you are not rooted in hope, you retreat into yourself, detach, and disconnect from others. When you have hope, you see the world as a source of meaning; you see endless possibilities for a better future that allows you to collaborate with others to bring these futures about."

What Parents Struggle With

Reading this, some might get the impression that—aside from having to decide when to allow a child to quit an instrument or back off on a sport—the adults whom I interviewed found parenting comparatively easy. But I clearly saw that while they all loved being parents and spending time with their children, they also struggled. Dealing with their children's schools, creating space to let their children fail, and being "different" parents were recurring themes in my conversations.

School Issues

As we've seen, reading in these families was valued highly as an end in itself, a form of discovery and play, not as a means to the end of doing well in school. You'll recall that the rule in the Phelps household was that the children all had to read an hour a day, but not books that were assigned for school. Some parents had to resist teachers' efforts to force their children to read. They also had to frequently define and defend their children's "differences" with school authorities. I found Leslie Lee's story of her son Mac's struggles with learning to read to be especially poignant:

"When the children were young, the custom in our house every night was for each kid to pick a picture book, then it was into bed, and I'd read to them. They all loved books, loved stories. But when Mac got to first grade, he couldn't grasp the idea of symbols on paper. [He was attending one of the most highly regarded elementary schools in the suburbs of Chicago.] The school wanted to test him for ADD (attention deficit disorder) because he wasn't reading the way other young kids were, but I observed that he was always asking questions, and so my thinking was that he didn't have ADD—he just didn't want to read the books the school gave him. I said to Mac, 'It's okay, you can get reading later.'

"I went to talk to his first-grade teacher and explained that he loved books and I knew he'd be a good reader someday, but that forcing it now would make him hate books. She burst into tears. Then she said, 'I can't tell you how glad I am that you said that. Most parents yell at me because I haven't taught them how to read yet.'

"The next year, Mac was in second grade in rural Michigan. Again, I had to explain to the teacher: He will read someday—not to worry. We flew to Hawaii for spring break, and on the plane, Mac pulled a copy of *Popular Science* out of a seat-back pocket. The cover had a picture of a submarine leaving the water, flying, then landing like a car. Mac looked for the article in the magazine, found it and said, 'Mom, I can read this!' You could not peel a book off that kid's face after that. By end of second grade, he'd read more books than any other kid."

Some parents had issues with their children's schools' expectations for obedience to authority. When I first began working on this book and shared some of my thinking with Annmarie Neal, she sent me the following e-mail about her son Tucker's experience at a highly regarded charter school outside Denver, where he'd just been accepted into first grade.

> My son is five and attended Montessori for most of preschool and kindergarten. He was recently accepted into the first grade of a charter school nearby—which is free and very academically rigorous. I took Tucker over for his entrance exams [for placement purposes]. The teacher gave him the test booklet and had him work through the math and writing exercises. She monitored as I read him the instructions.
>
> He finished the test in 20 minutes. He brought the test to her—remember Montessori schools don't test—so the idea of being tested is a unique concept to him, and she said, "You can't be finished—you have 40 more minutes. Go back and check your answers." He replied, "I did and

I think they are right." She scanned the test and said, "Hmm, they are all right." He told her that at Montessori he gets to go to the 2nd grade class to do multiplication and division. She said. 'Lower your voice,' and he stopped telling her the story.

The teacher then said, "Let's see if you can read as well as you do math," and proceeded to have him read a story. He did ok, but made a few mistakes. She said, "Now let's see if you can answer some questions." She went into a series of questions about air—do you know what it is, how do you know it is around you, how do you know it changes? He started talking about the earth versus other planets—about oxygen versus gas, about living creatures, about wind, and then he went into a story about how his yogurt top was picked up by the wind. And he told her of a moral dilemma when he was at Montessori about chasing the top—because he littered—versus staying at the picnic table, which was the rule. The teacher said, "You broke a rule?" Tucker replied, "Yes, but I told the teacher, and I did not want to litter." The teacher told him to lower his voice again. He was very excited about his story, as most 5-year-olds are, but he was certainly not yelling.

This is the public school mindset—even at a top-rated charter school. Answer the questions, comply with the rules—and lower your voice. He went back to his Montessori class later that day, and when his teachers asked how the testing went, he said "I did great on the test, but I did not feel so good after it." I was heartbroken.

Annmarie concluded her e-mail to me with the following observation:

Juxtapose this [Tucker's experience] to your book concept. Innovation is all about creating a culture for ideas to foster—good ones and not so good ones. And learning how to manage risk associated with experimentation of these ideas. How do we teach children to collaborate, disrupt, innovate, and adapt to a world that is rapidly changing, while developing their sense of mastery and self-esteem? Give them rich experiences and develop their confidence to explore, question, test, experiment, and

> push on the boundaries of relevance? The test in corporate life won't be how much you know—but how well you collaborate with others to bring strategic relevance to your firm.

Annmarie and her husband elected to send Tucker to a private school for first grade, rather than to the charter school.

Parents' struggles with their children's schools often centered on the conflict between learning for a test or a grade versus learning as an expression of their children's intrinsic interests—especially as their children grew older. Leslie Andresen said, "There is a tension between my own goals for my kids as learners versus the public schools' goals for them. I don't care what their MCAS scores are [the Massachusetts tests that are given for accountability]. I won't encourage my children to spend more time studying for the tests because I'd rather see them use the time to go further in a subject that really interests them. But it's a struggle for me.

"It's also challenging for me to keep my concerns about learning and success from being transferred to the kids. As a student, I used to worry about getting an eighty on a quiz. I don't want to put that anxiety onto my children. They have to want to do well because they love to learn, not for the grade."

Rich Lynch, Susan Lynch's husband and another focus-group participant, is president and CEO of Celticare Health Plan, a start-up business whose goal is to provide affordable health-care coverage to lower-income families. He said, "As parents, we try to balance a concern for our children getting decent grades versus being who they are, comfortable in their own skin and getting along with others. Emotional intelligence, EQ, is more important than IQ."[3]

Susan Lynch talked about how important it is to recognize that her three children learn differently from how she did, and that each has his or her own style of learning. "School was easy for me, and I was high achieving," Susan explained. "But I'm recognizing that things which were easy for me are not the same for my kids. We have three very different personalities, and it's important for us to understand that what works for one, or what worked for me, won't necessarily work for the others. It's not about us, we've already been to school, and it's not about the school. It's about them. Most of my work and social set are insanely pressured about achievement. I want my children to enjoy their childhood. I'm trying to resist all the craziness around me."

Robin Chase is cofounder and former CEO of Zipcar, the largest car-sharing company in the world, and GoLoco, the first company to combine ridesharing with social networks. She and her husband, Roy Russell, who is chief technology officer at GoLoco and held the same position with Zipcar, have two children in college. They were also "resisters" who refused to engage in the common parenting practice of managing their children's young lives to position them for admission to the "right" college. "We didn't tee them up for college, didn't push them to fill their résumés," Robin told me. "We felt it was much more important to teach our kids to be learners and to know where to go for learning. Besides, where they go for graduate school will matter more than what college they went to."

Tom Kelley, managing director of IDEO, described a tension in his aspirations for his high school–age children. "I want them to color within the lines of regular school, then go find the interesting and important stuff out of school," where, in Tom's view, the most significant learning happens.

Leslie Lee took a radical stance about how best to support her son when he was in high school.

"Mac spent a lot of time on the computer all through middle school—he was a pretty geeky kid. One week into high school, he discovered that girls were real and announced, 'I've decided to become more social.' Football, ski team—high school was a time for him to forge relationships, have fun, go to parties, and he had a pretty good time.

"He was going to a small-town high school. He had a few good teachers, a lot of really bad teachers, and a lot of mediocre teachers. He was a terrible slacker—often not even making an effort in his classes. But what I wanted to know was 'What are you enthusiastic and curious about?' If he still had both—even though it wasn't in the classes he was taking—then I wasn't worried.

"His biggest problem was being bored in class. I told Mac, 'If you are bored in class, don't be mean or rude, hide the book you want to read behind the text, and keep yourself interested. Your learning is your responsibility.'"

When I interviewed Jeff Hunter, he was transitioning from his job as vice president for human resource solutions at Dolby Labs, where he was responsible for talent acquisition, to his new position with a firm on the East Coast. Previously, Jeff worked at Electronic Arts and was cofounder and CEO of his own company, Euphorion, which he sold in 2003. Jeff also has his own award-winning blog, Talentism.com. In all of these endeavors, his focus has been on how to better define, recruit, and develop the talent needed by highly innovative companies. As a parent of three teenagers between the ages of thirteen and seventeen, he is acutely aware of the conflict between what his children must do for school success versus what skills they will need as future innovators. One of his 2007 Talentism.com blog entries, "My Son Won't Do His Homework," expressed this conflict most forcefully:

> I am going through hell with my son. He is twelve, and no matter what I do, no matter what my wife or my oldest daughter do, he won't do his homework. We ground him, we take away all his gadgets, we prevent him from going to birthday parties and other social events that he loves. Other than corporal punishment (which is a place I won't go), we have tried everything. It doesn't matter . . . he doesn't care. We can't force him to do something he thinks is wrong. And my personal hell is . . . he is right.
>
> My son can listen to the radio and pick up his saxophone and play whatever he is hearing. Or, if his sax isn't handy, he picks up whatever other musical instrument is around and plays that.
>
> But he doesn't do his homework.
>
> I bought him a book about drawing and he gets up at night and reads it and sneaks around the house sketching things. The portraits he does are incredible. The comics he produces are funny, insightful and engaging. Everyone asks him to draw for them.
>
> But he doesn't do his homework.
>
> My son is rarely if ever unhappy, and people are naturally drawn to

him. He has a great delivery on jokes and has a photographic memory for any piece of pop culture he has seen. We riff on *Simpsons* lines all the time, cracking each other up in the process. Then he'll tell me movies he saw three years ago, shot by shot, line by line.

But he doesn't do his homework.

My son is intellectually curious. He loves to learn new things and is always asking me, "Why does something work this way?" or "What about that?"

But he doesn't do his homework.

My son loves video games. I work at a video game company [Jeff then worked at Electronic Arts] so I know how long it is supposed to take to finish all the missions in your average next gen video game. My son takes half that time. He holds competitions with his friends where, after he beats them, he shows them all the tricks that he has figured out about how to beat the game.

But dammit, he doesn't do his homework.

The other day I insisted that my son finish a piece of homework. I sat down next to him and taught myself math that I never learned in all my years of high school and college (remember, he is twelve). I stayed up until midnight with him, browbeating him the entire time, my anger unchecked. Finally, we completed the problem, which had to do with plotting the parabola of a quadratic equation and reducing the result set to a graph of the system of inequalities. The project was about finding the cross section of a river based on a given quadratic equation.

The next morning my son woke early and went down and made his project interesting to him. He put in cartoon characters exploring the depth of the river, and drew a shark (which he labeled with his teacher's name) about to eat a happy little duck (which he labeled "My Grades"). He drew a fisherman packing gear and assorted other fish and life. These were not just doodles—he actually helped clarify some of the information that he had been struggling with. By drawing the characters he was helping himself understand what the lesson was trying to teach.

My entire family was completely enthralled by what he had done. It was not only artistically creative and engaging, it actually helped clear up the very nature of the project. Justly proud, we anxiously looked forward to hearing how his teacher responded.

My son returned home from school downcast, shuffling his feet. I asked him what was wrong. "My teacher didn't like the project, because I put it on the wrong size paper."

I don't have much hair, but I am ready to tear what little I have out at the roots. My son doesn't do his homework because his homework is stupid. I have spoken to educators and principals and academicians and grandparents and probably a hundred other people, and nobody has given me a decent answer to this question: "Why are you so convinced that my son is going to be an academic or an investment banker?" Because as far as I can tell, those are the only two things that schools prepare kids to be.

As a parent I am caught between two worlds. I am 100% certain that school is doing great damage to his future prospects, but I also know that the game is rigged to be in favor of kids who get the right grades. . . .

I want to focus on what will make my kids successful, on what will allow them to provide the most possible value to their clients, their society and themselves. But I have to focus on what will get them work, even if that will hurt them, society, the companies that hire them and everyone around them. This is the very definition of a broken system, the very epitome of how we are driving ourselves off a cliff all in the name of safe driving.[4]

Taking Risks

Allowing children to take risks was another recurring theme in my conversations with parents, and their philosophies are in sharp contrast to those of many "helicopter" and "tiger mom" parents. Many of the parents whom I interviewed said that it is important to allow their children to make mistakes and to not protect them from failure.

You'll recall that Leslie Lee gave her son Mac a box, some rope, and some sticks for a birthday. She lamented that many parents would not buy these kinds of things for their children today. "Parents today are so risk-averse. Kids can't have a stick or a rope. But I never found him or any of his friends tied up, and nobody ever got hurt. But there were lots of booby traps!"

Robin Chase and Roy Russell talked about the idea of introducing risk at low levels. "We gave our children progressive walking and biking privileges," Robin told me. "When our kids were eight, they could cross the street and go to the park a block away by themselves. When they were nine or so, they could go to the library a couple of blocks away. When they were eleven, I would let them go to the food co-op by themselves. And when they were thirteen, they could take the subway into town.

"But when we tell this to parents who live in the suburbs, they are shocked. I was reading an article about kids walking to school, which had an interview with a parent who would not let her nine-year-old child walk *four houses* down the street to school. The article also talked about other parents berating the mothers who let their children walk to school. I understand the fear about kidnapping, but I also understand probability and statistics. How many children are kidnapped by strangers in this country in a year?"

Zen Chu said something similar: "Our kids get autonomy to do things—riding bikes or taking the subway to places—it's a huge confidence-builder. But it also points to a tension—how much freedom and when? It's the right tension, though."

"Kids need practice at perseverance and resilience—bouncing back," said Rich Lynch. "We need to give them opportunities to take a chance and to fail. I don't want the first time they have that sick-in-the-gut feeling after a major setback to be when they are twenty-six."

"You have to help your children see 'failure' as part of the process," Roy Russell suggested. "So you didn't get the job. What are you going to do about it? Or what new opportunities could you pursue?"

With respect to risk-taking, parents told me that you have to understand who your children are. Some are more capable than others of assuming responsibility and being independent at an earlier age. "It can be different for different kids," Roy Russell explained. "Some kids can be clueless as to what's going on around them."

Robin Chase told the story of her independent and confident daughter who, at the age of ten, told her parents that she wanted to go live with a family in Mexico and learn Spanish. "We took it very seriously," she said. "We couldn't find anything for her then, but a week after her fifteenth birthday, she flew to Guatemala City by herself, then took the bus to an intensive Spanish school, where all the students were in their twenties and thirties. She also regularly took a bus to a small Mayan village an hour away to give English lessons to the kids.

"I believe that if you are going to develop your children's entrepreneurship skills, then you have to allow them opportunities to take initiative, and that invariably means some risk," Robin added. I interviewed Cameron Russell, Robin and Roy's daughter, to see "how the story turned out." Cameron, now twenty-four, is a highly successful fashion model, an economics and mathematics major at Columbia, and a writer and videographer. She is also a political activist, and in 2009 she organized a group of models to do a benefit video on behalf of the environmental organization 350.org, founded by Bill McKibben. Their YouTube clip has been viewed nearly 1 million times.[5]

"Parents want to think there's no risk in life," Leslie Lee said. But the life force is always at risk. If you are bringing someone into the world, you might lose them. You can't keep your children from it."

Being "Different" as Parents

In interviews with parents who are innovators or who are the parents of young innovators, I was struck by how frequently many mentioned their own struggles with being a different kind of parent from those around them.

Lea Phelps was the first to mention the challenge of being different as a parent—what she and Cord valued in education, the rules they set, and how much time they spent with their children. Christine Saunders, you'll recall, struggled with giving her children many fewer dolls than other children had and wanting her daughters to have more time to use their imaginations, but she felt that she was "swimming against the tide." Susan Lynch mentioned the criticism of other soccer moms who thought that, by not taking her daughter to away games, she was not encouraging Megan to be as good a player as she might. Susan worried about how many parents see their children as "trophy possessions" that are "programmed to succeed." Leslie Andresen said that she was sometimes criticized by other parents for seeming to allow her children to "dabble." Leslie Lee observed how "risk-averse" many parents are today. Robin Chase and Roy Russell talked about how aghast some parents were at how much independence they gave their children. And most of these parents' views on education were at odds with those of other parents who are more concerned about credentialing than learning. Unlike so many suburban parents, these "different" parents also refused to "hover" and protect their children.

To be the parent of a young innovator and an entrepreneur today requires confidence and courage. I don't know where these parenting qualities come from, but I do know that the teachers of young children—such as those whom we met at Bing—can and do make an enormous difference in helping parents understand how best to support their children's learning and development. And I hope that many parents can take heart in reading these interviews and realize that they are not alone in their views of what is right for their children.

Ultimately, to parent in the ways that I have described requires trust: First, trust in yourself as a parent—your intuitions, judgments, and values. Then trust in your child—in his or her unique interests and talents, in the hunger to learn and create, and in the innate drive to realize one's full potential. It also requires a reconsideration of your authority as a parent. This is no longer a "father knows best" world. What limits to set; when to say no versus letting a child decide; when to protect versus let go; when to push the homework versus when to support learning out of school; when to trust a child's "wisdom" versus your "better judgment" as an adult—all these are decisions that successful parents of young innovators struggle with daily.

The future of innovation depends on developing a deeper understanding of this new role for parents. But parents and teachers cannot create an innovation economy by themselves. Innovators also need a different kind of mentoring and management in the workplace in order to thrive.

Leading and Developing Young Innovators in the Workplace

You will recall that one of the recurring themes in our interviews with the STEM innovators was their skepticism about working for a large corporation. Jodie Wu talked about all the inefficiencies that she saw at the large multinational corporation when she interned her second year; she was also concerned about what kind of impact she could have doing engineering projects in a large company. Despite her initial doubts about working for a corporation, Shanna Tellerman accepted a job at Autodesk, but she made it quite clear that she was only there so long as the work was innovative and she had opportunities to learn and grow. Jamien Sills has consistently refused to take a management position in a corporation and stayed true to his vision of running his own company. Kirk Phelps left Apple to work for a small start-up. David Sengeh is still in school, but he has a highly entrepreneurial spirit and so is unlikely to end up working for a larger company. And our three social innovators are far more likely to work in the nonprofit sector than in a corporation.

This lack of enthusiasm for working in a large corporation is common among the Millennial Generation—and is likely to be a growing problem for companies. Attracting and retaining highly creative and innovative individuals is vital for companies whose lifeblood is creating new products and services—and, increasingly, that will be *all* companies. As Jeff Hunter, former vice president for human resource solutions at Dolby Labs, told me, "In the coming years, there won't be a single job in the US that doesn't require innovation." Thomas Friedman and Michael Mandelbaum make the same point in their new book, *That Used to Be Us.*

Much has been written about what companies must do to become more innovative, and I cited several of the more recent and popular books in chapter 1. My purpose is not to write another tome about how to innovate in businesses. What particularly interests me is the challenge corporate leaders face in attracting young innovators and developing their creative capacities. In other words, what management practices might need to change for young innovators to thrive in corporations? The successful and innovative business leaders whom I interviewed on this subject were quite passionate and consistent in their answers to this question.

Business Leaders Speak Out

Tom Kelley is not only a senior executive at one of the most innovative companies in the world, IDEO, he has also consulted extensively to corporations who want to become more innovative and so has a unique vantage point from which to view the kinds of changes that are required.

"At the senior management level in far too many companies," Tom said, "there is this top-down attitude—the belief that all the worthwhile ideas are created at the top of the organization, and everyone else is just an implementer. The CEOs believe that they are better at everything than anyone else, and if only they had enough arms and legs, then everything would be more successful.

"The free flow of information up and down the organization is critical for innovation, but a top-down management style tends to severely restrict the emergence of any new ideas and inhibits the development of the 'collective wisdom' of the company."

According to a recent article in the *Wall Street Journal*, "In many highly innovative companies, great ideas come from all levels of an organization, not just from the top, experts say. At most companies, the problem is, employees have little input. Research has found that the average U.S. employee's ideas, big or small, are implemented only once every six years..."[6]

Jeff Hunter told me, "The management systems in many companies are broken and are a relic of the past. Just creating more efficiency doesn't work. And you can't manage innovators the way you used to manage folks in manufacturing—with command and control. Innovators don't want to be managed. They want to work with a group of people whom they respect and solve customer problems that are intrinsically interesting to them."

Ellen Kumata, who does a great deal of executive coaching as part of her job at Cambria Consulting, is a keen observer of the kinds of leadership that do—and do not—produce innovation. She consulted to Apple in the 1980s and saw how Steve Jobs had organized Apple in ways that were quite different from most corporations. "There is often a contradiction between the corporate environment and what innovators need to thrive," Ellen said. "Corporations are concerned with return on investment, but the process of innovation is not linear and will not likely produce a short-term return. Jobs knew this and so he, and other smart corporate leaders, carved out protected spaces in their companies for innovation.

"When we interviewed people at Apple," Ellen added, "what was most striking was that problem solving or getting your hands wrapped around an interesting issue was really important to everyone. Most managers in traditional companies get further and further away from their area of expertise—but not at Apple.

"The world is changing so quickly that if you don't think forward, by the time you figure out what is happening, someone will have beaten you to market. We need people who can think out of the box, see the future in a different way, but organizations aren't built to accommodate this way of thinking. Corporations try to hire in the talent they need, but many creative people are reluctant to go into large organizations, so larger companies frequently don't get the most talented individuals."

Like Jeff Hunter, Ellen observed that the "industrial" model of management simply won't work in a world that requires constant innovation. "The idea that you can manage and organize companies in Western-centric ways is based on a rational and linear logic. But that logic doesn't exist anymore. Today, the process of improvement and innovation is discontinuous and happens by jumps."

One of Annmarie Neal's primary responsibilities at Cisco Systems is talent development. She, too, talked about how the old-style linear approach to business challenges is no longer effective. "The work problems in previous generations were easy. They were about replication, scaled efficiencies, making things predictable and reliable. [In the words of Joel Podolny, 'how to get more juice out of the orange.'] Through linearity [steady progress over time] an organization would achieve success. In today's environment, companies compete with fundamentally different business models. If you are sitting in Bangalore, you can buy a cell phone for a dollar. So what happens to T-Mobile, which is trying to sell their cell phones for two hundred and fifty dollars? Or BMW, whose cars cost forty thousand dollars, while Tata makes one that sells for twenty-five hundred dollars? The solutions to these new business challenges are, for the most part, nonlinear, and they are not going to be solved with the traditional tools that we've used in business in the past. So the question becomes, how to teach, recruit, and reward the flexible, creative, nonlinear thinking that is required?"

According to Annmarie, innovation demands "an organizational shift from a system focused on driving for large-scale efficiencies to driving for much more flexibility and creativity in how people work. It's no longer about individuals pushing widgets through a system. It is about how to manage for collaborative, creative outputs."

Throughout this book, we have learned how young people are creating innovations that require a high degree of expertise, as well as creativity and initiative. All have had at least some college. But I believe that every young person can and must become an innovator, not just those who work for high-tech companies such as Cisco, and going to college will not necessarily enable you to be a better innovator. Noted Harvard economist Larry Katz, who coauthored the recent book *The Race between Education and Technology,* told me, "There are two sources of value-added [or innovative] jobs: (1) high-end analysis and the creation of new products and services; and (2) anything requiring empathy—lower-wage manual work done in person—from haircuts to driving taxis to child care. Traditional middle-class routine jobs have become commodities which can be replaced by machines or done overseas, but there are many valuable—and value-added—things that can be done in the 'in-person' sector. You can run an old-age home with Walmart minimum-wage kinds of employees who basically keep the elderly restrained in their beds, or you can have highly trained [and much better paid] employees who understand Alzheimer's and how to give the elderly a better life. There is innovation in this kind of work as much as there is in designing the next iPad."

A full discussion of innovations in the "in-person" job categories lies beyond the scope of this book. However, I found the story of Best Buy, the big-box electronics retailer, to be a powerful illustration of how a different approach to management can free the energies of employees to become innovators.

I first learned about Best Buy from Tom Kelley, who told me the story of how, back in 2000, the company wanted to expand from being a big-box retailer to having a shopping-mall presence with smaller stores. So the company acquired Musicland because it was the biggest seller of CDs and DVDs. But by then, eighteen-to-thirty-year-olds were no longer buying CDs. When Best Buy was finally able to unload Musicland, Best Buy had lost $1 billion. "The really sad part of the story," Tom said, "was that most of Best Buy's employees are between eighteen and thirty. If they had been asked about their music-buying habits, Best Buy might have avoided such a costly mistake. Their new CEO, Brad Anderson, has told people, 'You will see my company make many mistakes, but you won't see us make that mistake again.'"

Brad Anderson served as CEO for Best Buy from 2002 to 2009, having worked his way up the corporate ladder from salesclerk. When I interviewed him, I asked him to elaborate on how he had tried to use the talents of his young employees to create innovations in his business.

VIDEO CUE:

Anderson on Best Buy's Innovations

Go to www.creatinginnovators.com
to watch the video.

"For most of my years in retailing, once a company had multiple stores, your goal was to dumb down the operations so as to reduce the number of variables. [Joel Podolny would call this a strategy for getting the most juice out of the orange.] Now we have this extraordinary and singular opportunity to remake the workplace and dramatically improve productivity.

"With the new communications tools, you can have a much deeper engagement with people who work for you. Line-level employees at Best Buy can now have access to the same kind of knowledge as the CEO, but they also have access to knowledge the CEO doesn't have because of their direct contact with customers. And with the increased competition, you have to find competitive breakthroughs. So you now can, and must, engage your employees in much more creative ways, as opposed to telling them how you want customers to be dealt with. Henry Ford used to say that he wanted his employees' hands, but not their minds. Retailing was the same way through the nineties. Now we have to differentiate and adapt to customers' needs, using what we learn from our line employees, while also realizing the economies of scale." (Grow new oranges and get more juice.)

I asked Brad to give an example of how he has used his employees' knowledge to improve the overall customer experience, and he described how some of the younger employees had noticed that few women ever came into their stores. It turned out that many women were turned off by the technical talk about the number of megapixels in a digital camera, for example, when all they wanted to know was how to e-mail their friend a picture they'd taken. So Best Buy has worked with its employees to help them better understand different customers' needs and interests.

"Most people have something unique to contribute in the workplace, but it takes the right environment and leadership. You have to engineer the business around the individual who works for you, rather than around the system you use."

Brad described some of the "strength-finding" tools that Best Buy used to help individuals find out what their particular gifts were. He also dramatically increased the range of the kinds of jobs in the stores. "There are people who love to solve technical problems, people who enjoy being on the showroom floor interacting with lots of customers, people who prefer going to customers' homes to do installations. In every case, they have to solve problems, but the nature of the problem and the work environment varies significantly between these jobs. The greater the range of skills among your employees, the more you can offer the customer. At the same time, you provide more opportunities for employees to do what they love to do. You have to use the latent talents in your workforce as a competitive edge. You become not just a retailer, but also a service company."

"What did you find most challenging in making this transition?"

"The hierarchy," Brad answered emphatically. "Once you promote someone to executive rank, the vision of what it means to be an executive is so often counterintuitive to the idea of listening to your employees, developing them, and using their expertise. It was hard to find people who were authentically inspired by wanting to lead, and developing the people they were leading—as opposed to the financial rewards and the belief that they succeeded because they were smarter than everyone else."

Innovators for the Army

Chain-of-command hierarchies and command-and-control leadership are common in businesses—and are the targets of much criticism by my interviewees, as you've just read. But these have long been a way of life in the military—in fact, that's where the term *command and control* comes from. However, even the military must now innovate and rethink its traditional organizational structures. Through several conversations with General Martin Dempsey and Lieutenant General Mark Hertling, and after spending time at West Point and the US Marine Officer Candidates School in Quantico, Virginia, I came to learn how the US military is transforming its training programs to develop soldiers' capacities to innovate on the battlefield without having to rely on command and control to tell them what to do.

When I first met General Dempsey, he commanded the US Army Training and Doctrine Command (TRADOC), with responsibility for all the training that takes place in the army, and Lieutenant General Mark Hertling was his deputy commander in charge of all initial training. Both men have had long and distinguished careers in the army. General Dempsey was recently appointed US Army chief of staff and chairman of the joint chiefs, and Lieutenant General Mark Hertling was promoted to commanding general of the US Army in Europe.

"When I was commander of TRADOC, I used to give a talk to all new rising battalion brigade commanders" (usually soldiers who have recently been promoted to the rank of colonel and who will command a force of three thousand to five thousand soldiers), General Dempsey told me. "And I made three promises: one, we are not going to give you an organization that is perfectly fitted to your needs; two, we are not going to give you the equipment that is exactly what you'd like to have to accomplish your mission; three, the guidance you get is likely to be late to your need. They'd all scratch their head and say, 'What the hell,' and I'd say, 'The answer is you—you the leader—have to figure this out. You have to find ways to be both adaptive and innovative to accomplish the mission. The nation is counting on you.'

"The enemy is not predictable," General Dempsey continued. "A second lieutenant in a mountain pass in Afghanistan can often do more to advance the mission in a very strategic way than can a four-star general in Kabul. So the requirement is there, but we haven't yet figured out how to produce that outcome. West Point cadets, and I was one, want to know what the answer is, what are you looking for. 'Tell me what you are looking for, and by God, I will produce it.' We know how to build tactical leaders, but how do we develop strategic leaders?"

General Dempsey initiated a process to better understand what knowledge, skills, and attributes a strategic leader needs in the army today. He tasked his team to then map those results back to figure out what various army training programs were delivering and what needed to change. He chose 2015 as the target date for full implementation. The resulting document, "The Army Learning Concept for 2015," makes a compelling case for a radical overhaul of all army training programs. The opening paragraph sets the context for these fundamental changes:

> The U.S. Army's competitive advantage directly relates to its capacity to learn faster and adapt more quickly than its adversaries. The current pace of technological change increases the Army's challenge to maintain the edge over potential adversaries. In the highly competitive global learning environment where technology provides all players nearly ubiquitous access to information, the Army cannot risk failure through complacency, lack of imagination, or resistance to change.[7]

The paper includes specific recommendations for immediate change:

> The objectives in ALC 2015 will require substantial changes in infrastructure and policy; however, the urgency to build a competitive Army learning model cannot wait until 2015. It must begin now. Many of the actions necessary to achieve ALC 2015 goals are within reach, and the first steps must begin immediately to establish a more competitive learning model. All course proponents can start now by taking the following three steps.
>
> (1) Convert most classroom experiences into collaborative problem-solving events led by facilitators (vs. instructors) who engage learners to think and understand the relevance and context of what they learn.
>
> (2) Tailor learning to the individual learner's experience and competence level based on the results of a pre-test and/or assessment.
>
> (3) Dramatically reduce or eliminate instructor-led slide presentation lectures and begin using a blended learning approach that incorporates virtual and constructive simulations, gaming technology, or other technology-delivered instruction.[8]

TRADOC is now completely reshaping all training programs in the army—from basic training to advanced officer training. Hertling, who was in charge of revamping Basic Training, gave me an example of the kinds of changes he's pursued to develop the skills of soldier-innovators. "I have asked trainers to force people to make decisions [rather than just obey orders]. Recently I observed training in first aid which had been combined with an obstacle course and physical fitness. The instructors had put mannequins on the course with a variety of injuries. The soldiers not only had to treat the different wounds, but they then had to carry the wounded mannequins to the end of the obstacle course. At every position along the course, four soldiers carrying a litter were faced with requirements to get over a wall or get under a wire or through a doorway or window. We are trying to teach soldiers the basics of innovation—that it's a thinking man's game, where you are never going to be given the right solutions."

In these conversations and in reading the "Learning Concept" paper, I was particularly struck by the stark contrast between the sense of urgency the army leadership has about transforming training in order to produce soldiers and officers who can innovate versus the sense of complacency in too many of our schools and corporations. For the army, transforming training is literally a matter of life and death. Imagine how different things might be if our nation's leaders talked and acted as though transforming education was a matter of life and death for the economic future of our country—as, indeed, I think it is.

And imagine if our secretary of education had the clarity that was evident in the army paper about what needs to change immediately in our education system. Imagine how different our schools and colleges could be if they all simply made the same three changes that the army is implementing: "Convert most classroom experiences into collaborative problem-solving events led by facilitators; tailor learning to the individual learner's experience and competence level; dramatically reduce or eliminate instructor-led slide presentation lectures." All of the outstanding educators whom you have met in this book have made these three changes in their classes.

This is not to suggest that the changes have been easy to implement in the army. "The institutional anxiety around changing a learning model is monstrous, far worse than I imagined when we began this journey," General Dempsey told me. "There is too much comfort with the status quo—learning ain't broke, don't try to fix it. I worry that we have lost the instinct to be inquisitive, creative, and innovative."

Cisco's Action Learning Forum for Future Leaders

Most teachers teach in the ways that they were taught, most managers behave in the ways that other managers did before them, and most drill sergeants train in the ways that they were trained. If you have always been "commanded and controlled," first in school and then in the workplace or the army, how are you going to learn how to teach or manage or lead differently? We saw how High Tech High and the Upper Valley Educators Institute are creating new models for the preparation of educators that disrupt traditional ideas of what is good teaching and model a different kind of teaching and learning. To overcome this "legacy" problem in management and disrupt the conventional hierarchies that so vexed Brad Anderson, Annmarie Neal and Robert Kovach, director of the Cisco Center for Collaborative Leadership, have worked with colleagues to create a radically new model of executive development called the Action Learning Forum.

VIDEO CUE:

Cisco Innovates Executive Education

Go to www.creatinginnovators.com
to watch the video.

Teams of eight or nine young Cisco executives work together over sixteen weeks to create new businesses or products, based on concepts that have been vetted by senior management. The teams meet in person several times, then meet "virtually" from the diverse places around the world where team members live and work. The goal is for each team to write a plan for a potential new Cisco business, which they present to senior executives at the conclusion of the program. About half of the new businesses then receive start-up funding from the company.

Most recently, the teams meet in Bangalore for an orientation, which might better be called "disorientation" because Robert and Annmarie's goal is to disrupt the thinking of these successful young executives by exposing them to the chaos and alternative reality of a developing country. "When you see the mothers of young children walking down the street barefoot and carrying babies with no diapers, but they all have cell phones, it disrupts your view of the world. You experience how consumers in different markets have diverse needs and priorities," Annmarie explained. "So we 'teach' executives about emerging-market dynamics in Bangalore and Beijing by actually taking them on field trips out into communities, where they will spend time working in a soup kitchen, a school, or hospital. Our challenge is to create environments that provoke new thinking."

"The typical executive-development program is ninety percent 'taught' through textbooks and cases," Robert went on. "Ours is ten percent taught and ninety percent learned in the context of creating new businesses and solving real problems."

"Another important element of the Action Learning Forum is teaching executives how to be reflective," added Annmarie. "If you are going to develop yourself as an executive, some of that is about learning more, but much of it is also about reflecting on who you are as a human being, what's important to you, why you are on this earth, and then how you translate that deeper understanding into a leadership platform."

Robert elaborated, "The cut and thrust of business is a hard game. You have to be very tough to succeed in business, but the more you know yourself—your own biases and those of the culture in which you were raised—the better decisions you are going to make. More reflective executives are better able to assess their impact on the lives of people they are leading and so make decisions that are more deliberate and less reactive."

At the end of the sixteen-week training program, each team presents its business plan in great detail to a group of senior managers for assessment. As part of the final review, every team member receives extensive feedback from his or her teammates in a "360 review," as well as comments from a psychologist who has observed the team carefully.

The training, then, has several objectives. Clearly, one goal is to develop leaders who better understand the realities of doing business in countries very different from their own—not by reading books, but through experience. Another is to hone participants' new-business-creation skills. A third equally important goal is to create a new kind of leader, one who is much more self-aware, reflective, and collaborative, traits that are essential not only for innovators but also for leaders of innovators.

Conclusion: Redefining Authority

Rebels such as Huck Finn are some of the great heroes in American literature. Many of our most popular novels and movies celebrate the rebels who defy authority, a theme that likely has its roots in our country's origins as a rebel colony. This unique aspect of our history may be why we have tended to tolerate more outlier innovators than most other countries, which profess far more respect for traditional authority. But the Huck Finns of the world are usually portrayed as an exception—court jesters to perhaps be admired but not to be emulated. Most American children are still socialized to obey authority. As a teacher, parent, executive, or ranking officer in the military, you are assumed to be "in charge" and to have all the answers. Your job is to "command" the people under you to do what you think best, and their job is to listen and to obey. Your authority comes with your position or title or rank and is generally not questioned—at least not to your face. The smooth functioning of society depends on some compliance to authority.

The problem is that the highly disruptive nature of innovation creates new challenges to traditional authority, and successful leadership of an innovative enterprise requires a different kind of authority. Clayton Christensen's classic, *The Innovator's Dilemma*, documents how supremely confident CEOs in some of America's industry-leading companies have often refused to invest in promising new innovations because they thought their products were good enough. Most of those companies are gone today. Innovation demands that both assumptions about what is necessary or possible, and the authority that defends those assumptions, be challenged. As Semyon Dukach—a successful innovator, entrepreneur, angel investor, and parent—told me, "You can't separate innovation from disobedience." If you are an innovator, compliance is not in your nature.

We have seen how essential it is for teachers of innovators to give up a measure of their authority and control in order to transition from being the "sage on the stage" to the "guide on the side," as we heard several say at Olin. And, as we learned earlier, parents of innovators relinquish traditional authority in much the same way to allow their children the space to explore, to make their own discoveries and mistakes—and even to fail. We have also seen how innovative companies share information with line employees and seek their input. Even today's army has to recognize, as General Dempsey said, that the second lieutenant in the mountains may be in a better position to make strategic decisions than the general who is far away and so must have a different kind of training and more authority for decision making. Finally, we have learned how Cisco sets out to disrupt their most promising executives' assumptions about the world and to create a far more open, collaborative, and reflective kind of leader.

Authority still matters for successful innovation, but it is not the authority that comes with a position or title. It is the authority that comes from having some expertise, but it also comes from the ability to listen well and empathetically, to ask good questions, to model good values, to help an individual more fully realize his or her talents—and to create a shared vision and collective accountability for its realization. It is the authority that empowers teams to discover better solutions to new problems. Whether you are a parent, teacher, commanding officer, or employer, to enable individuals to become innovators, you must rethink the sources of your authority. The word *coach*—rather than mere *facilita-*

tor (the army's term)—describes this new kind of authority at its best. Innovators need excellent coaching at every age and stage.

The questions are, can those of us who have positional authority develop this different kind of earned and enabling authority? Can our institutions of learning and work recognize and promote a new kind of authority? Can we move from top-down, compliance-based systems of accountability in our schools and companies to forms of accountability that are more face-to-face—reciprocal and relational? And, finally, are we prepared to not merely tolerate but to welcome and celebrate the kinds of questioning, disruption, and even disobedience that come with innovation?

Developing better answers to these fundamental questions is essential for "growing" innovators and will likely determine the extent to which America prospers in the future.

VIDEO CUE:

Since the Book Was Published . . .

Go to www.creatinginnovators.com
to watch the video.

Epilogue

Letter to a Young Innovator

Dear young (and young at heart) innovator,

I write to you not just as someone who has researched what enables young innovators to flourish, but also as a person who has, in some modest ways, tried to be an innovator in his own life's work. So this letter to you comes from both my head and my heart.

First, you must understand how important it is that you remain true to your vision and that you persevere in the pursuit of your particular passion—whatever it may be. It is vitally important that you do this for several reasons.

The first reason is because you will likely not be happy if you do not. If you give up or give in to convention, you may please some family members and others who are made uncomfortable with your being different, but there will be a cost. You may lose your self-respect. You may become depressed. You have a calling, a need to create something, to "put a ding in the universe," as Steve Jobs said. I know how hard it often is to believe that you can do this thing you are called to do—and that it's worth doing. But your creativity, rooted in your curiosity and imagination, is what gives your life meaning and direction.

Martha Graham, one of the great dancers and choreographers of the twentieth century, once said:

> There is a vitality, a life force, an energy, a quickening that is translated through you into action, and because there is only one you in all time, this expression is unique. And if you will block it, it will never exist through any other medium and it will be lost. The world will not have it. It is not your business to determine how good it is nor how valuable nor how it compares with other expressions. It is your business to keep it yours clearly and directly, to keep the channel open.[1]

The second reason is that, quite simply, your country needs you. I know that you are not motivated mainly by the idea of wanting to grow America's economy. Money is less important to you than it may have been for your parents—and that's fine. You want to do things that will make a difference in the world. You want to make a contribution to a more sustainable planet. You want to reduce the growing gap between the rich and the poor, both in this country and around the world. You want to enable people to have healthier and more satisfying lives. And I am grateful because we are in desperate need of all these changes. But please understand that the incremental and breakthrough innovations that you create in pursuing these goals will also create jobs and add to the wealth of our country, and I encourage you to embrace that goal, too.

Innovators and the things they create are the lifeblood of our economy, and now more so than ever before. We no longer make very many things in this country. Most manufacturing can be done far more cheaply elsewhere. Many other kinds of routine jobs—both white-collar and blue-collar—are rapidly being either off-shored or automated as well. And we cannot sustain our standard of living just by providing more and more goods and services to consumers who are too debt-burdened to keep on buying. As you probably know, nearly one-sixth of our country's workforce is now either unemployed or underemployed—and has been so for a longer time than at any point in our history since the Great Depression. So your country needs you to create new ideas, products, and services that are sought after around the world and that will generate jobs and wealth and enable happier, healthier lives in this country and elsewhere.

Without you, our country is likely to see a continuing economic decline and ever-widening income disparities.

Many of your parents were consumers, unknowing consumers of our planet's wealth and your future. So now it is your turn and your choice: You must, first and foremost, be a creator. Now let's talk about some of the things that make your life as an innovator hard and what you can do about them.

I know that you are sometimes—or perhaps often—lonely. You think differently, you see the world differently. You believe and say and do things that are unconventional and often not understood by the people around you. So a sense of separateness and loneliness is inevitable. But you need to have faith that, as you grow more confident and disciplined in the pursuit of your passion, you will find others who share that passion or perspective and who respect you precisely because you have the courage not to give in to conventions. When you do find those kindred souls, you must stay in touch and support one another. Better still, form a team. Don't give in to the temptation of thinking that you can do this thing you want to do all by yourself. You can't.

School. Oh, boy. Another tough one. A wise person once told me, "When you pick your school, you pick your complaint." Unless you are fortunate enough to go to someplace like High Tech High or Olin or the Media Lab, you will likely experience much of your schooling as boring or irrelevant. I want to say, "Don't let your studies interfere with your education," but it's not that simple, is it? Sometimes we learn important or useful things in school, and we often need the credentials and credibility that a degree gives us in order to accomplish the things we want to do. At times, too, learning something new is truly exciting.

So my advice is first to seek out teachers who have a real passion for their subject—no matter what it is. It is often inspiring to be around other people who have a passion for something, and you will likely learn far more from them than someone who merely has deep expertise. Spend time on—and get good grades in—the subjects that engage you, and try not to worry too much about the others. Get what you can from those courses, and take any assignment you are given for a class and try to make it your own. Adapt or adopt the requirement as much as possible to fit your needs or interests, even if that means having to seek some kind of special permission. Finally, in or out of school, study things that you care about in depth and develop an area of expertise. A tremendous sense of exhilaration comes from mastering something that is intellectually hard through a sustained effort over time. This kind of pursuit develops your capacity for discipline, and the muscles of concentration and perseverance that you will need to succeed. People will also listen more closely to you if it is evident that you really know something.

Another hard thing: You are going to fail—and likely more than once. If you don't fail, then you are probably playing it too safe. Failing hurts like hell—especially failing in public. But you will learn some of your most valuable lessons from failure—far more than from your successes. As you reflect on the causes of your failure(s), you will come to better understand yourself—your strengths and weaknesses—and you will adjust your aspirations accordingly. You will also become clearer about what it is that you are trying to do and what is required to make it work. Think of failure as iteration, as learning.

One of the hardest and most important things you need to do is believe in yourself and your vision. It is especially hard to maintain that self-confidence in the face of failure. But without the inner certainty in the rightness of what you are trying to accomplish, you cannot persist. Some people may confuse your confidence with arrogance, and they will often tell you that you are just plain wrong. Don't listen to that kind of static.

But do work at staying modest. If you are successful, people will flatter you, feed your ego, tell you how great you are. Don't listen to that noise either.

Practice listening to many different kinds of people and ideas, though. As that would-be do-gooder Karl Marx once wrote, "To make the frozen circumstances dance, you have to sing to them in their own melody." Listen for the melodies around you. Become an anthropologist to better understand the economic, social, and cultural influences that promote or inhibit the changes you are trying to make. Read history and good novels to understand culture and character. Ask lots of questions, and observe carefully. Listen to advice and then take it with a grain of whatever. Be passionate, but not dogmatic. Be both a believer in and a skeptic of your own ideas. Stay curious. Seeking to understand and appreciate many different kinds of people—their backgrounds, ideas, and beliefs—is fascinating and often fun.

Speaking of fun, make sure to have some. Take time off. Take walks and do other things to be in nature. Get exercise regularly. Listen to music. Study paintings and photographs. Volunteer. All this will help you to stay more centered and balanced and give you both creative and physical energy, as well as more stamina.

Enjoy your fun pursuits, but also know that you will need to cultivate several kinds of disciplines. One is the discipline of plain hard work. In his book *The Outliers,* Malcolm Gladwell writes about the importance of putting in ten thousand hours in order to get really good at something. Don't hang around waiting to be inspired. I think it was Thomas Edison who said that the creative process is 1 percent inspiration and 99 percent perspiration. You will likely need to develop a regular schedule and a routine for your work.

Another discipline is focus. Because you are naturally curious and creative, you'll be tempted to explore many things and go in several directions at once. That's important to do for a while, especially in the early years of college. But at some point you will have to get and stay focused. While you don't want to wear blinders or become maniacal, you will not achieve anything significant without a sustained focus. Focus and finish, then move on to a new project that captures your interest.

The final discipline you need to cultivate is self-reflection. It can be through meditation or by writing in a journal regularly or walking or yoga. Many different ways exist to listen to what the Quakers call "that still, small voice within." However you do it, you need to practice regularly and not wait until the mood strikes you. As we heard Annmarie and Robert at Cisco Systems say, the better you know yourself, the wiser your decisions will be. It will also help you to develop your capacity for discernment: knowing when to listen and when to block out others' voices, as well as whom to listen to and whom not to, what company to work for and which ones to avoid.

Being an innovator and an entrepreneur is a blessing and a curse. The blessing is that you have the capacity to see and do things that others around you may not. The curse is that to realize your potential and the potential of your creation, you have to work hard at a lot of different things. But you can and you must persevere. Your personal sense of satisfaction and the future of your country and our planet all hang in the balance.

Afterword by Robert A. Compton

Spending so much time with the talented young innovators profiled in this book—as well as with their parents, teachers, mentors, and employers—has been an extraordinary experience. My thoughts on parenting, educating, and mentoring have changed in profound ways.

Feeling the passions these innovators exude was inspiring and energizing. It's easy to get excited being around them. It was disheartening, however, to know that so much of what animates them came in spite of, not because of, our traditional institutions and approaches. Although expensive for our society, school was hardly a stirring experience.

A Different American Dream

The American Dream has always been that each generation would be better off than the previous. All it took was a little more education, working a little harder, and innovating a bit more.

In an economy made up of domestic companies inventing, producing, and hiring locally, that dream was attainable. But this generation lives in a world radically different from that of their parents. It is now a global economy, interconnected and highly competitive. Capital, production, and jobs rapidly move to wherever they are most productive and efficient.

Achieving the American Dream for this generation, in Tom Friedman's view, means doing everything "twice as hard, twice as fast, twice as often and twice as much."

But I don't see these young innovators buying into being the "twice as" generation. They are defining their own, different American Dream—one that values passion and purpose, in which their priority is making a difference more than making money. As one young innovator said, "I want to live a meaningful life with just enough money to support myself and a family."

Can this different American Dream support a sustainable economy where most people lead satisfying lives? My own experience as an entrepreneur and venture capitalist leads me to believe there must be a middle ground between "twice as" and "just enough."

Can Passion Pay the Bills?

"The world is filled with new ideas," explained one mentor, "the test is whether an innovation can be turned into something valuable."

I sensed this one blind spot in these young people—the lack of a clear understanding of how their innovations can be converted into value that sustains their enterprises, their communities, and themselves.

While they have seen entrepreneurial successes, they haven't fully learned how new wealth is created. Clearly, the free enterprise system is not taught in schools, and the concept and processes are hard to learn on one's own.

I think this will be the biggest hurdle for this generation of innovators—making passion pay the bills.

They'll Just Figure It Out

"I'm not teaching a subject. I'm here to teach a process for learning," explained one Olin professor. "I want my students really to learn only one thing from me and that is how to teach themselves."

Learning to learn was a theme with everyone I interviewed. The explosion of new technologies and the blazing speed with which they are commercialized means one simply can't learn enough in college to call it quits with education.

What impressed me most about these young people is that they're unafraid to try new things, to explore the world, and to face unexpected problems. They are unafraid to fail because they see it as just a step in the process of learning. They have become adept at teaching themselves, using the Internet to learn, to find and contact people with knowledge specific to their project.

What makes this generation of innovators unique, and what ultimately gives me faith about their future, is that no matter what they encounter in life, they will find a way to figure it out.

A Letter from Tony Wagner to Business Leaders

Since *Creating Innovators* was first published, I've had opportunities to meet with hundreds of you at events sponsored by leading corporations and most recently, the Business Council, where I spoke to a large group of Fortune 200 CEOs.

I've heard from many corporate leaders struggling to find employees who can bring innovation skills to your businesses and are worried that current education reforms are not addressing your needs. At The Business Council meeting, I asked how many of the CEOs present were concerned about their new hires' lack of skills, and nearly every hand in the room—more than 100—went up. When I asked how many believed current educational reform efforts were successfully addressing this problem, I spotted just one hand. I then asked how many had concerns about the quality of education their children and grandchildren are receiving, and once again every hand shot up.

In one-on-one conversations, I've heard an all-too-common refrain about this problem and what is required to solve it. Your view of the education dilemma is understandably colored by your business experience, but unfortunately the kinds of solutions that work for businesses don't often work in education. However, some of your best hiring and promotion practices have extraordinary relevance for how we can and must transform education, once we redefine the problem. Let me explain.

Many of you believe that the essential problem in education is lack of competition. Public schools are a monopoly, and so you support charter schools in the hopes of deregulating the education industry. I, too, support charter schools and helped start one of the first in Boston. At their best, charter schools provide vital educational research and development for new models of learning, teaching, and assessment. Still, while competition often does improve products and services and lower costs in the business world, it does not work this way in education. Only a small percentage of charter schools are truly different from and better than comparable public schools in the same area. And the very best advances in education developed at these charter schools don't get adopted broadly.

The latest national charter school study, conducted by Stanford's Center for Research on Education Outcomes, found that 25 percent of charter schools had significantly stronger growth than comparable public schools in reading, 56 percent were about the same, and 19 percent of schools underperformed. In math, the results show that 29 percent of charter schools had stronger growth than their public school counterparts, 40 percent did about the same, and 31 percent did worse.[1]

While these outcomes are better than those from the same group in a 2009 study, they nevertheless offer a poor assessment for a twenty-year experiment that has consumed an enormous amount of money and generated bitter controversy. I have to ask you: As business leaders, are you really satisfied with the return on this investment?

Many of you also share the prevailing belief that teachers' unions, in addition to lack of competition, are the root cause of our country's education mediocrity. I'm no fan of teacher tenure, and I agree that in the past unions have been far too protective of poor teachers. I support greater accountability for teachers, but abolishing unions or severely weakening them has not resulted in significantly better education results.

Right-to-work states, where union strength is at its weakest, perform most poorly on national education assessments. And most charter schools, which do not have unions or tenure, do no better than their public school counterparts, as we've seen. In my experience, even teachers in elite private schools are often mediocre, adhering to obsolete teaching practices and priorities. By contrast, in Finland 96 percent of teachers are unionized in one of the highest performing education systems in the world.

If competition and unions aren't the main culprits in our underperforming education system, then what are? I've identified three: childhood poverty, poor teacher preparation, and an obsolete accountability system that measures the wrong outcomes and incentivizes mediocre teaching.

The relationship between childhood poverty and educational achievement is well established. The childhood poverty rate in highest-scoring Finland is a little over 3 percent, while ours is more than 22 percent. Analysis of data from the National Assessment for Educational Progress shows that more than 40 percent of the variation in reading scores and more than 46 percent of the variation in math scores across states is correlated with a variation in childhood poverty rates.[2] According to a recent analysis conducted by the Organization for Economic Cooperation and Development, "Currently the United States is one of only three OECD countries that on average spend less on students from disadvantaged backgrounds than on other students." The report went on to state that the most talented US teachers rarely work in disadvantaged schools, while the opposite is true in countries with high-performing education systems.[3]

Great teachers and great schools can and do overcome the effects of poverty, but only at considerable effort and expense. Poverty is not an excuse for an underperforming education system, but we must recognize the significant contribution it makes to students' capacity to learn. A serious debate in this country about reducing childhood poverty and ameliorating its effects is long overdue.

For nearly a quarter of a century, our education reform debate has focused almost exclusively on ways to improve the most disadvantaged students' schools. However, mediocre teaching affects almost all of our children—rich and poor alike. In the United States, many teacher-training programs admit almost all applicants because the programs are cash cows for large universities. Students graduate with very little teaching experience and then are often placed in classrooms in front of the most challenging types of students. Once hired, teachers rarely receive effective supervision—even in the best private schools. Compounding these challenges is the unfortunate place of teaching in our value system. Teaching is not a respected profession in this country. No small wonder that more than half of all new teachers quit after five years. How long would you stay in business if you had a turnover rate like this?

By contrast, countries like Finland, Singapore, and South Korea have made massive investments in and radically improved their teacher preparation programs. All Finnish teachers, for example, have been required to earn an academic master's degree since the mid-1970s. Their program obliges them to conduct real research and spend a year apprenticeship with a master teacher. Only the very best universities in Finland offer teacher preparation programs; all others have been closed down. Because teachers in these countries have been so well prepared, they are both trusted and respected as professionals. Teaching is a sought-after profession. Only 10 percent of education-school applicants in Finland are accepted.

You might argue that there is very little that business leaders can do about the problems of childhood poverty and teacher preparation. But business leaders like yourselves have an enormous influence on our politicians and media, when you choose to exercise it, and I urge you to push policy makers on these underlying causes of the failure of our education system. These changes will take time, but there is one thing that all of you can advocate for right now that would have a rapid and profound payoff.

Before I made my presentation at the Business Council, a senior executive from the Conference Board reported on their recent survey of CEOs. Among the questions asked was what skills executives are looking for when they make hiring decisions. The results tracked very closely with what I learned while researching my book *The Global Achievement Gap*. Critical thinking, communication, collaboration, and creative problem-solving skills continue to top the list, along with agility, adaptability, curiosity, and imagination.

But how many of these skills correspond to those for which we test kids and hold teachers accountable? The answer: none! There is no correlation between what is examined on our predominantly multiple-choice, factual recall, computer-scored tests versus the education outcomes that matter most to you in your businesses. The new common core curriculum assessments, which forty-five states have agreed to use, will be tougher, but they will still be mostly tests of academic content knowledge, with the addition of critical thinking and more writing. And they will test content knowledge—like advanced math—that almost no one will ever use in their lives. When was the last time you—or any of your employees—had to solve a quadratic equation or factor a polynomial?

The value of explicit content knowledge, which is so much of what we test, has rapidly dropped to zero, as you know. Knowledge has become a free commodity. The world and all of you do not care about how much your employees have memorized to pass a test—answers that can be googled in a nanosecond. What you care about is what they can *do* with what they know. We cannot assess a child's ability to ask a good question, apply what they've learned, or create new knowledge on the basis of the cheap tests we use.

How many of you make important hiring or promotion decisions on the basis of a test score? None that I know of. Even Google, which was a company known for hiring only students from name-brand colleges with the highest GPAs and test scores, has come to understand there is no correlation between these data and employee excellence. Two recent interviews with Google executives suggest that the company now looks for individuals who have a sense of mission in their work and personal autonomy. Even having a college degree is no longer considered essential. Fifteen percent of employees in some Google teams have no degrees.[4]

I know that you make important personnel decisions on the basis of collective human judgment informed by evidence. You conduct multiple interviews and want to see evidence of what a prospective employee has done in the real world—problems they tackled and times that they have been both successful and have failed. If this is the best system for corporations, then why shouldn't it be for schools, as well?

I think the simple reason is that you do not trust teachers. I understand that. It's hard to trust someone who appears to have a job for life with no accountability. So the real explanation for all the constant testing we do in this country is that it is an attempt to hold teachers accountable. The problem is: What gets tested is what gets taught. Or in your terms, what gets measured is all that matters. But having the wrong metric is worse than having none at all because it incents the wrong behaviors. And that's exactly what's wrong with our education system today.

Our accountability system motivates teachers to create a test prep curriculum focused heavily on memorization and repetition. And with the US Department of Education's recent Race to the Top effort, which requires participating states to evaluate teachers on the basis of test scores, this problem is going to become even more severe. We will drive the best teachers out of the profession, and we will continue to bore our students with mindless test prep. As a result, our education outcomes are likely to get worse, not better.

You, collectively, can do something about this. Indeed, nothing is likely to change without your leadership. In the mid-1990s, the pressure to create what I call the Accountability 1.0 System originated from business leaders. Courageous CEOs like IBM's Lew Gerstner and Xerox's David Kearns called for a national summit on education where they and other CEOs put pressure on governors to raise academic standards and accountability. Incidentally, a handful of educators were invited to that summit in 1996—but only in an observer capacity. The accountability systems that were created had no real input from educators. Can you imagine a system where your performance as a CEO would be evaluated by teachers who knew absolutely nothing about your business?

Here's what I'm asking you to do: demand an Accountability 2.0 system. First, be very clear about the educational outcomes that matter most. Find more public opportunities to talk about the skills you need and what you find lacking among high school and college graduates whom you interview. But when you do so, I urge you to also talk about the importance of these same skills for active and informed citizenship in the twenty-first century. Teachers will be much more attentive to what you have to say if they perceive that you are not merely talking from your own self-interest.

Next, I want you to pressure the US Department of Education and state governments to create an assessment system aligned with the outcomes that matter most. To do that, we will need to use an auditing strategy, where we test sample populations every few years—instead of every child every year. This will free up money needed to pay for dramatically better assessments like the College and Work Readiness Assessment and the international PISA test,[5] as well as the training teachers will need to prepare students for these new tests.

Another essential part of this Accountability 2.0 System is requiring all students to have a digital portfolio where they collect work that is evidence of progressive mastery of the skills like critical thinking, oral and written communication, collaboration, and creative problem solving. Some of your employees should work with college teachers in appropriate departments to audit random samples of these portfolios to ensure that they meet your performance standards. You should also ask to see them as a part of your hiring process. More than 8 in 10 of you have already indicated an interest in doing this in a recent survey conducted by the Association of American of Colleges and Universities.[6] You are increasingly skeptical of the value of transcripts and GPA's in the hiring process—and for good reason!

What about holding teachers accountable? The best educators and union leaders I know welcome accountability—not based on results of a single standardized test for which students themselves have no accountability but rather on evidence of growth and effectiveness as a teacher over time. All teachers should also have digital portfolios for initial licensure and for recertification. These portfolios would include videos of their teaching, sample units of study, student work, and student course evaluations. I think teachers can and should be evaluated on the basis of evidence of improvements in their students' work over a school year, and school faculty can be held collectively accountable for attendance and graduation rates. Incidentally, most teachers agree. You can—and you must—forge trusting and respectful relationships with the education leaders who welcome these forms of professional assessment and accountability.

For years, the talk is been about holding teachers, parents, and students more accountable. Now it's your turn to shoulder some of the responsibility for radically improving our education system. Without your intervention, your businesses and the American economy will be in jeopardy.

Innovator Updates

When I have a speaking engagement for Creating Innovators, *the question I hear from audiences the most is, Where are they now? The innovators, that is. As I prepared the new edition of the book, I asked each of the innovators I featured to send me an update on his or her current projects. The responses are fascinating, and I'm excited to share them with you here. (Responses were edited slightly for length and clarity.)*

—Tony

Jodie Wu

Hi Tony,

Quick update from me . . .

I'm building a network of village entrepreneurs who sell disruptive technologies to their communities.

Since we last spoke, I've gotten another $100K in investment and $150K in grants, and I've moved into our new workshop.

I will be heading to the TED Fellows Retreat this coming weekend, and SupporTED [a mentoring service offered to TED Fellows] has been amazing, giving me the leadership thinking to ensure success.

I definitely have some new acts in the pipeline.

Zander Srodes

Tony,
I am employed this summer at Denali State Park in Alaska. In September I will be returning for my senior year at Marshall University.

I am continuing my work in Guatemala with Akazul. I spent two weeks sleeping in a hammock and living in a dirt floor hut last March. I will be returning for a week this fall and over the holidays. My work continues to evolve. I'm doing more with sustainable living for the village and trying to design a prototype for other underserved communities. A year ago I established a youth soccer league and this spring created a children's library.

At school last semester I received a Maier Award for a paper I had written for a class that traces my emotional struggle in Guatemala. My professor submitted it to the competition without my knowing. I would have worked harder on it if I had known in advance!

It is reassuring to know that there are adults that have a vision for education in the future. Hope that you will recruit some followers who can see the big picture beyond the boring black and white textbook.

Laura White

Hi Tony,
After graduating from Tulane in Spring 2012, I accepted a position on Ashoka's Empathy Initiative and became the builder and manager of the Changemaker Schools Network. The Empathy Initiative's goal is to make empathy as fundamental in elementary education as reading and math. The purpose of the Changemaker Schools Network is to highlight the leading elementary schools in the United States that are valuing empathy and other "changemaker" skills like leadership, teamwork, and entrepreneurship, and to tell stories of how these schools are educating their students as innovators. By lifting up these schools, we are striving to build demand among parents, teachers, and community members for schools to provide a "changemaker" education.

On a day-to-day basis, I am researching innovative elementary schools across the United States, speaking with teachers and principals interested in the network, evaluating school applications with the Ashoka team, and working with our current Changemaker Schools on collaborative projects to amplify their impact. I also assist with Ashoka's middle school, high school, and college programs, because it's important that our entire education system supports students' development as innovators. Since the Changemaker Schools Network demands so much of my attention and entrepreneurial energy, I don't have any side projects right now. However, I am a passionate early childhood education advocate and spend a lot of time thinking and talking about how we can set young children and families up to be changemakers.

I hope to see you again soon!

Syreeta Gates

Hey Tony,

I'm thankful that a lot of really awesome things have happened and are in the works since *Creating Innovators* was published. The most important for me is that I released my own first book, *Just BE Cause: Ah Ha Moments to Inspire the Next Generation of Change Makers*, a chronicle of social entrepreneurship for the millennial generation. The book is available on www.justbecausebook.com or Amazon. I also graduated with the first degree in Urban Youth Culture in the world, so that's pretty cool. I won a few awards, such as the Point of Light Award. It's also super cool to have my first film credit in Nelson George's film *Finding the Funk*.

In other news I recruited for the first national Chief Dream Director Officer, Sallomé Hralima, for the Future Project. And have been featured in a book by John Schimm titled *Stand Up*. Lastly I launched my new website, www.syreetagates.com, so if you're looking for a speaker please reach out.

Shanna Tellerman

Hi Tony,
I spent a little over two years at Autodesk following our acquisition. It was a very interesting time to be part of that company. The transition to cloud has been a huge undertaking, and the company is in a state of unprecedented transition. Our team joined at the right time and we were part of the core of this transformation from the inception. I spent time running the product management team that launched the Autodesk Cloud initiatives, including the cloud platform and several web and mobile applications. The ride was a bumpy one for everyone. It was an entrepreneurial experiment in a large company, and we moved at a speed that was uncommon. At times we had a blast and other times we ran up against the big machine. Watching such a large organization make such a massive transition was very revealing, and the growing pains were highly visible.

Personally this was an incredible time of growth for me. I had the chance to see the workings of a big organization while still maintaining an entrepreneurial role and spirit. However, as two years neared their end I felt the itch to get back into the world of startups. Although I loved the people at Autodesk I found myself longing to be on the bleeding edge again, inventing the future. So with the support of everyone at Autodesk I took the leap back into the unknown with a plan to spend several months investigating what I should do next. During this transition I spent time reconnecting with my Silicon Valley network, advising several start-ups, and I briefly joined an old investor's fund as an Entrepreneur in Residence.

Only a few weeks into my new life I got a message out of the blue over LinkedIn from a recruiter at Google Ventures. The message was somewhat cryptic, but before I knew it I found myself talking to them about a role on their investing team. The decision was quick and easy. It was clear that there would be no better place in the world to explore what comes next than to be on the investment side at one of the best companies in the world and one of the most innovative venture firms. Since joining Google Ventures as a partner this May I have had the chance to meet with the most incredible entrepreneurs, dive deep on several areas of interest, gain a much deeper understanding of how investors evaluate businesses, and work alongside amazingly smart and successful people.

It is a bit jarring to have left the creative side and to no longer be building a product, company, or team, but I am guessing the next entrepreneurial endeavor is just around the corner for me.

Kirk Phelps

After three years at Sunrun, a residential solar utility based in San Francisco, California, I am currently consulting for a number of tech start-ups and for Kleiner Perkins, a local venture capitalist, as I look for my next adventure.

Jamien Sills

The last three years of my life have been the most trying and difficult of my thirty-four years. In this period, I have been evicted, sued, lost everything financially, married, and now divorced. Through it all I have learned some invaluable life lessons and strengthened my resolve as a person and as an entrepreneur. I have tried, even announced on several occasions, that I was giving up Neimaj, and returning full-time to the workforce, but I simply cannot quit. I have realized that Neimaj—what it has become—is bigger than me, and that I must endure the trials and tribulations to continue my mission. After so much loss, and facing what I thought were my greatest fears and surviving and enduring, I have a much better sense of who I am and what is really important in life.

In 2011, after returning from China, I relocated from Memphis to the campus of Mississippi State University to begin an MBA program. I moved Neimaj to the school's Entrepreneur Center incubator. It was a perfect fit for the company as well as for myself. The people at Mississippi State were very gracious and helpful, but in retrospect, my financial timeline did not line up with the timeline needed to execute the program. Eventually, I had to leave school and return to Memphis. In the three weeks prior to leaving, I had been working tirelessly to complete a seventy-plus page business plan to enter in the MillerCoors Urban Entrepreneurship Business Plan Competition. I submitted it the day before I left. As I was driving back to Memphis, I received an email saying my submission had been rejected because they could not open my file (Mac and PC stuff). So, I pulled over on the side of the highway and called them, and they were gracious enough to allow me to resend. I pulled my laptop out right there, reformatted the file, then drove to a nearby McDonald's, using their Wi-Fi to re-submit my plan.

Upon returning to Memphis, I needed quick employment and returned to my "work home," Champs Sports. Three months later, the store shut down and left us all unemployed. Just as the Champs staff closed the doors for the last time and we went for a last lunch together, I received an email from the MillerCoors competition stating that I was one of the winners and would be receiving a $25,000 grant. That was a sign to me in that moment that I could never quit, that there was always a way as long as I didn't give up. I am forever grateful to the MillerCoors corporation and staff for their generosity and willingness to reach out to young entrepreneurs. They saved me and my company.

For the past two years, I have been restructuring the company as well as myself. Before I was completely focused on making cool-looking products, but I realized that no matter how cool or innovative a product is, it will not sell without belief in the brand. So now the focus is on the ethos or heart of the company . . . THE EVERYDAY HERO. All of the products will be dictated and derive strictly from the EVERYDAY HERO concept. We are on the brink of moving into our factory in Louisiana and working with Southern University in Baton Rouge to develop our concept for manufacturing footwear in the US, utilizing 3-D printing and our proprietary manufacturing process, which we have titled Qi™. Qi will revolutionize the shoe industry. We are also continuing work on the EXO safety boot, which has now been tested and approved by ASTM standards. We have found a new manufacturer in China that can produce the

EXO with great quality, lower quantity, and more manageable costs. We are exploring various modes on distribution, and are in talks with several entities to carry and launch the EXO.

I am thankful for all of the hardships and pain I have endured, all the mistakes I have made, and all of the people that have wronged me, and especially those that have been there for me. I would especially like to thank my mother: without her example, teachings, and love, I would not be strong enough to endure everything that I have and will have to in the future. Everything good and bad has made me stronger and wiser, and I am now ready to grow and lead Neimaj toward the vision I had when I first imagined it.

David Sengeh

I finished my master's at the MIT Media Lab in 2012. My project was a novel 3-D-printed multimaterials prosthetic socket. I tested it and was able to show that it reduced pressure on limbs. I published the work and was accepted into the PhD program at the Media Lab.

In 2012, I got the idea of starting a high school innovation challenge in Sierra Leone. I wanted to bring creativity, not products, to my country. So we launched a National High School Innovation Challenge. I wanted to do it big—to get a lot of people involved. The Media Lab supported my nonprofit, Global Minimum, as did a couple foundations. Three hundred students applied in the first year. We invited the eight finalists to a "camp" where they critiqued one another's work and refined their prototypes. The winner received cash to develop their prototype, as well as mentors and a network of peers to work with. At the same time, we developed two innovation labs in two high schools.

In 2013, four hundred kids in Sierra Leone, four hundred in Kenya, and three hundred kids in Cape Town applied to the High School Innovation Challenge. We'll go to Botswana next year. We recently won the Rockefeller Next Century Innovators Award for this work, and I was also invited to participate in the Clinton Global Initiative. We made a video of the experience of one of our young innovators from Sierra Leone, which has been viewed five million times: http://bit.ly/1a0kAnu.

This past July, I gave a keynote at the UN Economic and Social Council in Geneva. That was a great experience! I called for leaders to think about innovation as a national development strategy.

I started a clothing company two years ago—T-shirts with my designs, which are based on traditional Sierra Leone art. I have ten employees in Sierra Leone. I'm also doing a little bit of rap music.

I'm on an expedited track for my PhD. Hope to finish two years early, in May 2014. We have one patent and are working on another for new types of prosthetics.

I want to figure out how create innovation labs in high schools. What do they look like? How do we make them available to every kid?

Note to Readers: This brief note from David does not begin to cover all of the things that he's doing. Check out his website: http://cargocollective.com/sengeh.

Launching a New Movement to Reimagine Schools

Several years ago, Ted Dintersmith, one of the most successful high tech venture capitalists in the 1990s, sent me an email. He had read my 2008 book, *The Global Achievement Gap*, and wanted to talk. We haven't stopped talking since. Ted shares my conviction that our education system is obsolete and needs reinventing, not reforming.

Working with a team of colleagues, Ted and I have formed Learning Innovation.US to catalyze a movement to reimagine US education. Our first project is producing a feature-length documentary—the *An Inconvenient Truth* of education. The documentary showcases learning in reimagined classrooms in places like High Tech High and makes a compelling case for change through interviews with thought leaders like Thomas Friedman and Sir Kenneth Robinson. For the past fifteen months, award-winning filmmaker Greg Whiteley and his crew have been filming in extraordinary schools and colleges around the country, and, as of this writing, are in the final stages of editing the footage.

With a coalition of partners supporting us, we'll launch the film in spring 2015. We believe it will catalyze a national reassessment of our country's education goals. The film's call to action will impel communities to reimagine the role of schools in producing graduates with the passion, skills, and grit to become self-fulfilled adults who can make meaningful contributions in their communities and places of work. We will support the film with an integrated set of initiatives to reach communities all over the country and provide ways for groups to share ideas through our website: www.learninginnovation.us.

Acknowledgments

I have asked for and received a great deal of assistance with this project because of its complexity. Thanks go first to the more than 150 people who gave generously of their time for the interviews and conversations that are the heart of this book: Young innovators and their families, mentors, and teachers, as well as business and military leaders—all welcomed my interest and offered invaluable insights. Without their full cooperation, this book would never have been possible. I am also most grateful to have Bob Compton as a collaborator on this project and producer of the videos that accompany the book. I deeply value the help I received from two retired business leaders, Stan Sharenson and Dennis Hunter, who critiqued drafts of chapters and offered suggestions of resources. Matthew Bundick as well reviewed much of the book and offered many useful ideas. Rose Else-Mitchell also reviewed portions of the book and offered a valuable perspective as a business executive. Other helpful suggestions and leads for interviews came from Annmarie Neal, Dwight Gertz, Clay Christensen, Paul Holland, Linda Yates, and Charles Fadel. Paul Bottino offered me a valuable institutional affiliation at the Technology and Entrepreneurship Center at Harvard and many informal conversations while I was working on this project.

I also want to acknowledge the contributions of the young research associates who provided important insights and Millennials' perspectives on my ideas: Niha Jain, Allie Kimmel, Chike Aguh, Laura White, Kirsten Hill, and Michael Klein. My agent, Esmond Harmsworth, was tremendously helpful in developing the proposal for the book, placing it with the right publisher, and commenting on drafts along the way. At Scribner, Samantha Martin and Paul Whitlatch split the editing work, and both offered excellent critiques and advice; and Steve Boldt did a superb job of copyediting the manuscript.

Finally, and most important, I am deeply grateful to my wife, PJ Blankenhorn, who was a true collaborator on every part of this book, discussing and critiquing ideas, carefully and patiently reading many drafts of chapters. I doubt that this book could have been written without her strong and unswerving support.

Notes

Introduction

1. Tamar Lewin, "Burden of College Loans on Graduates Grows," *New York Times*, April 11, 2011, accessed September 23, 2011, http://www.nytimes.com/2011/04/12/education/12college.html.
2. Richard Arum and Josipa Roksa, *Academically Adrift: Limited Learning on College Campuses* (Chicago: University of Chicago Press, 2011).
3. You can find out more about Bob Compton, view trailers, and order copies of his films at his website: www.2mminutes.com.

Chapter One

1. David Wessel, "What's Wrong With America's Job Engine?," *Wall Street Journal*, July 27, 2011, accessed September 12, 2011, http://online.wsj.com/article/SB10001424053111904772304576468820582615858.html?mod=djemITP_h.
2. Hope Yen, "Census: Recession Takes Big Toll on Young Adults," Forbes.com, September 22, 2011, accessed September 23, 2011, http://www.forbes.com/feeds/ap/2011/09/22/general-us-census-recession-apos-s-impact_8696311.html.
3. Robert Pear, "Recession Officially Over, U.S. Incomes Kept Falling," *New York Times*, October 9, 2011, accessed October 12, 2011, http://www.nytimes.com/2011/10/10/us/recession-officially-over-us-incomes-kept-falling.html?_r=1.
4. Sabrina Tavernies, "2010 Data Show Surge in Poor Young Families," *New York Times*, September 19, 2011, accessed September 23, 2011, http://www.nytimes

.com/2011/09/20/us/poor-young-families-soared-in-10-data-show.htm?_r=1&adxnnl=1&adxnnlx=1316815137-EOmdk98v6pfzbGyIgDcrmg.

5. US Census Bureau report, "Income, Poverty, and Health Insurance Coverage in the United States: 2010," September 2011, accessed September 15, 2011, http://www.census.gov/prod/2011pubs/p60-239.pdf.
6. Thomas Friedman and Michael Mandelbaum, *That Used to Be Us: How America Fell Behind in the World It Invented and How We Can Come Back* (New York: Farrar, Straus and Giroux, 2011), 138.
7. "Rising Above the Gathering Storm, Revisited: Rapidly Approaching Category 5," Members of the 2005 Committee, prepared for the presidents of the National Academy of Sciences, National Academy of Engineering, and Institute of Medicine, accessed May 3, 2011, http://www.nap.edu/catalog/12999.html.
8. Information Technology and Information Foundation, "The Atlantic Century: Benchmarking EU and U.S. Innovation and Competitiveness," 2009, accessed May 15, 2011, http://www.itif.org/files/2009-atlantic-century.pdf.
9. "The 50 Most Innovative Companies," *Bloomberg Businessweek*, April 10, 2010, accessed May 14, 2011, http://www.businessweek.com/magazine/content/10_17/b4175034779697.htm.
10. "Ready to Innovate" (New York: Conference Board, 2008).
11. McKinsey & Company, "Innovation & Commercialization, 2010," accessed May 7, 2001, http://www.mckinseyquarterly.com/Strategy/Innovation/Innovation_and_commercialization_2010_McKinsey_Global_Survey_results_2662.
12. Members of the 2005 Committee, "Rising Above the Gathering Storm, Revisited."
13. Mr. Y, "A National Strategic Narrative," accessed May 4, 2011, http://www.wilsoncenter.org/events/docs/A%20National%20Strategic%20Narrative.pdf.
14. Accessed May 13, 2011, http://abcnews.go.com/Politics/State_of_the_Union/state-of-the-union-2011-full-transcript/story?id=12759395.
15. "GE Global Innovation Barometer, 2011," accessed May 10, 2011, http://files.gereports.com/wp-content/uploads/2011/01/GIB-results.pdf. Emphasis added.
16. From "The Creativity Crisis," accessed May 1, 2011, http://www.newsweek.com/2010/07/10/the-creativity-crisis.html.

17. Ibid.
18. Melissa Korn, "Dean in London Champions Innovation," *Wall Street Journal*, May 4, 2011, accessed May 5, 2011, http://online.wsj.com/article/SB10001424052748704740604576301181974037002.html.
19. Richard K. Miller, "How Do You Recognize and Cultivate Potential Innovators?" (paper prepared and presented at Olin College, May 9, 2011).
20. Teach For America fact sheet, accessed May 13, 2011 http://www.teachforamerica.org/newsroom/documents/2010-11_Press_Kit_Updated_04.29.11.pdf.
21. Tony Wagner, *The Global Achievement Gap: Why Even Our Best Schools Don't Teach the New Survival Skills Our Children Need—and What We Can Do About It* (New York: Basic Books, 2008).
22. IDEO website, accessed May 11, 2011, http://www.ideo.com/about/.
23. Tim Brown, "Design Thinking," *Harvard Business Review*, June 2008, 3.
24. Jeffrey H. Dyer, Hal B. Gregersen, and Clayton M. Christensen, "The Innovator's DNA," *Harvard Business Review*, December 2009, 62.
25. Ibid.
26. "50 Most Innovative Companies," *Bloomberg Businessweek*.
27. 2011 survey reported by Tech Pluto, accessed September 12, 2011, http://www.techpluto.com/most-desired-employer-2011/.
28. Brown, "Design Thinking," 4.
29. Dyer, Gregersen, and Christensen, "Innovator's DNA," 67.
30. Bronwyn Fryer, "How Do Innovators Think," *Harvard Business Review* blog, September 28, 2009, accessed May 11, 2011, http://blogs.hbr.org/hbr/hbreditors/2009/09/how_do_innovators_think.html.
31. Robert Sternberg, "Creativity Is a Habit," *Education Week* Commentary, February 22, 2006, accessed May 11, 2011, http://www.edweek.org/ew/articles/2006/02/22/24sternberg.h25.html?r=192032759.
32. "Generation M2: Media in the Lives of 8- to 18-Year-Olds," Kaiser Family Foundation, 2010, accessed May 20, 2011, http://www.kff.org/entmedia/8010.cfm.
33. Teresa Amabile, "How to Kill Creativity," *Harvard Business Review*, September–October 1998.
34. Ibid., 79.

35. Alison Gopnik, "Your Baby Is Smarter Than You Think," *New York Times* Op-Ed, August 16, 2009, accessed May 16, 2011, http://www.nytimes.com/2009/08/16/opinion/16gopnik.html.
36. Alison Gopnik, *The Philosophical Baby* (New York: Farrar, Straus and Giroux, 2009), accessed May 16, 2011, http://us.macmillan.com/BookCustomPage.aspx?isbn=9780312429843#Excerpt.
37. "Excerpts from an Oral History with Steve Jobs," Smithsonian Institution Oral and Video Histories, April 20, 1995, accessed May 17, 2011, http://americanhistory.si.edu/collections/comphist/sj1.html#advice.
38. Dyer, Gregersen, and Christensen, "Innovator's DNA," 66.

Chapter Two

1. From Phillips Exeter's "Facts" publication, accessed December 14, 2011, http://www.exeter.edu/documents/facts_2011WEB.pdf.
2. Steve Jobs's 2005 Stanford University Commencement Speech, *Stanford University News,* June 14, 2005, accessed May 30, 2011, http://news.stanford.edu/news/2005/june15/jobs-061505.html.

Chapter Three

1. More information can be found at http://www.wildpockets.com.
2. Information about the center and its interdisciplinary degree program can be found on their website, http://www.etc.cmu.edu/site/.
3. Through his book *The Last Lecture* and a YouTube video with the same title, Randy has gained international recognition. More information about Randy can be found on his website, http://www.cs.cmu.edu/~pausch/.
4. The company's website is http:// www.globalcyclesolutions.com.
5. More information about the D-Lab can be found on their website, http://d-lab.mit.edu/.
6. Accessed August 12, 2011, http://www.time.com/time/specials/packages/article/0,28804,1984685_1984745_1984806,00.html.
7. The MIT $100K Challenge is a student-managed entrepreneurship competition that is overseen by the MIT School of Engineering, accessed June 10, 2011, http://www.mit100k.org/.
8. Information about Global Minimum can be found at http://www.gmin.org/.

9. Information about Lebone Solutions can be found at http://www.lebone.org/about/.
10. Information about the Idea Translation Lab can be found at http://thelaboratory.harvard.edu/.

Chapter Four

1. David Bornstein, *How to Change the World: Social Entrepreneurs and the Power of New Ideas* (New York: Oxford University Press, 2004), 1.
2. More information on Ashoka can be found at http://ashoka.org/.
3. More information about TED and videos of many presentations can be found on the website, http://www.ted.com/.
4. Quoted from the Ashoka U website, accessed July 6, 2011, http://ashokau.org/getting-involved/changemaker-campus-initiative/.
5. Syreeta's portfolio can be seen at http://sgclifeexperience.wordpress.com/.
6. Lutheran HealthCare website, accessed July 9, 2011, http://www.lmcmc.com/CommunityPrograms/Support/YouthandAdolescentServices/.
7. Accessed July 9, 2011, http://theswtlife.com/.
8. More information on StartingBloc and its programs can be found on their website, http://www.startingbloc.org/institute.
9. His presentation can be viewed at http://www.youtube.com/watch?v=hZR214wjIfA.

Chapter Five

1. See, for example, the extraordinary video interviews of Harvard and MIT graduates who struggle to explain basic concepts such as the reasons for the four seasons or how to complete an electrical circuit, produced by the Harvard-Smithsonian Center for Astrophysics, Science Education Department, Science Media Group, accessed October 17, 2011, http://www.learner.org/sphider/search.php?search=1&query=private+universe&x=0&y=0.
2. Quoted from the Art Start website, accessed July 9, 2011, http://art-start.org/.
3. Friedman's column can be found at http://www.nytimes.com/2010/03/21/opinion/21friedman.html. More information about the Intel science competition can be found at http://www.intel.com/about/corporateresponsibility/education/sts/index.htm.

4. As quoted from Salman Khan's TED Talks video, accessed October 22, 2011, http://www.ted.com/talks/salman_khan_let_s_use_video_to_reinvent_education.html. More information on the academy can be found at its website, www.khanacademy.org.
5. Amy Harmon, "It May Be a Sputnik Moment, but Science Fairs Are Lagging," *New York Times*, February 4, 2011, accessed October 17, 2011, http://www.nytimes.com/2011/02/05/us/05science.html?_r=3&hp.
6. Mark C. Taylor, "End of the University as We Know It," *New York Times*, April 26, 2009, accessed July 19, 2011, http://www.nytimes.com/2009/04/27/opinion/27taylor.html?scp=1&sq=the%20end%20of%20the%20university%20as%20we%20know%20it&st=cse.
7. Accessed August 7, 2011, http://moneywatch.bnet.com/saving-money/blog/devil-details/debt-in-america-students-buried-in-education-loans/4972/.
8. Richard Arum and Josiah Roksa, *Academically Adrift: Limited Learning on College Campuses* (Chicago: University of Chicago Press, 2011).
9. "Scholars Test Web Alternative to Peer Review," *New York Times*, August 24, 2010, accessed July 19, 2011, http://www.nytimes.com/2010/08/24/arts/24peer.html?_r=1&pagewanted=all.
10. Ibid.
11. Olin College website, accessed July 17, 2011, http://olin.edu/about_olin/history/olin_history.aspx.
12. Ibid., http://olin.edu/about_olin/overview.aspx.
13. For a syllabus and more information about how Jon Stolk evaluates his students, see the course website, http://faculty.olin.edu/~jstolk/failure2008/index.html.
14. More information about the SCOPE requirement can be found at http://scope.olin.edu/about/.
15. More information about the survey can be found at http://nsse.iub.edu/html/about.cfm.
16. For more information, see the Olin website, http://www.olin.edu/about_olin/olin_news/olin_press_release.aspx?id=409.
17. Accessed October 22, 2011, http://www.nga.org/cms/home/news-room/audio--video/page_2011/col2-content/main-content-list/2011-winter-meeting-audio-and-vi.html.

18. Vivek Wadhwa, "Engineering vs. Liberal Arts: Who's Right—Bill or Steve?," Techcrunch blog, March 21, 2011, accessed October 22, 2011, http://tech crunch.com/2011/03/21/engineering-vs-liberal-arts-who%e2%80%99 s-right%e2%80%94bill-or-steve/.
19. Isaacson, Walter, "The Genius of Steve Jobs," *New York Times,* October 29, 2011, opinion column, accessed December 4, 2011, http://www.nytimes. com/2011/10/30/opinion/sunday/steve-jobss-genius.html?pagewanted=all.
20. Vivek Wadhwa, "Career Counselor: Steve Jobs or Bill Gates?," *New York Times,* March 20, 2011, opinion column, accessed October 22, 2011, http://www. nytimes.com/roomfordebate/2011/03/20/career-counselor-bill-gates-or-steve-jobs.
21. Vivek Wadhwa, "Engineering as Liberal Arts."
22. More information about the program can be found at http://www.etc.cmu .edu/site/program/.
23. Accessed July 28, 2011, http://www.media.mit.edu/about/academics/.
24. Accessed July 28, 2011, http://www.media.mit.edu/about/mission-history.
25. Accessed July 29, 2011, http://admissions.media.mit.edu/admissions/research.
26. Accessed July 29, 2011, http://www.media.mit.edu/research/groups /biomechatronics.
27. d.school course listings can be found here at http://dschool.stanford.edu/ classes/.
28. Accessed August 4, 2011, http://dschool.stanford.edu/our-point-of-view/# innovators.
29. Linda Tischler, "Ideo's David Kelley on 'Design Thinking,'" *Fast Company,* February 2009, accessed August 4, 2011, http://www.fastcompany .com/magazine/132/a-designer-takes-on-his-biggest-challenge-ever .html?page=0%2C4.
30. Ibid.
31. High Tech High website, accessed July 30, 2011, http://www.hightechhigh.org /about/.
32. UVEI website, accessed July 30, 2011, http://uvei.org/images/stories/pdf _downloads/uvei%20m.a.t.%20program%20description.pdf.
33. More information on the competencies for each certification area can be found at http://uvei.org/.

34. Team Academy's website, accessed September 8, 2011, http://www.tiimiakatemia.fi/en/.
35. The trailer and ordering information are available at http://www.2mminutes.com.
36. The 2009 OECD PISA results are summarized at http://nces.ed.gov/pubs2011/2011004.pdf. More information on the OECD PISA testing program is in chapter 3 of my book *The Global Achievement Gap*.
37. The two most widely cited global innovation indexes rank Finland ahead of the United States, accessed September 7, 2011, http://www.globalinnovationindex.org/gii/GII%20COMPLETE_PRINTWEB.pdf or http://www.bcg.com/documents/file15445.pdf.

Chapter Six

1. From the school's website, accessed August 13, 2011, http://www.stanford.edu/dept/bingschool/.
2. I had several long interviews with Mac, his mother, and two of his teachers, but I could not include his profile in the book because of space limitations. You can find out more about Mac's innovations at http://diybio.org/.
3. *EQ* is a reference to Daniel Goleman's groundbreaking work on what he termed "emotional intelligence." See his several books on this topic.
4. Jeff Hunter, "My Son Won't Do His Homework," accessed August 22, 2011, http://www.talentism.com/business_talent/2007/06/my_son_wont_do_.html.
5. Accessed August 18, 2011, http://www.youtube.com/watch?v=kdz555JBIwY.
6. Rachael Emma Silverman, "How to Be Like Apple," *Wall Street Journal*, Online Addition, August 29, 2011, accessed August 29, 2011, http://online.wsj.com/article/SB10001424053111904009304576532842667854706.html?mod=djkeyword&mg=com-wsj.
7. "The Army Learning Concept for 2015," TRADOC Pam 525-8-2, accessed August 28, 2011, http://www.tradoc.army.mil/tpubs/pams/tp525-8-2.pdf.
8. Ibid., 8–9.

Epilogue

1. Agnes de Mille, *Martha: The Life and Work of Martha Graham—A Biography* (New York: Random House, 1991), 264.

A Letter from Tony Wagner to Business Leaders

1. National Charter School Study 2013, CREDO, Stanford University. http://credo.stanford.edu/research-reports.html, Accessed August 21, 2013.
2. As reported by Helen Ladd and Edward Fiske in their article "Class Matters. Why Won't We Admit it," *New York Times,* December 11, 2011, http://www.nytimes.com/2011/12/12/opinion/the-unaddressed-link-between-poverty-and-education.html?pagewanted=all&_r=0. Accessed August 21, 2013.
3. Quoted from OECD Economic Surveys: United States, Paris, June 2012 (p. 30). http://www.keepeek.com/Digital-Asset-Management/oecd/economics/oecd-economic-surveys-united-states-2012_eco_surveys-usa-2012-en. Accessed August 21, 2013.
4. See Steve Lohr's column, "Big Data, Trying to Build Better Workers," in the April 20, 2013, *New York Times* (http://www.nytimes.com/2013/04/21/technology/big-data-trying-to-build-better-workers.html?pagewanted=all) and Adam Bryant's interview with Google senior vice president Laszlo Bock in the June 19, 2013, *New York Times* (http://www.nytimes.com/2013/06/20/business/in-head-hunting-big-data-may-not-be-such-a-big-deal.html?pagewanted=all&_r=0). Both accessed August 21, 2013.
5. PISA or Program for Student Assessment, is an international testing program established by the Organization for Economic Cooperation and Development and is currently used by more than sixty countries.
6. "It Takes More Than a Major: Employer Priorities for College Learning and Student Success," The Association of American Colleges and Universities, 2013, http://www.aacu.org/leap/documents/2013_EmployerSurvey.pdf. Accessed August 21, 2013.

Index